book of
enlightenment

book of
enlightenment

anadi

MANTRA
BOOKS

Winchester, UK
Washington, USA

First published by Mantra Books, 2014
Mantra Books is an imprint of John Hunt Publishing Ltd., Laurel House, Station Approach,
Alresford, Hants, SO24 9JH, UK
office1@jhpbooks.net
www.johnhuntpublishing.com
www.mantra-books.net

For distributor details and how to order please visit the 'Ordering' section on our website.

Text copyright: Anadi 2013

ISBN: 978 1 78279 667 1

A CIP catalogue record for this book is available from the British Library.

Printed and bound by CPI Group (UK) Ltd, Croydon, CR0 4YY

We operate a distinctive and ethical publishing philosophy in all
areas of our business, from our global network of authors to
production and worldwide distribution.

contents

opening

introduction

The purpose of this book is to reveal the multidimensional evolution of human consciousness from the state of ignorance to complete enlightenment. It is a book of spiritual guidance directed to uncompromising seekers of truth and wholeness, a precise elucidation of the deepest secrets of the spiritual realm and the path to self-realization. We do not offer it as a manual of enlightenment, for the ultimate truth of awakening cannot be reduced to a conceptual model. Rather, this book should serve as a guiding light for those mature enough to apply conceptual knowledge towards a non-conceptual apperception of reality. Accordingly, the explanations and tools presented here point beyond words to the realm of direct experience and pure understanding.

Although we aspire to unravel the many steps of the awakening process in a clear and comprehensive way, the revelations of this book can be easily misinterpreted and misunderstood. There is an immense chasm between theoretical knowledge and real understanding; concepts with the power to illuminate the truth of our inner reality can also obscure it, depending on their interpretation. In most cases, to awaken complete understanding and penetrate the conceptual constructs set forth herein, a seeker must have the support of a fully qualified teacher. Ultimately, to truly understand the teaching, its experiential essence must be realized through the unfoldment of one's own evolution and enlightenment.

Due to the inherent limitations of spiritual vocabulary, the meanings of certain words and phrases that we use overlap and interpenetrate each other, and therefore must be read with imagination and sensitivity to the context in which they are presented. For instance, the notion 'I am' most often signifies the soul, our essence of pure subjectivity, but at times it refers to the inner state. 'The self' points to the supreme reality of universal I am; however, when written as 'self', it refers either to the personal I, or ego, or in another context, to one's true subjectivity, or I am. The term 'ego' usually denotes our false identity, but it sometimes relates to our inborn sense of me in the mind, the natural reflection of the soul's consciousness. Other frequently used terms with variable meanings are 'being' and 'presence'. 'Being' should generally be understood as the fundamental aspect of the inner state that links the soul to the dimension of the source, though it can also represent one's true essence and basic identity. The term 'presence' is sometimes used to describe a general sense of presence, but most often signifies pure awareness. The nuances of the many terms presented here should be thoughtfully considered so that the understanding and spiritual insight intended will be aroused.

Although it is indeed a long journey from ignorance to complete self-realization, the way to truth is far more than the attainment of progressively higher spiritual states. It is not a linear path in the sense of being goal-fixated, because from the standpoint of the soul, each step of the journey is complete and thus whole in and of itself. Neither is it a finite path, for there is no end to enlightenment. That which we are everlastingly realizing, yet can never fully attain — the unknown heart of the beloved's presence — is eternally beyond and ever ahead of the intelligence that pursues it. Although the god state can never be entirely grasped, our evolution towards its divine radiance is the very meaning of our existence. It is indeed the journey, not its culmination, that is the essence of our spiritual unfoldment. Honoring this, we should regard the ineffable mystery of the spiritual path with humility and wonder, its majesty with a sense of awe.

This book is a response to the deepest need for true understanding that lies within the consciousness of every seeker. It is a vital compendium of spiritual knowledge addressed both to those commencing their inner journey, as well as those who have already reached higher levels of spiritual realization. The teaching presented here is not a personalized interpretation of spiritual reality, but a reflection of truth with the power to broaden understanding of the inner dimension and assist in navigating the intricacies of the inner path.

It is essential that the material presented here be studied in the context of real inner work, for without a foundation of practice that yields experiential knowledge of the inner realm, a reader will not be able to grasp the true meaning of the teaching or, worse still, will create the illusion of understanding. When not based on spiritual realization, intellectual knowledge is but a hollow substitute for real experience. The reality of the awakening process is extremely complex and must be illuminated gradually from within. To approach this material solely from the standpoint of the mind would defeat the very purpose of its presentation.

the goal of spiritual wholeness

Crowning the principal aims of evolution — human completion, emancipation from suffering, the end of ignorance, and reunion with the self — is its supreme purpose: expansion into the state of wholeness. While it is true that liberation is the highest goal of all traditions of enlightenment, from the viewpoint of the teaching, liberation that is not based on wholeness is no more than a denial of human existence. True liberation includes transcendence, but is not defined by freedom from ignorance, which we consider to be a 'negative' type of enlightenment. Enlightenment is not release from the false, but evolution into the true, at the heart of which lies the state of wholeness founded upon the complete awakening of the soul's original identity. The state of wholeness cannot be captured by the earthly mentality; it is beyond the imagination of the human mind. In fact, it does not belong to the human reality at all. Only by transcending the dimension of forgetfulness can we access the truth of our future self.

The realization of wholeness is unique for each individual, but the awakening of the inner state is the existential foundation all souls require to become whole. It is only by expanding into the states beyond the mind that the soul can actualize her multifaceted existence beyond the limits of her human identity. Abiding in the inner realm, she gradually merges with the timeless ground of existence, the womb from which she gives birth to her complete presence. We cannot even speak about wholeness and soul-realization in separation from this notion of the unity of the soul with the absolute reality. It is only by the power of her union with the supreme self that the soul finally awakens her ultimate subjectivity.

Although our journey towards wholeness is rooted in expansion into the realm of the inner state, we must not confuse abidance in states beyond the mind with wholeness itself. The one who becomes whole is not the state we abide in, but the individual consciousness that embodies it, our pure subjectivity. To realize her ultimate potential, the soul must not only reach unity with the beyond, she must also awaken her multidimensional body of I am.

Wholeness is a pure reflection of universal perfection in the heart of an individual being. For the soul to become whole, she must reach completion in her human existence and align her human identity with her awakening process. She has to reach maximal integrity within her human personality before she is free to realize herself, for unless the personality matures to the highest level of wisdom and purity, she cannot integrate her human incarnation with her eternal essence. The human consciousness of the soul must be refined to the point that it can serve as a suitable vehicle for her awakening and transcendence.

The state of wholeness is the flowering of a multidimensional awakening through which we evolve into the states beyond the mind, human completion, soul-awakening, ego-transcendence and, finally, surrender into the beyond. We enter the path to wholeness when we remember our evolutionary goal and begin to consciously serve our soul and her enlightenment. From here, the process unfolds as an energetic expansion into the realm of pure subjectivity that is actualized through the opening of the inner state and the awakening to me. Next comes the awakening of the soul, in which our sense of identity shifts from ego to I am. At the culmination of this process, self-realization, the mind is surrendered and one's relative consciousness merges with the inner realm. The soul reaches the state of transcendence and, liberated from identification with her human personality, returns to the abode of her origin. Dwelling in her primordial home-state, she re-embodies her original condition of wholeness, her eternal identity actualized at last. To become whole is to become a divine being, free of any sense of incompleteness, emancipated from the personality and absolutely one with existence.

the frontiers of enlightenment

Is enlightenment freedom from the mind? Is it the realization of pure consciousness? An awakening to the dimension of love? The ability to abide in being? Is enlightenment multidimensional or can it be reduced to a single state or realization? Does it imply a complete understanding of reality? What do we really mean by enlightenment? In spite of being a central concept in the realm of spirituality, enlightenment remains a secret reality. Although certain past traditions do present valid information on the subject, their understanding is generally fragmented, and therefore can be a distorting influence. Rarely, if ever, do they point to complete self-realization and the state of wholeness. Due to their limited vision, they tend to compound rather than resolve seekers' confusion and projections with ambiguous and conflicting interpretations, often twisting earnest yearning into pure fantasy. With so many incomplete teachings saturating the spiritual scene, how can we reach the clarity of mind necessary to grasp the true nature of enlightenment?

The teaching is unique in that it does not consider enlightenment to be the static climax of spiritual evolution, but an eternally expanding movement of intelligence and consciousness that is unique for each soul. Although rooted in the inner realm of universal subjectivity, the enlightened reality can only be accessed through the awakening of our individual subjectivity; the presence of the personal I am is what makes awakening to the ultimate possible. It is our individual essence that journeys through the process of evolution, progressively shifting through states of awakening and levels of surrender that lead ever deeper into the supreme beyond.

How far we can expand the frontiers of our enlightenment depends upon our spiritual capacity, inspiration, knowledge and intelligence. However, of equal consequence is the limiting factor of our own unconsciousness. Because it exists only as the reversal of its opposite, not only must we see enlightenment in relation to unconditional truth, but also to the depth of human ignorance. Our expansion into enlightenment is not only an evolution of human consciousness, but a process of breaking through the gravity and resistance of the unenlightened reality. It is the power struggle between the forces of the inertia that bind us to the plane of forgetfulness and our ability to transcend them that ultimately defines the territorial boundaries of our human awakening.

The more our consciousness evolves, the more its potential expands for a further, more complete enlightenment. By 'complete' we do not suggest the end of enlightenment, but our relative completion in the realm of human enlightenment and the realization of wholeness. The concept of complete enlightenment must be seen from the perspective of the infinite and eternally evolving truth of creation, unfathomable by individual consciousness. No one can be said to be completely enlightened in a literal sense, for to apply the notion of completion to the realm of truth presumes its finitude. We must treat the idea of enlightenment with a humility born of an understanding of our human limits within the limitlessness of the divine mystery. Our personal enlightenment is only a point of entry into universal evolution and awakening.

Now that the relative nature of 'complete enlightenment' is clear, we can look at it in the context of our earthly dimension and human identity. Not all souls are destined to reach exactly the same level of realization, but we can make the generalization that although there are many stages of awakening, the ultimate frontier of enlightenment for a human soul is her liberation, the point at which she transcends her personalized identity and earthly consciousness. Liberation does not end the soul's evolution, but it does end the human journey of the soul. When she transcends the plane of lower intelligence, the soul merges with the realm of pure subjectivity, leaving the human ego behind. In doing so, she becomes one with universal evolution, supporting the evolutionary purpose of creation through her own existence and everlasting enlightenment. For the soul, our universal self, the expansion of light and consciousness into further enlightenment is eternal — beyond enlightenment and beyond.

the map of awakening

Although many traditions and schools of enlightenment have attempted to draw objective maps of awakening, from our standpoint these maps do not reflect a true model of wholeness, for they fail to accurately describe the stages of our evolution into the inner state, the awakening of the soul, and the soul's multidimensional movement into the beyond. Not only do most available teachings lead to a partial realization at best, they create imbalances by stressing particular aspects of evolution while ignoring others. Certain schools point to an awakening in which only one aspect of the inner state is embodied, while others overlook the realization of the soul and focus exclusively on transcendence. Some even misconstrue abidance in the inner state or the realization of one of many mystical states for enlightenment. Perhaps the most misguided of all are those who suggest that everyone is already enlightened.

Incomplete teachings can seriously limit or even cripple our spiritual vision. Without a holistic and complete map of awakening that clearly reflects the fundamental laws of human evolution, a seeker has little chance of finding his way towards the fulfillment of his ultimate potential. The plane of enlightenment is so vast and intricate that unless a new, higher level of conceptual detail is brought to bear on its description, it will never be seen for what it truly is: a relevant and tangible reality directly connected to our natural growth towards wholeness.

Although we often use the terms 'enlightenment' and 'awakening' interchangeably, it is important to note that they do not signify the same level of spiritual attainment. When we refer to an enlightened state, we point to self-realization — transcendence and the actualization of wholeness. 'Awakening', on the other hand, indicates a singular expansion beyond the mind within the total course of one's evolution. To have arrived at one of the many states beyond the mind is far from enlightenment in the ultimate sense of the word. It is only by traversing various dimensions of awakening that one finally arrives at complete, multidimensional enlightenment.

One must also be clear that after experiencing an awakening to one of the various states beyond the mind, there is a need to stabilize and then integrate that state. Seldom, if ever, does sudden awakening result in a lasting inner realization. Unless the state we have awakened is stabilized, its fluctuations prevent it from becoming a permanent foundation of our existence. Once stabilized, the state must also be integrated so that it can reach its final depth and purity and become energetically and existentially attuned to the body, mind and other aspects of our whole being.

The map presented below is a condensed description of the awakening process that is explicated extensively throughout this book. Although the states of realization described do not always manifest in exactly the same sequence, the model presented here provides the necessary framework to grasp the fundamental laws of the awakening process.

the state of presence

The realization of the state of presence — consciousness without content — is the foundation of our awakening, for without it there is no way to transcend the mind. The state of presence is the center of the soul's intelligence and the true nature of awareness. Until we regain the essence of I am in the mind, we will remain forever imprisoned in the shell of personality, with no solid existence, no center of identity, no soul. Only by awakening pure awareness can we break through our false personality and meet ourselves beyond the mental dimension, putting an end to the ignominy of forgetfulness.

Because few teachers and seekers are able to pinpoint the exact energetic location of pure awareness, it is often confused with the experience of being, or an overall *sense* of presence. It is essential, therefore, to understand that the correct realization of the state of presence is experienced exclusively in the headspace. The state is initially recognized as the sense of I am in the area in the middle of the head when the eyes are closed, and in the depths of the head when the eyes are open. As it matures, the state naturally expands to fill the entire headspace and the area around it.

The state of presence is awakened either through self-enquiry or initiation by a spiritual guide, and then stabilized through the practice of self-remembrance, which eventually yields an unbroken continuity of pure awareness. The awakening of awareness is of immense significance, for it represents the soul's entry into the realm of pure subjectivity and her freedom to begin the process of extricating her existence from the collective state of unconsciousness.

being

Awareness alone cannot enter the inner realm unless it becomes absorbed in the stillness of being. Being is that which enables us to rest in existence — the intermediary space that links consciousness with the source and maintains the gravitational equilibrium between creation and the original void. As both the impersonal ground of the beyond and the true foundation of meditation, it is being that allows the depth of reality to be divulged to our consciousness.

Being is felt all over the body as an energetic expansion, with its main energy flowing downwards. The primary means to reach and deepen the experience of being is the practice of meditation in the mode of 'non-doing', or 'just sitting', which opens us to the gravity of the now so that the energy of the soul can be absorbed into a state of repose. This practice can be supported by belly breathing, which balances our energy and assists the sense of I am to descend towards the unmanifested.

Although it anchors us in the now, the experience of being does not have the quality of complete, unconditional rest prior to the realization of the absolute.

the absolute state

In the realization of the absolute, the soul transcends the fluctuations in her experience of being and moves into a state of unbroken rest. In the pure rest of the absolute, the motionlessness of being reflects the perfection of universal stillness. The absolute state represents our union with the unborn, uncreated source. It is the ground of oneness through which we reach unconditional absorption in the beyond.

In the absolute state, one experiences unity with reality only within the being aspect of I am; the mind and the consciousness of the soul have not yet merged with the source.

heart

The heart belongs to the realm of the beloved, love and grace. No one can reach completion without actualizing its essence. While the opening of the spiritual heart is necessary to reach wholeness, it is impossible before we have first solidified our identity beyond the mind and become absorbed in the source. This is why paths that limit their view of spirituality to love and devotion cannot serve as a bridge to reality unless they are grounded in awareness and being. Without the foundation of the inner state, the heart has no reality apart from emotion. In order to open us to the dimension of the soul and the divine, the heart must be met beyond emotion in a space of clarity and stillness.

The initial phase of our journey into the heart's essence is its energetic opening, which brings us closer to the experience of oneness with creation. The complete enlightenment of the heart requires the purification of one's intention and the realization of the soul.

transparent me

The awakening of the soul begins in the heart, but its further deepening occurs through the realization of transparent me, a holistic experience of unity with existence reached through expansion into

13

the whole of oneself. The state of transparent me represents the true awakening to the pure subjective existence of the soul. It is the fusion of our existence with the inner state coupled with the embracing of our complete identity.

the state beyond polarities

The state beyond polarities is the first step of transcendence. It is the meeting of oneness and non-separation — the heart and the absolute — that manifests when consciousness enters the realm of surrender. Through a radical integration of awareness, heart and being, in which all the three aspects of I am merge into a single state, one moves beyond the polarities of inner and outer, here and now. By the power of this unification, a deeper surrender and absorption in the beyond takes place.

The state beyond polarities is a transitional state between presence and absence. One has stepped into the beyond, but not yet moved fully to the 'other side'.

the transcendental state

In her first entry into the absolute, the soul reaches unconditional absorption in the beyond through the gateway of being. Her consciousness, however, still remains outside the absolute. The transcendental state can be seen as the second entry into the absolute, for here the consciousness of the soul, her I am in the mind, shifts into the dimension of absence. The mind, ego and sense of separate identity are uprooted so that the soul, as pure me, can move freely into the divine realm.

There is still a long journey between the initial shift to the transcendental state and its complete realization. The shift into the realm of absence is not transcendence itself — it is merely the initiation of the complex process of ego dissolution through which the soul gradually renounces her human personality and surrenders her existence to the beyond. In order to reach transcendence, the soul must fully extract her true identity from the construct of her subconscious me.

Only then does she have enough force to cross over into the realm of absence with her whole existence and re-embody her original state.

The transcendental state is the ultimate frontier of our human expansion into the inner plane — the final portal through which we pass to liberation. Yet, as mere abidance here can divert us from our ultimate goal, it can also be seen as the last barrier. In the transcendental state, the soul reaches her deepest absorption in the beyond, but the human is still bound to the earth; he maintains his grip on the soul, blocking her complete release from the dimension of forgetfulness.

samadhi: the state of surrender

Prior to realizing the true goal of the transcendental state — liberation — the relative me of the soul has not yet merged, and continues to exist as a separate entity within our consciousness. To fully embody the transcendental state, one has to reach the supreme state of surrender, samadhi. The state of surrender transcends all states, as here not only awareness but our very me becomes absorbed in the realm of absence. Samadhi is a unity of being and non-being, the consciousness of the now and the void of the beyond, I am and the absolute. It is an exalted union of the two primary aspects of soul-realization — complete awakening and ultimate surrender. Culminating the process of the soul's re-absorption into reality is the unconditional fusion of her me with the heart of the beloved. Samadhi is the true foundation of our liberation from separate consciousness, the ground of our dissolution into the source of creation.

liberation

Liberation is the ultimate fruit of samadhi: the very merging of the personality with the soul. It is the total dissolution of the I-construct in the mind. Far more than the attainment of another, deeper energetic state, it is our radical transcendence of illusion and the end of incarnations — the state of no-return. Liberation is the end of the process of the soul's transcendence, for here she fully exits the plane of the forgotten self at last. Emancipated from her human identity and earthly consciousness, the soul returns to the abode of universal intelligence and, from the depths of original absence, reclaims the light of her primordial presence.

the measure of evolution

It must be noted that one's level of evolution cannot simply be seen as a linear progression through various states of inner expansion. The inner state is merely the internal space requisite for the awakening of the soul. It is the consciousness that embodies the inner reality that is the true measure of the evolutionary value of any awakened state. Hence, someone with a profoundly realized state of presence may in fact be more conscious and evolved than someone abiding in the absolute state. It is not what has been attained that matters most, but *who* has attained it. This 'who' is the quality of our consciousness and intelligence, the existential depth of our very soul, the subject of all stages of awakening.

evolution into wholeness

The map of awakening we have described applies strictly to the internal evolution of the soul. The purpose of evolution, however, is not only to reach self-realization, but to become whole, which must also include completion in the human dimension. Far from being an escape from the difficulties of human life, the way to wholeness involves the completion of many aspects of our human existence: purification of the subconscious mind, emotional healing, psychological maturation, the development of a harmonious connection with the world, the fulfillment of core desires and the ending of karma.

Purification and healing are essential in order to release the burden of the past, and accompany the entire course of our inner awakening. These extremely delicate processes cannot be completed by willpower alone; one has to be in touch with the light of the soul and open to the dimension of grace. Only the creator of the soul can fully transform and ultimately remove the many layers of subconscious tendencies, blocked energies and emotional wounds that exist within us. Still, each soul does have the capacity to develop ways to deal with those areas of her existence that are incomplete. She must take responsibility for her own growth, facing all the suppressed, unconscious and immature areas of both her internal and external reality with courage and wisdom. By exercising her free will and cultivating qualities that reflect a dignity of intelligence, true sincerity, purity of intention and honesty, she prepares the ground to receive assistance from the beyond.

As the weight of the past gradually lifts and we continue to evolve through further life experiences, the soul gathers enough internal space for her intelligence and emotional body to reach the necessary degree of maturity and fulfillment in the human dimension. To arrive at this relative psychological completion is imperative for any seeker on the path. Only when she has been freed from the grip of her human identity and the pull of earthly existence can the soul fully expand into her potential and become her eternal self once again.

The psychological evolution of the human and the internal evolution of the soul are mutually supportive along the path. To reach psychological completion as a human, one must awaken the states beyond the mind and the soul, and for the soul to expand into the beyond, one must reach a deep sense of completion in one's human life. Only a human who is over and done with the earthly dimension is ready to experience the freedom of the soul; and only when the soul is free can she embody an awakened human existence.

17

pitfalls on the path

Whenever there is a progression towards light and truth, opposing forces and energies will naturally be present. In the dimension of forgetfulness, we are constantly being diverted as we move towards truth, pulled by forces of unconsciousness that would hamper or even jeopardize our awakening. A seeker should thus be aware of numerous pitfalls that may await him on the path.

Although they can indeed threaten our progress, these obstacles are not inherently negative, for moving through and beyond them is a natural part of the maturation of our intelligence and consciousness. There are countless types of pitfalls, but we can regard them as falling into three primary domains — understanding, practice and ego.

understanding in action

Sadly, the vast majority of seekers get spiritually stuck the moment they step onto the inner path. This is due to either their ignorance, or to the fact that they follow teachings that present a shallow vision of spirituality and enlightenment. They perform all sorts of practices in the name of self-realization, but get no closer to truth. True understanding is essential to avoid such stagnation. One has to enquire into the essence of spirituality as well as investigate the complex science of spiritual evolution as embodied in high teachings. Only in this way can a seeker discover the real purpose and significance of the path. True understanding of the inner dimension is a flowering of our intelligence and spiritual intuition, and reflects our maturity and sensitivity to the inner realm.

Spiritual practice is understanding in action based on the science of the inner states. At the heart of true practice lies insight into the nature of pure subjectivity — awakening to I am — the primary means through which a seeker cultivates the subtle art of becoming increasingly established in the realm of the self.

18

In order to experience real progress, one has to focus in a precise manner on the particular dimension of expansion that corresponds to one's present level of evolutionary development. Unless we have a clear understanding of the state we are in, there is a danger that we will miss the intermediate steps of awakening necessary to bridge us with the far deeper levels of realization we are capable of reaching. If we try to move too quickly, our efforts will bear no fruit, for we cannot reach depths that we have no means to access. For instance, to aim at the dissolution of self or the actualization of oneness prior to first establishing the state of presence would be a misguided effort, for without a continuity of pure awareness, practices of surrender only result in even deeper unconsciousness. The inner work is progressive in nature; each phase of expansion must become stable and permanent so that it can serve as a solid foundation for the ensuing awakening.

The inner realm is such an unknown land, that without the proper conceptual tools and guidance, one is simply unable to navigate the process of expanding into and within it. The ability to correctly identify what is still incomplete in oneself, and to recognize the next step to be taken, reflects a well-refined attunement to the natural evolution of the soul towards her wholeness. In the absence of this inner clarity, one must receive support from a competent teacher.

errors in the verification of attainment

There are three common problems in the evaluation of one's inner realization: first, one may mistakenly believe that one has arrived at an awakened state when none whatsoever has been reached; second, one may have arrived at an awakened state, yet due to a lack of sensitivity, be unable to register it; and third, having experienced a real awakening, one may not grasp its true nature and significance due to the fact that intelligence has not yet integrated with the newly awakened state. We find the first problem to be the most common.

Many seekers abandon the inner work altogether having arrived at only a superficial spiritual realization. This is especially true in the case of those who follow the simplistic paradigm of sudden awakening or believe that in order to reach enlightenment it is sufficient to have a purely intellectual insight into the nature of reality. Premature claims of enlightenment often lead to false spiritual confidence or even arrogance. To be caught in the delusion that one has reached enlightenment when one has not, only wastes the evolutionary energy one has already accumulated, and can easily block one's further evolution.

attachment to conceptual understanding

Right understanding is a bridge between the plane of unconsciousness and the true reality. Superior concepts are not merely intellectual metaphors — they resonate with the energy of the truth they represent. Conceptual understanding of ideals such as 'self', 'oneness' or 'enlightenment' can even inspire us to initiate the spiritual search. Still, there is always a danger that by becoming overly attached to intellectual ideas we will find ourselves living in a virtual reality of mental constructs that actually separates us from reality as it is. Concepts are only representations of reality in the mind; reality itself is non-conceptual.

One can become convinced that 'there is no self' or 'there is only the self' and actually mentally experience existence as such, yet still not be established in any state beyond the mind, as ignorant to one's true self as ever. This is the case of a false, intellectual 'enlightenment', in which one has been programmed to perceive reality in an 'enlightened' way through pseudo-sophisticated ideas and spiritual slogans.

True understanding is a direct and pure knowing of reality that reflects the soul's blueprint and unique angle of perception. It is not a product of personal knowledge, ideas or philosophies, but an expression of the wisdom of universal intelligence seeing the truth of creation and evolution through the eyes of an awakened soul.

evolutionary imbalance

One of the most serious pitfalls on the path is an imbalance between one's inner and outer evolution. Some misguided seekers suppress their psychological issues, fears and natural desires in the name of the quest for enlightenment. They see their outer reality as a threat to inner peace and stillness, and neglect their emotional development by spending too much time in meditation and solitude. If one becomes overly attached to the peace and calm of meditation, or spends excessive amounts of time alone, one tends to develop an unhealthy fear of the world, with its many challenges and distractions. The completion of the human personality requires that we engage in a well-balanced relationship with the world, for one can never be truly whole without psychological stability and emotional maturity.

In addition to becoming imbalanced in our relationship with the world and our human existence, we can also develop imbalances in our internal growth towards the self by becoming too extreme or one-sided in our practice. For instance, some over-crystallize awareness and neglect the expansion into being, while others deepen being but fail to address the work with awareness. Perhaps the most common imbalance we come across is a disproportionate development between the mind and heart. On one side, many on the path of love disregard the evolution of their intelligence and awareness and become trapped in emotional states devoid of clarity and inner stability; on the other, those who strictly follow the path of awareness and understanding tend to repress their sensitivity and, in consequence, remain alienated from their divine essence. To become integrated and whole, one has to follow the principle of harmonious evolution and possess a complete and holistic vision of oneself.

the snare of ego

Due to their simplistic nature, traditional models of enlightenment do not offer sufficient conceptual protection against the menace of ego. Because enlightenment is commonly misunderstood as occurring through the annihilation of the ego, it is assumed that after awakening, no challenges on the level of our ego-identity remain. However, even though the supreme goal of evolution is transcendence of the mind and personality, the ego cannot be entirely dropped before our final liberation. Rather, the ego, as the intelligence of our relative consciousness, naturally accompanies us through each stage of our growth, witnessing the awakening of the inner states, consciousness, intelligence and the heart. In actuality, its purified presence supports our internal awakening.

The nature of ego is twofold. The aspect of ego that surrenders to the soul's intent is in fact the very energy that the soul uses for her evolution towards light. However, as long as the ego is lost in the past and holds on to its ignorance, it inevitably hinders our evolution by continuing to rule our consciousness as host. Most seekers, irrespective of their relative awakening, experience the ego, or false me, as their center of identity. They are egos, not yet souls. Prior to soul-realization, the ego claims awakening, believing that *it* owns the inner state and the knowledge of I am. As it matures in its evolution, it begins to recognize that it was originally created to serve our awakening, and that its final destiny is to surrender itself to the soul. However, until the ego has been sufficiently cleansed with the light of higher intelligence, it will resist its own dissolution. Even after realizing its own unreality, it will continue to return through the back door to assert supremacy. This is the point where one usually proclaims: "I am enlightened!", "I am a master!", "I have reached...", "I... I... I..."

Until the mind surrenders, we remain vulnerable to the ego's impure tendencies. In the initial stages of its inner quest, the ego's immaturity leads it to treat spirituality as a playground for its basic emotions. It uses spiritual practice to wallow in feelings of self-pity, lack of self-worth, guilt and shame; or alternately, to inflate itself with pride, arrogance and competitiveness. The spiritual ego is in fact quite worldly. Entering the path has not changed its basic neurotic nature, only the sphere of its activities. Now, instead of wanting fame or fortune, it wants to reach god or attain enlightenment. In both cases we encounter the same bogus ego displaying its vanity.

In its madness, the ego constantly seeks ways to sneak into spiritual territory. It tries to make itself special in one way or another by taking on 'spiritual' roles — holy man, rebel, eccentric, even redeemer. The idea of being holy may appeal to the ego because it craves respect, if not from others, at least from itself. Or perhaps it is more attracted to rebelliousness and prefers the role of an unholy character, enjoying the chance to show off how original it is. Maybe it wishes to become a healer or great master, for it finds the idea of helping others exciting. It might even believe that it has a unique role to play on earth and has been chosen for great things. But perhaps the most insidious way that the ego can assert itself is by assuming a stance of humility and devotion to magnify a false sense of piety. No matter what role the ego chooses to play, its performances are no more than pitiful attempts to maintain its fundamentally empty identity.

The more conscious we become, the more cautious we must be, for the ego's games become increasingly sophisticated as we evolve. Letting go of the ego is not only the final goal of the inner path, but an unremitting act of becoming real inside. As cunning as it is, the ego ultimately has no way to succeed in manipulating the spiritual path for its own purposes. Sooner or later it must relinquish itself at the altar of our original self, for it has no essential reality — it does not exist apart from the illusory image it projects.

misconceptions of enlightenment

Not all teachings point to the highest truth, just as not all seekers seek the highest knowledge and realization. Traditions of enlightenment reveal varying levels of understanding, as they reflect the particular intelligence and capacity of their founders. If we seek complete clarity and illumination, we must exercise caution as we explore the many existing interpretations of enlightenment. To cut through naïve views, spiritual clichés, and false ideas, we need to sharpen our intelligence, develop true understanding and pass through the fire of necessary experiences.

Below we explore the major misconceptions of enlightenment in relation to their four sources: preconceived notions, a philosophical basis of a teaching that inaccurately reflects reality, an incomplete vision of the path, and oversimplifications of enlightenment. Although inextricably tied to one another, we draw the distinction between these issues for the sake of making a clear presentation.

Preconceived notions: One can argue that objective truth does not exist at all; that what we call 'truth' is only a matter of subjective perspective and interpretation. On some level this is indeed correct, since our universe is composed of innumerable interpenetrating viewpoints and angles of perception. However, the more we evolve, the closer we come to universal intelligence and understanding, and the higher our standard for truth becomes. When we speak about truth in this context, we are pointing to the understanding that serves our particular soul so that she may realize wholeness and fulfill her destiny.

Enlightenment is by definition a complete absence of personal interpretation and mind-based perception. Nevertheless, to reach it, we must possess a sound conceptual knowledge of the evolutionary process. Whether the philosophical tenets of a particular tradition can support our evolution towards enlightenment depends not only on their legitimacy, but also on our ability to discern whether the truths they contain are absolute or obsolete. For this reason, throughout this book we analyze a variety of different views of spiritual evolution and address some of the most common misconceptions they propagate which, taken as truth, can easily confuse a seeker on the path to wholeness.

Our primary concern here is not to debate conceptual theories of reality, but to address those perspectives that can have a practical impact on the nature of our realization. It is irrelevant whether a spiritual tradition labels the ultimate reality as 'no-self', 'self' or 'neither self nor no-self', for it is the same reality being pointed to, only through different means. This is not to say that how we perceive certain concepts is unimportant; in fact, it very often determines the core energy of our approach to the path, thus affecting the depth of our enlightenment.

The problem arises when we unimaginatively cling to preconceived notions of reality, for in so doing we run the risk of missing the objective truth of our evolutionary purpose. For instance, if our spiritual vision is conditioned by the concept of emptiness, the very notion itself can prevent us from realizing the soul, because our insight into reality is bound to bypass the essence of our pure subjectivity. If we believe that the ego is non-existent and refuse to see its significance in the evolution of our intelligence towards human completion, we are likely to fall into spiritual denial and remain unwhole, for we have not embraced an essential part of ourselves. Or, if our realization of the ultimate reality is limited to non-identification and non-suffering, we will stagnate in a partial awakening to impersonality and fail to get in touch with the divine aspect of the absolute existence. If we assume that we can reach liberation and wholeness through devotion alone and refuse to take responsibility for doing the inner work, we will miss the opportunity to engage the vital qualities of human will, discrimination and discipline.

Preconceived notions about the path affect not only the nature of our experience, but can also lead us to misperceive our attainments. For example, having realized the state of presence, an adept following a tradition that regards awareness as the ultimate attainment may falsely believe that he has reached his destination, while he in fact remains stuck in a horizontal expansion of consciousness, unaware of the need to merge with the source of the now. Similarly, a seeker who arrives at the state of being, but lacks any concept of wholeness and multidimensional evolution, may naïvely interpret his shallow realization as the final goal. Due to an imbalanced identification with the universal, one who is strongly influenced by non-dualism may reach the state of transcendence and realize himself on the energy level, yet still not know who he is as a soul. All of these examples show us that despite having positive inner experiences and even true awakening, we can fail to perceive them correctly.

We must be mindful that insensitive readings of existing concepts can easily distort our vision of the path. Two different seekers who have arrived at the non-conceptual state may in fact abide in two entirely different realities. To reach a non-conceptual condition represents only one aspect of spiritual realization; it does not presuppose enlightenment.

A philosophical basis that fails to reflect reality: Some of the most common misconceptions on the spiritual scene relate to notions about the nature of the universal self, the soul, and the role of ego. Traditions of non-dualism in particular offer an impersonal interpretation of reality that tends to negate not only our ego-identity, but also our individual soul. In their desire to express the truth of universality, they overlook the significance of our sacred individuality. Rigidly applying the idea of non-duality, they miss one of the defining features of reality — the dynamic interplay of truth and consciousness between the individual and the universal. Enlightenment is perceived as no more than the removal of the false self, when in fact, experiential clarity reveals that it cannot exist without the individual, who must not only transcend his own ignorance, but whose presence is necessary to actually experience the state of truth.

We may wonder why extraordinarily deep teachings of non-duality founded by seers of the highest order have repudiated the existence of a personal essence. It is not that the conclusions of these masters sprang from incomplete realizations, but rather that their perceptions of reality were conditioned to express their experiences in a purely impersonal way. The traditions we are referring to were created in times when humanity was not yet ripe enough to embrace the consciousness of the soul. They may have been revolutionary in their time, but from the viewpoint of the now, their spiritual vision is outdated. At its conception, any new tradition of enlightenment naturally reflects the unconscious evolutionary needs of the contemporary collective mind; otherwise it is rejected and forgotten. It is in fact the will of the divine cause to express truth at a level in accordance with the evolutionary capacity of humanity at any particular stage of its development.

Traditions of the past were not designed to reveal the subtle dimension of the soul; their objective was the strict realization of impersonal peace and freedom. Their teachings were not incorrect, only incomplete — and not in their time, but from the present perspective of the expanded potential of human consciousness. Even though enlightenment is a timeless realization pointing to the changeless principle of the absolute reality, insight into that reality eternally evolves as the subject of illumination becomes increasingly whole. Ancient questions about our true identity and the nature of self have to be revisited in order to unravel the ultimate mystery of me within.

An incomplete vision of the path: Teachings that do not point to the dimension of pure subjectivity in a clear way fail to offer a tangible link between practice and realization. The idealistic vision of enlightenment prevalent today appears so abstract — so remote and incredible — that even the most sincere seekers easily become lost in the jungle of their practices, unable to cut through ignorance.

There are teachings that *do* point to the essence, but because they ignore the complexity of gradual evolution towards deeper states of awakening, we consider them to be one-dimensional oversimplifications of the path. Even traditions that acknowledge the need for gradual evolution are difficult for seekers to relate to experientially, due to their ambiguous terminology and imprecise descriptions of the various levels of realization.

In addition to a clear explanation of sudden versus gradual awakening, a teaching must also present a balanced vision of the relationship between practice and grace. Some teachings emphasize the important role of grace in awakening, but offer no intelligent connection between one's personal effort and the possibility of receiving that grace. They create the illusion that enlightenment is merely the result of transformative forces descending from above, disregarding the importance of one's conscious cooperation in the evolutionary process.

The oversimplification of enlightenment: Oversimplification of the awakening process is a phenomenon particular to so-called 'sudden-enlightenment' schools. A seeker must be aware that although the term enlightenment describes the simple reality of the natural state, it also reflects the complex reality of our multidimensional awakening as realized through a long and arduous process that involves the actualization of many different aspects within our consciousness. Hoping to inspire awakening, teachers sometimes apply concepts that point directly to the ultimate reality, such as 'you are already that', 'there is nothing to attain', 'when the seeker is no more, the search is over', 'being is enlightenment' and 'all is consciousness'. These ideas can be useful teaching devices, but when taken as absolute truths or ends in themselves, they can warp a realistic vision of the spiritual path. If a student thoughtlessly identifies with the declaration of a non-dual teacher that 'everybody is already realized', without seeing its figurative character, he simply ends up confused.

The responsibility of an intelligent teacher is to precisely describe the nature of enlightenment and the complex reality of the path, and to dispel the various misconceptions and myths of self-realization. Although many of the simplistic statements about enlightenment popular on the spiritual scene carry some element of truth, they must be seen in relation to the path as a whole in order to prove constructive. Simplistic teachings that absolutize fragments of truth in the name of enlightenment do not promote true awakening, but in their lack of complete vision, keep indiscriminate seekers in ignorance.

the verification of attainment

We should not assume that a state of awakening is automatically self-evident to the one who has reached it. This may be so in the event of complete transcendence and liberation, but not before. Unless one possesses the necessary understanding of the spiritual realm and receives precise guidance from a competent teacher, it is quite easy to evaluate one's inner realization inaccurately.

To assess our awakening is challenging at any stage, but the more deeply we enter into the inner realm, the more difficult it is to precisely appraise the nature of our experience, for the inner territory becomes progressively more subtle and transparent. Initially, progress is measured by the level of our inner expansion; next, by the degree of the transformation and purification of the ego; and finally, by our transcendence and dissolution into totality.

There is always a chance that one may believe one has arrived at a particular stage of awakening when in fact there is no existential basis for such an assumption. One may confuse an experience of strong concentration for the state of presence, or imagine oneself to have reached the absolute state, mistaking a deep sense of being for the actual realization of the source. Expanding into a state of emptiness or boundless consciousness, a seeker may think that he has transcended, blind to the fact that his ego has neither been dissolved nor purified. Conversely, one may experience a real awakening, but disbelieve it, due to an inability to see it in the proper conceptual frame. For example, sincerely following a model of impersonal enlightenment, an adept who has shifted into one of the awakened states may doubt his attainment due to the continued experience of his relative personality, unaware that the presence of his ego does not negate his realization. All of these misinterpretations and their consequences can be avoided if one has a clear vision of the inner realm and sufficient understanding of the complex nature of multi-dimensional awakening and ego-transcendence.

We often come across seekers who presume that they have arrived at an enlightened state after having had an experience of a radical shift of consciousness, such as a sudden sense of oneness or a feeling of ecstatic union with the divine. How can they know the difference between what they believe they experience and what they actually experience in reality? How can they know if their shift into an altered state of consciousness has anything to do with enlightenment? What someone chooses to translate as a realization of oneness, or even enlightenment, may in fact be any one of numerous relative experiences that do not reflect an existentially valid or permanent state of awakening at all.

The fundamental cause of inaccuracies in self-assessment is the fluidity, generality, imprecision, and even inaccuracy of spiritual terminology. Terms like 'oneness', 'emptiness', 'self', 'cosmic consciousness' or 'absolute' have become clichés so packed with significance that the mind, unable to contain the potency of their true meaning, actually renders them meaningless. To make these terms more useful we must bring them into sharper focus so that a seeker can relate them to his experiential reality with clarity and precision. The teaching seeks to imbue these overused concepts with new relevance so that they can inspire, explain and verify any awakening experience. In this way, what were once abstract concepts become practical instruments of spiritual illumination.

In presenting a detailed conceptual model of the inner realm, describing the various stages of the awakening process step by step, and strongly emphasizing the importance of the processes of stabilization and integration, we offer indispensable tools for the verification of attainment. However, as we have pointed out, no matter how extensive our conceptual knowledge may be, extreme caution must be exercised in evaluating any type of inner realization. No amount of theoretical knowledge can completely safeguard us from

misinterpreting our spiritual state. For this reason, in addition to study-
ing the science of the inner states, we must also create a foundation of
inner experience through practice and develop our spiritual sensitivity,
intuition and discriminative wisdom. We are fortunate indeed if we are
also blessed with the assistance of a living spiritual guide.

realm of entry

In the dimension of forgetfulness, a human being lives fully locked within the claustrophobic walls of his psychological reality, his true nature veiled by mental states and emotional moods. He knows nothing beyond body and mind. He knows not reality. He knows not the way. The unreal is his domain. He lives in a dream state, tethered to the constant fluctuation of appearances, painfully disconnected from the unconditional refuge of the absolute principle. His desperate striving to find satisfaction and security in the realm of illusion only reinforces his self of separation and perpetuates his alienation from the source. Unless he starts to question the unreal and seek the real, he will find no way out of ignorance and no way into the consciousness of truth.

Beyond the turmoil of our phenomenal existence, beyond our insatiable search for happiness, lies hidden the great way, the inner way to our original state of wholeness and completion. Discovering the way, we finally realize the purpose of our creation and the meaning of our life on earth. Our true life as conscious existence dawns only the moment we awaken from the dream of the human mind and begin our journey into the heart of the self.

The great way is an opening in the plane of illusion through which the soul can return to a state of unity with the light, love and perfection of the god state. The great way is the inmost river of pure intelligence through which we journey into the infinite depth of universal subjectivity. It is the way of the self, by the self, through the self, to the self.

awakening to the way

The inner search begins in complete darkness. To enter the path is to take a risk on the level of our very existence, for initially we have no real way of knowing what we lack or what we seek — we are entering the unknown. No matter how much knowledge we gather, how much reassurance we receive from others, how much we are inspired by the teachings of great masters — until we awaken to the way we simply cannot know if there is any substantial reality behind the search for spiritual enlightenment.

Awakening to the spiritual path is not an expression of a conclusion reached by the linear mind, for the intellect is unable to fathom the truth of the inner dimension. It is an existential opening to the beyond, a major breakthrough in our evolution as a human being. We make the decision to enter the path from a place of higher wisdom — the intuitive realm of the soul, the timeless intelligence of our inner self.

the inner call

From a superficial standpoint, entering the inner path is a choice, a positive exercise of free will. But seen from a higher perspective, we actually have no choice. The spiritual path is the only antidote to the fragmented, unconscious and painfully ignorant state of human existence. To be imprisoned in the human mind in complete identification with the collective psyche defines spiritual amnesia and existential death. The mind may *think* that entry onto the path is elective, but the soul knows that the inner search is the only intelligent response to the indignity of unconsciousness.

The unconsciousness of each individual reflects the unconscious condition of humanity as a whole, and can be transcended only through the initiative of one who becomes conscious of his capacity to evolve beyond the collective mind. This shift in the perception of our purpose on earth emerges from the core of our primordial consciousness. We cannot enter the spiritual path unless we are summoned by our soul, called by a remembrance of our destiny arising from the innermost recesses of our being.

Although eternally present, the inner call is remembered and actualized in our conscious mind only when our spiritual intelligence is awakened. Spiritual intelligence — the highest kind of intelligence — is not mind-based, but rooted in our sensitivity to the realm of pure subjectivity. It is this silent wisdom of the self that allows us to recognize the call of the soul. Only our essence can hear the inner call and reveal the innate knowing of our evolutionary purpose.

the role of suffering

The experience of suffering can serve as a major stimulus in our search for transformation and freedom. While it is true that in the hierarchy of truth, suffering is inferior to the inner call as an incentive to awaken, it nonetheless can serve as a powerful motivational force.

Suffering is a fundamental characteristic of the earthly dimension. It does not occur exclusively during times of misfortune — it is the permanent shadow of the unawakened self. We may disagree, citing the example of those who appear to be content within the confines of their human existence. However, like most humans, these people just do not recognize their suffering. It is an existential condition so chronic in nature that their unawakened minds simply cannot detect it. The deep and pervasive anguish of true suffering can only be viewed from a conscious perspective. From this standpoint, it is obvious that most people who seem 'normal', or even 'happy', are only satisfied on the surface, and that humanity as a whole actually lives in a collective state of suffering due to its complete ignorance.

Existential suffering only becomes an issue when consciousness has matured enough to experience its condition as painful and dissatisfying. Awakening to the true root of this suffering represents a crisis of ego through which our mind begins to doubt the precon-

ceived vision of reality it has absorbed from the collective unconscious. It is this shocking recognition of our suffering that gives rise
to a sense of evolutionary emergency and compels us to seek a way
out of it. Seen in this way, suffering is in fact a passage between our
past bondage and future freedom. If not for suffering, in most cases
there would be no real incentive to break through the spiritual inertia
of the collective mind.

Suffering is also an important tool in the development of spiritual sensitivity. Existence uses suffering to awaken the recognition of
the gap between our present state and our potential. The existential
sense of discontent that comes from feeling our own incompleteness
awakens in us the need to realize our future self. The end of suffering
cannot be reached by abolishing the causes of our anguish, since they
are infinite; it can only be achieved through expansion into spiritual
light and transcendence of the realm of illusion.

longing for light

When the inner call is recognized, it naturally gives rise to spiritual
longing. To evolve to the point where we can identify our longing
for the self is itself a sign of awakening, because it indicates that we
have matured enough to rebel against our fundamental unconsciousness. A profound thirst for spiritual fulfillment has been activated —
a thirst not of the earth-plane, but of the beyond.

This dimension has been designed to veil the true reality and
seduce the soul into a state of forgetfulness. All our thoughts, con-
cerns, disturbed emotions and infinite desires are actually the tenta-
cles of lower intelligence holding us captive in the plane of ignorance.
We begin our spiritual journey in this darkness and gradually move
towards light. Even though our inner longing initially lacks clarity, it
sets in motion our future split from the realm of forgetfulness.

The light of the self has a magnetic force that naturally pulls
all souls to its source; however, it is our yearning and our yielding
to that light that make the miracle of illumination possible. In its

nascent stages, our inner yearning is vague and fragile, and can easily be disturbed, if not obliterated, by the forces of ignorance. Only
with practice, guidance and the passage of time, can this spark of
spiritual intuition be transformed into the light of clarity, true understanding and unbroken certainty.

conscious seeking

There is often a significant gap between the awakening of inner longing and the conscious commencement of the spiritual journey. Even
after longing arises, most seekers grope around in darkness for pro-
longed periods of time, with no clarity whatsoever about the nature
of their search. Such is the sad truth revealed by a careful examination of today's spiritual environment. Spiritual seeking seems to
have become just one more expression of the collective unconscious.

Most seekers are inauthentic and fragmented, lost in pursuit of
an *idea* of enlightenment that lacks any connection to the reality of I
am. Locked in the unconscious mind, they seek in a fantasy world,
totally unable to relate their quest to the truth of the self. Unconscious
seeking is one of many ways that the real meaning of the spiritual
path is distorted by the collective mind. Seeking that is not anchored
in a connection to our essential nature is simply another expression
of ignorance, and has no relevance to the soul's purpose.

What does it mean to begin the inner search in a truly conscious
way? The heart of conscious seeking is the deep recollection of the
fundamental truth that enlightenment signifies our return to the state
of pure subjectivity. Conscious seeking by its very nature must point
directly to the essence of consciousness, the light of I am.

meeting a spiritual guide

For many seekers, the spiritual search is equivalent to finding a master.
The true purpose of the inner search, however, is not to seek a master
to surrender oneself to, but to seek oneself. To seek an outer master
without being in touch with the essence of the path is no more than an

attempt to avoid taking responsibility for one's own awakening. It is the self that is the supreme master — and this master is within, not without.

While it is true that the spiritual search essentially takes place in our aloneness, we very often do need the support of a spiritual friend. Our progress rests on our ability to intelligently balance receptivity with self-reliance, vigilantly avoiding overdependence on a teacher at one extreme, and willful independence at the other. An intelligent seeker is never closed to receiving help and guidance, because he clearly recognizes what a great blessing it is to meet a true teacher in human form. Those who believe that they do not need a guide are most often caught in idealistic or naïve notions of enlightenment, or have an overblown sense of self-importance.

A spiritual friend is an experienced guide who has already traversed the inner territory of the unknown and embodies self-realization. Because he holds the secrets of the path and the key to the inner realm in the very molecules of his being and consciousness, he not only has the power to transmit conceptual understanding of the path, but also the ability to energetically initiate the soul of a seeker with the seeds of awakening.

A student should not relate to his teacher through energies of unconscious devotion or imbalanced surrender, for they distort the reality of the inner work with spiritual projections. It is important to bear in mind that such a relationship is not personal, but takes place on the inner plane of truth and light. Still, a sense of sacredness, respect and gratitude should pervade the connection to a spiritual guide. What matters most is that one possess a natural openness to learn from someone who has completed the path, or a large portion of it.

Most seekers find it extremely difficult to discern whether a particular teacher is genuine and offers the necessary tools of awakening. Although open-mindedness is essential in the search for a guide, we must also be judicious. The clearest indicator of whether or not we are receiving the proper guidance is our progress, or lack of it. It is through our own awakening that we gradually develop trust and confidence in a teacher.

realm of entry

The manifestation of a spiritual guide on our path is the natural response of existence to our passion for truth and our dedication to the inner work. Our depth of aspiration, intensity of longing, capacity of intelligence and purity of intention are the factors that determine the quality of the spiritual guide who comes our way.

the true seeker

If the spiritual search begins within the state of ignorance, how can it possibly yield truth? How can reality emerge from illusion?

The pre-cognition of our spiritual purpose is a revelation that arises from the encoded knowing inherent to our original nature. To be in touch with this knowing is in fact what makes one a true seeker. In the absence of this sensitivity, our whole perception of the path is disconnected from any existential or evolutionary truth. The authenticity of a true seeker is reflected in the depth of his connection to the light of the soul; he seeks from the soul, not the mind. That which gives reality to his inner quest is the presence of his higher being, which, even prior to the actualization of his awakening, eternally knows the goal of his evolution. To begin the search for truth, we must feel its essence within our existence. Unless the one who begins the inner journey is in touch with the realm of I am, all efforts to awaken will be futile.

becoming a seeker

To become a seeker is to begin serving the light by taking responsibility for the realization of one's evolutionary purpose. It is to use all of the resources given to us by existence — the mind, heart, intelligence, and the powers of energy and will — to penetrate and ultimately transcend the thick veil of ignorance. For a true seeker, not a single moment passes that the inner work is not in progress. His life is completely dedicated to that which is real, and to renouncing, with courage and complete attention, that which is false. To become a seeker is to acquire a new identity — not of the ego, but of the soul. It is not just one of the many roles that we play in our life or something we do in our free time, but our very reason to live.

Awakening is the call and command of each individual soul, but it has universal implications as well. Our inner quest is not merely a personal affair with spirituality, but part of a much greater plan of universal evolution. Anyone who does not move towards the light actually hinders the universal expansion of consciousness; our individual contribution as a conscious seeker serves the universal movement into the fathomless wisdom and mystery of the creator's supreme presence.

the essential qualities of a seeker

To seek is the most challenging endeavor in human existence. While striving for illumination, not only do we have to face the challenge of cutting through innumerable layers of our own unconsciousness, we must also cope with the complexities of living in the world and the ignorance of the collective mind. Last, but certainly not least, we must face our personal psychological issues and often conflicting desires and fears. In order to meet these challenges and ultimately realize our higher being, it is critical that we develop certain essential qualities:

Sincerity: Sincerity is truthfulness to oneself and others. It expresses our purity of intention and the deep honesty of the soul. Sincerity is the only true remedy against the ego's games and manipulations, and can be seen as the virtue that connects our human identity with the integrity of the soul. When there is a lack of sincerity, the ego becomes arrogant and succumbs to the impurities of the mind. The presence of sincerity proves that the soul has already purified the mind and heart to a significant degree.

Self-awareness: Self-awareness is the aspect of sincerity that guards against self-deception. A typical example of self-deception can be seen in a seeker who pursues the path of renunciation while still having significant desires to fulfill. Such a radical approach is entirely inappropriate, even counterproductive. Lacking self-awareness, the seeker mistakes his willingness to make sacrifices for what he believes to be a superior way of life for true readiness to transcend his human existence. In another classic scenario, a seeker deceives himself by intellectually indulging in spiritual matters, while refusing to actually do the inner work. He believes himself to be 'spiritual', but lacks the honesty and integrity to face his own fragmented state of being.

Maturity: The level of maturity of a seeker can be seen as the measure of his evolution through many lifetimes. One of the clearest indicators of spiritual maturity is the ability to take responsibility for the realization of one's own spiritual potential. Another is the capacity to discriminate between one's lower and higher nature, and serve the latter. However the keystone of maturity is the sensitivity through which one identifies the dimension of pure subjectivity, the state of I am, as the essence of the path.

Inner strength: There can be no true progress on the spiritual path unless one has the necessary inner strength. Inner strength is the power of will we call upon to prevail over the major obstacles on the path. Without it, we cannot transcend the darkness of unconsciousness and overcome the hindrance of the mind. Furthermore, inner strength is absolutely crucial in order to be able to hold to our own truth in the face of the collective ignorance. A seeker must be completely dedicated to the inner work — like a warrior — courageous and one-pointed in following that which is real.

Patience: Because the evolution of consciousness takes many turns and progress is mostly gradual, a great deal of patience is required as we tread the inner path. Patience can be seen as an aspect of inner discipline, an opposing force to our subconscious tendencies. Essential to meditation, patience pacifies frustration, restlessness and mental agitation. We cannot cultivate the inner state without the endurance and inner softness of complete patience. Patience develops from the growth of our humility, spiritual maturity and trust in our perception of the path.

Determination: To grow on the path and persevere in the face of difficulties, one must have steadfast determination. Determination is founded on the awakening to one's evolutionary purpose; it is total conviction in the truth of the inner work. When one sees that there is no choice but to walk the path, regardless of the many obstacles, one unwaveringly persists with the work of awakening.

Discriminative wisdom: Most seekers remain half-asleep, functioning in a semi-conscious state, not making an effort to truly *understand*. Through the evolution of intelligence we begin to comprehend the significance of the path and the truth of enlightenment. Born of spiritual intelligence, discriminative wisdom enables us to discern not only that which is true, but also that which is false, guarding us against various pitfalls on the path.

Sensitivity to the realm of I am: Sensitivity to the realm of I am, the dimension of pure subjectivity, is the very marrow of a true seeker. Unfortunately, sensitivity to the realm of I am is the quality most lacking among the majority of seekers. Unless one can recognize I am as the fundamental nature of the spiritual dimension, one will compulsively cling to the objective side of reality.

The ability to meet oneself: The ability to meet oneself is a complementary quality to sensitivity to the realm of I am. Many seekers are lost in artificial forms of self-enquiry, unable to touch the core of their existence. Their difficulty lies not in an inability to awaken the inner state, but in the fact that they lack the maturity required to meet their souls. The ability to meet oneself is either an expression of wisdom acquired from past evolution or the result of present awakening. However, even if we lack this maturity, spiritual inertia is not justified, for awakening is ultimately a function of the present. How can we mature without sincerely facing the challenge of awakening in this very now?

Due to the intangible nature of the spiritual search, even if we intuitively recognize the essence of the way, we cannot truly know our final destination. Like a seed that cannot foresee its future destiny as a tree, a seeker entering the path cannot grasp his ultimate goal. Only by possessing the virtues we have described here can we persevere in the face of the unknown and unravel our final destiny.

commitment to the path

It is better not to begin the spiritual journey if we are not ready to complete it — better not to open the wound of unconsciousness if we are not determined to heal it fully. Many seekers give up their search having reached only a partial awakening. Some prematurely assume the role of teachers, while others simply idle, believing there is nowhere further to go. Both are mistaken, for there is always more to be realized before becoming truly complete on all levels. Unless we harbor the deepest commitment to the path, we will lack the necessary strength and determination to accomplish our evolutionary purpose. It is our burning desire to understand and expand into light that inspires us to move forward in spite of all obstructing forces.

Commitment to the path is an absolute requirement for all seekers. It assures our steady progress and safeguards us from relinquishing the inner work prematurely. Among the many temptations that can lead us to abandon the path are errors in the verification of attainment, a sense of stagnation, lack of progress, the inability to recognize the next step, or an overwhelming sense of futility. One can become hopeless and lose inspiration, beset by doubts, or even succumb to the skepticism of the collective mind with its utterly unconscious perception of spirituality. Regardless of these and any other difficulties, one should never desert the inner work under any circumstances.

living the path

The inner work takes place at all times. It is not something that we announce to others or even speak about, but our silent secret beneath the apparent reality, the inner jewel we treasure above all else. The inner journey is not merely a means to reach a degree of inner awakening so that we can move on with our 'normal life'; it is unbroken enquiry into the nature of reality and continuous awakening to the reality of the now. Entering the path, we should be aware that we are embarking on an adventure for our whole lives and beyond.

Living the path is the very essence of our existence. Some may choose to live the path in the mode of renunciation; others, by actively participating in the world. But ultimately, living the path is beyond the polarity of being in the world or renouncing it. It is an eternal love affair with the light of the self — the very meaning of life itself.

clarity about the path

It is so easy to become entangled in erroneous concepts or an incorrect vision of the inner work, that to unravel the true meaning of the spiritual path from within the plane of unconsciousness is truly a supreme achievement. Unless our intelligence reaches a profound degree of clarity and true understanding, we will never arrive at our spiritual destination.

The evolution of intelligence remains the most mysterious facet of the soul's awakening, reflecting her very consciousness and the frequency of her light. We have to mature over many lifetimes before we reach a level of intelligence that mirrors the truth of our blueprint. Our quest for clarity precedes all other steps of our inner journey.

the spiritual goal

To uncover the nature of our spiritual goal, we must ask ourselves what it is that we are truly seeking. Unless we bring focus to our inner search, our path will lack strength and clear direction. How can we summon the recollection of our evolutionary purpose? How can we avoid living in an illusion of spiritual fantasies and expectations?

Through knowledge imparted by superior spiritual teachings, the help of a spiritual guide, and our own enquiry, we need to intuitively sense the direction and aim of our internal evolution. Upon entering the path, this can be a great challenge, because we are moving into entirely new territory. Our initial task, however, is not to uncover the final purpose of the path, but its essence. True recognition of why we follow the path directly coincides with this discovery.

The inner way is indeed the great unknown, but within its intangibility we can intuitively sense its silent core, the light of I am. The spiritual search is not the pursuit of an abstract idea of enlightenment, but of our very self. Only by looking within and diving into the stillness beyond thought can we awaken the inner potential through which the light of I am can be reestablished as the heart of our identity.

encountering a true teaching

A mature seeker entering the path should by all means take into account the experiences of those who have reached self-realization. Many generations of monks, sages and mystics have explored the inner realm, and their testimony is an invaluable resource of spiritual understanding. Unfortunately, the extremely varied and often contradictory visions of the inner path presented by different individuals and spiritual traditions can make the process of finding the correct teaching and guidance extremely confusing.

Despite the considerable effort great thinkers have made throughout the ages to try to prove the unity of all religions and spiritual schools, the irreconcilable differences that exist between them simply cannot be denied. They are at odds not only in the practices they recommend, but also in their philosophies and interpretations of spiritual illumination. No one has yet arrived at an interpretation of spiritual evolution that would be universally accepted.

This difficulty is compounded by the fact that the interpretation of spiritual truth is not only a matter of philosophy and belief, but also an expression of the evolutionary level and spiritual potential of the individual or group of souls that seeks to convey it. Although truth is universal, its perception and reception are by nature subjective, determined by the capacity and point of view of the consciousness into which it is assimilated. For this reason, we cannot simply declare the superiority of one tradition over another, for such judgment is relative.

What are the criteria for choosing the most suitable tradition and spiritual teaching? Most seekers choose according to their karmic predisposition. They feel an immediate sense of familiarity and recognition when they encounter a tradition known personally from past incarnations and naturally gravitate towards it. However, feeling a connection to a particular teaching does not always indicate that to follow that tradition is in one's best interest. Often the soul needs to break certain connections in order to learn new lessons and decondition herself from her karmic past. It may be that an association with a particular tradition or teaching is a temporary affair, meant only to be experienced for the sake of learning a specific lesson before moving on. One has to use a very deep and sensitive discrimination to be able to truly feel which spiritual teaching is the proper vehicle for one's inner journey.

Through our commitment to the path we serve the truth of universal evolution, not a single interpretation of the spiritual dimension channeled through a human belief system. A spiritual tradition remains just one of many vehicles we use to journey within on the path to the self. Complete understanding cannot be expounded by any one tradition for the simple reason that truth is beyond traditions. Truth belongs to universal intelligence, which oversees the whole of existence, and to the intrinsic knowledge of the soul's blueprint encoded in the consciousness of our higher being.

Finally, we should note that in general, the light of truth needs to be dispensed appropriately and absorbed gradually. For some seekers, excessively high doses of truth are indigestible, even destructive. When the level of truth administered surpasses one's capacity to receive it, it is either missed or misused. As truth is none other than the highest frequency of light and understanding, in order to safely receive it, the ground of our intelligence and consciousness has to be prepared as a suitable container.

recognizing the next step

The inner way is an unbroken continuity of evolution consisting of many separate steps and gradual progressions. However, since we cannot possibly have a panoramic view of the inner realm at the outset of our journey, our advancement depends upon the lucidity of our present state and our ability to recognize the next step. We can liken the inner journey to the ascension of a steep mountain: in order not to slip and fall we focus not on the summit, but on each individual step we need to take to reach it.

The ability to identify and take each next step of our inner journey is an outcome of our spiritual knowledge and a clear insight into where we are in our process. But because it is often impossible to identify one's exact or even approximate place on the path, the majority of seekers need a qualified teacher to verify their state and provide guidance and support.

As we move deeper into the inner realm, the vision of our evolutionary purpose becomes increasingly apparent and we grow more independent. Our personal intelligence gradually merges with the higher wisdom of the soul, who timelessly knows her final destiny and recollects all the steps of awakening as the natural landscape of her evolution and blueprint.

the role of doubt

No true understanding can be reached without first going through the fire of doubt. Doubting supports the development of clarity and in many instances protects us from pitfalls on the path. The function of doubt is particularly critical at the outset of our search when we are faced with a vast and varied array of spiritual teachings; we must exercise doubt as we weigh our options. An intelligent mind does not subscribe to a teaching indiscriminately, but investigates and considers it thoroughly before making a commitment. Only a dull mind blindly accepts a teaching.

Naïve and immature seekers routinely become victims of teachers with inadequate or even questionable qualifications. The price they pay is grave, for they can become spiritually stagnant for long periods or, worse yet, regress in their evolution. To assure our forward movement, we must remain alert and critical in our perception of the path. We are not suggesting that one should be resistant or closed. On the contrary, constructive doubt serves as an intelligent test of reality that leaves the door open to all possibilities in choosing both a spiritual teaching and a teacher. Although our capacity to verify a teacher's qualifications and recognize the quality of a teaching is restricted by the level of our own maturity, within our limitations, we absolutely must practice discrimination with the highest level of clarity, wisdom, intuition and simple common sense. Choosing the right teaching and teacher is of the utmost importance and often determines the course of our whole life.

If the absence of doubt is coupled with insincerity and arrogance, a dangerous kind of spiritual ego that blocks the evolution of the soul can easily develop. One has to honestly question one's intention, spiritual direction and inner experience. Only with the emergence of complete clarity can doubt be abandoned.

Although the role of doubt is essentially positive on the path, excessive doubting can undermine the inner work. Doubting can become an addiction based on fear, insecurity and the inability to discern between right and wrong. For this reason, we must keep the doubting mind in check so that doubts will not erode our basic trust in the path and our courage to enter the unknown.

the role of trust

When our doubt exceeds our trust and faith in the path, we lose our spiritual force — we feel helpless and powerless. Trust is the quality that channels the doubting mind in a positive direction and maintains the basic balance of our intelligence.

Trust must be founded upon clear discernment. We must not believe with blind faith, but recognize the truth of the direction we have taken. Our trust should be rooted in the intuition and wisdom of the heart, for not everything can be verified by the mind. The mind, in fact, very often proves quite limited in its ability to find the right way. To trust is to follow a sense of rightness into uncharted territory. This does not mean that we are one hundred percent certain of what we believe to be true. In fact, once we have reached a particular point of inner certainty, there is no longer any need for trust — we simply know.

Trust also serves as the foundation of the student-teacher relationship. It grows as a student gets confirmation from his inner experience of the accuracy of the guidance received. Trust in a teacher is the natural outcome of a student's progress. In the process of seeking out and committing to a teacher, the initial degree of trust should be based on a sense of the quality of the teacher's heart and being. One should not look for eloquence, charisma or 'spiritual' gestures. A student has to feel genuine light and truth behind the presence of a teacher, his pure intention and wisdom.

cutting through confusion

Just as doubt can be caused by confusion, confusion can be the outcome of unresolved doubt. If we are unable to transcend our confusion because we keep feeding it with doubts, we may experience a major crisis in our evolution. However, the presence of confusion, like the arising of doubt, is a natural aspect of the spiritual path. If a seeker never experiences confusion or doubt, it suggests a serious lack of spiritual refinement and a gullible type of personality.

Confusion is a feeling of being lost, of lacking a clear sense of direction or satisfactory understanding of one's inner situation. It is not an enemy, but a challenge to be faced and overcome so that at a certain point the light of clarity can emerge. We need to accept confusion as an inevitable part of spiritual exploration, but also know how to break through it. To cut through confusion, we must call upon our passion for understanding, faith in the spiritual path and determination to see clearly.

There are two basic types of confusion: the natural and gentle kind of confusion that arises from the sheer impossibility of comprehending all the intricacies of the path, and the obstructive kind that arises from intellectual dullness and lack of imagination. It is the latter type of confusion we must be most wary of, for if it remains unresolved, it can seriously impede our spiritual progress.

Although the presence of confusion often serves as an incentive to strive for higher levels of understanding, we should never dwell on it or allow it to take root in our inner life. Confusion is fundamentally non-existent, and according to the law of reality, must eventually be dissolved by the light of truth and understanding. Sooner or later, a true seeker will triumph over any kind of confusion or doubt. He will *know*.

the role of practice

As we have pointed out, the conceptual models espoused by different traditions differ in their perception of the inner work. Some deny that to reach enlightenment is a process that requires effort; others emphasize the necessity for concentrated practice and meditation. In order to go beyond simplistic views and one-sided notions of self-realization, we must comprehend the complex nature of the laws governing the process of awakening. Only through critical examination and experiential knowledge can we grasp the reality of the spiritual path and embrace the sudden and gradual dimensions of enlightenment in holistic understanding.

the necessity of practice

We have already spoken about the need for clarity in understanding the basic principles of the path. We have also mentioned the importance of cultivating an enquiring mind and developing sensitivity to the realm of pure subjectivity. However, regardless of our level of inner preparedness and awakening, we are still certain to encounter numerous hindrances in our experience of the self on the level of its continuance, depth and purity. What we face here is the imperfection of our relative consciousness and our lack of inner integrity. Due to the gravitational force of unconsciousness — the primary obstacle in our ability to move beyond the mind and consistently uphold the light of I am — we simply cannot maintain that which we have awakened, nor can we establish its final depth. Before long we realize that without committed practice, even real experiences of awakening cannot bring us to a stable place within the inner realm. Only by seeing this clearly does our attitude towards practice become more humble and open.

Practice should be understood as an organic extension of understanding, self-knowledge and awakening. It should not be mechanical or based on exaggerated effort. It needs to be implemented in a very natural way so that concentration and other exertions initially necessary are eventually transmuted into an effortless flow of inner abidance.

The dynamics between effort and effortlessness should be carefully balanced according to the level of one's awakening and energetic expansion. For example, beginners cannot afford to be too relaxed and spontaneous, but must apply a great deal of mindfulness and discipline to skillfully deal with the disturbing nature of the mind and the strong pull of lower intelligence. As we evolve, our effort can become lighter and more transparent.

Although grace does play a vital role in our evolutionary progress, it does not diminish the necessity of the inner work. Practice manifests out of a deep command within the soul to use all means available to accelerate her spiritual enlightenment — it is an expression of our innermost collaboration with the divine will. If we fail to actively participate in our own evolution, how can we expect the divine to assist us? Waiting indolently for grace to do the inner work for us is an arrogant approach. It is no different than expecting water to spring from the ground without first digging a well. One needs to be ready to receive grace, and through conscious cooperation with one's evolution, to increasingly mature into that readiness.

the tools of the inner work

Across the vast spectrum of spiritual traditions, different methods and tools are offered as a means to reach inner awakening. However, in all mature schools of enlightenment, the heart of an adept's effort is the practice of meditation. Meditation, in the broadest sense of the term, denotes the effort of consciousness to maintain a focus on the self. For our meditation to be real, this internal concentration of energy and consciousness must be based on self-knowledge and a certain degree of awakening. We need to sensitively practice self-enquiry in order to turn consciousness back to its source; and for our awakened experience to deepen and become permanent, we need the regular internalization and concentration of energy and consciousness of sitting meditation.

The nature of the inner work changes as we focus on different areas of awakening: the work with awareness demands a great deal of concentration and mindfulness; the work with the heart is based on opening to sensitivity, prayer and the divine; the work with being is founded upon the art of letting go and the vertical expansion of energy; the work with the ego and the mind requires self-observation, non-identification and the cultivation of purity. Spiritual practice has to be applied intelligently, with both our potential and our limitations taken into consideration. Practice is not an end in itself, but a means to achieve a natural state, free of effort. The responsibility of a teacher is to prescribe a practice according to the specific needs of the student. The responsibility of the student is to understand the nature of that practice, and to recognize the point of its completion.

right effort

It is not enough to practice 'hard'. Practice has to be correct, and our effort has to be right. Practice that is not skillful can create the opposite of its desired effect — it can damage rather than help us. Unskillful practice is a serious problem on the spiritual scene that prevents many seekers from making real progress in spite of their sincere efforts. This is unfortunate, but an important lesson can be learned here: even our most genuine efforts go to waste when they are not founded on self-knowledge and real understanding. Lack of progress on the path and the suffering that results can be seen not only as a call to awaken, but also as a call to awaken from bad practice.

What is right effort? Right effort is a fluid response to both our general evolutionary needs, and the specific needs of the moment. Through right effort we are able to assist in the process of our own evolution in a highly effective and intelligent way.

We must be able to clearly see what we need to accomplish through practice and thereby determine the right effort to make. For instance, we apply self-remembrance in order to attain a continuity of presence, or we apply concentration to gain control over the mechanical mind. Only when we are clear about our target does our effort have the proper quality of energy and consciousness.

Right effort on the path directly coincides with our ability to meet our true self. It is an evolutionary movement towards our higher being rooted in the realm of pure subjectivity that reflects our optimal contribution to the awakening process.

realm of meditation

*Meditation is the way and the goal — the entrance to the inner realm
and the inner realm itself. It is both the state of objectless abidance
in the supreme reality and the self-contained presence of our true being.
In the plane of forgetfulness, meditation is the most powerful tool
we have to awaken our dormant self.*

*There are two gateways to the dimension of meditation: the inner gate of
the now through which we enter the pure subjectivity of universal I am,
and the gate of our individual essence through which we meet the pure
subjectivity of the soul. The first gate leads to the beyond; the second,
to the heart of our own existence. From the ultimate perspective, however,
there are not two gates, but one — upon entering the beyond we realize
our own soul, and upon awakening to our soul we merge with the beyond.*

an open secret

Meditation is an open secret. Its essence is hidden to those who are ignorant, but clear to those who have passed through the gateway to pure subjectivity. To meditate is to abide in reality, anchored in the ground of existence. It is a natural state of spiritual sanity and integrity. The path of meditation is not any particular way; it is the only way — the pathless path to the heart of the now.

the meaning of meditation

The common conception of meditation bears no relation whatsoever to knowledge of the inner realm. Most people incorrectly assume that meditation is a mind-based activity involving concentration upon mental, aural or physical phenomena. Pure meditation, however, is none of these performances — it is an entirely new dimension of existence and consciousness.

The original meaning of the term meditation was 'thinking about', suggesting some kind of conscious reflection, and did not refer to the reality beyond thought. To meditate was to use the power of the mind in a focused way to attain goals confined to the mental reality alone. To avoid associating meditation with deep thinking, some meditation masters used the term 'contemplation' instead of meditation. However, even the word contemplation, with its more mystical connotations, still points to the mental realm. To contemplate is to reflect upon religious, sacred or spiritual objects. The word contemplation, therefore, also imperfectly reflects the reality of pure meditation.

Unfortunately, because language has been created by the collective mind, which dwells exclusively in the reality of appearances, it cannot convey the essence of pure subjectivity. Consequently, throughout history, mystics and spiritual masters of various traditions have had to compromise, attributing uncommon meanings and explanations to common words, or otherwise inventing entirely new terms to try to communicate the true nature of meditation. So then, how to transmit the meaning of a completely new domain of being — the objectless realm of pure reality — to the ordinary mind, which itself cannot enter this reality? We have to go beyond words into silence to experience that to which all definitions and descriptions of meditation point: our very self.

sitting meditation

Meditation is a revolutionary withdrawal of the mind's energy from thought to pure awareness and being; it is total attention given to the source of the now. Because the force of ignorance is so strong, we have to use special means to shift the balance of power within our consciousness so that the state of meditation can manifest. Sitting in meditation is the basis of meditation practice, the sitting posture itself symbolizing our complete dedication to the inner state.

Sitting meditation has a profound impact on both body and mind, tuning our entire psychosomatic existence into the essence of our being. Through the practices of concentration and relaxation while sitting, we gradually establish ourselves in the state beyond the mind. The birth of the inner state signifies a quantum leap in our existence, and sitting meditation is the ground upon which this conversion takes place.

from illusion to reality

The paradox of meditation practice is that even though it points beyond thought, prior to our awakening it remains entirely confined to the mind. The one who begins to practice is in fact indistinguishable from the mind, for his essence lies dormant and his sense of self is completely identified with chaotic, compulsive thinking. How can that which is unreal, ignorant, false, and which itself must be transcended, attain reality? The saving grace of each meditator is his 'minimum soul', the trace of me that links him to the dimension of I am. This sense of me can be considered to be the minimum reality within the unreality of one's unconscious self. By empowering his subjective presence, crystallizing the observer and establishing his existence in the state prior to thought, an adept gradually moves his sense of identity from illusion to reality.

the practice of meditation

Before we can open to the state of meditation experientially, we need to face the fragmented condition of our mind — its restless and unconscious nature that blocks us from recognizing the heart of pure subjectivity. Meditation is an essential tool to integrate our mind with consciousness, solidify our presence, transcend mechanical thinking and move our existence into the inner state. Our work changes and evolves as we grow roots in the inner realm and become more aligned with the natural state of meditation. However, to enter the dimension of meditation in a real way and establish oneself in the realm of objectless consciousness, a beginner has to cultivate inner discipline and commit to formal practice.

Sitting: Although meditation ultimately transcends any bodily point of reference, to enter the state of pure subjectivity we must center our dispersed existence in the strict form of sitting meditation. We move beyond the body *through* the body, and therefore must respect the state of our energy and the condition of our physical form, for they greatly influence the ease of our entry into the inner realm.

Sitting meditation should be practiced by assuming a stable posture in which one sits elevated on a pillow to help keep the spine straight. If possible, one should sit with the legs crossed and the knees comfortably resting on the ground. If one is not supple enough to cross the legs in one of the variations of the lotus posture, one should seek another sitting position that assures an erect spine and physical stability. The placement of the hands and fingers in mudras bears little significance and thus is not indicated here. We should not concern ourselves with too many details, for they only burden our meditation with mental constructs.

63

As we gain more mastery in the art of meditation we need not follow the above recommendations literally, but can sit in meditation in any comfortable position, even on a chair. However, prior to becoming completely one with the state of meditation, formal sitting holds significant benefits. To sit with the legs crossed and spine erect instantaneously activates alertness, opens energy flow, generates inner strength, and offers solid, yet comfortable support for the physical body. The classical meditation posture exemplifies a perfect unity of relaxation and stability through which we can transcend bodily reference and enter the realm of being.

Time and length of meditation: There are no fixed rules regarding the length of each sitting, but in general, meditation should last up to one hour. One should certainly meditate daily, preferably in the morning and evening. Additionally, it is important to find time for a short meditation just before going to sleep in order to integrate the meditative consciousness with the subconscious mind.

Apart from daily practice, one must occasionally sit in the more concentrated form of silent meditation retreats in order to accumulate more energy to establish oneself in the inner state or deepen the state already present. A retreat can be done alone or in a group.

During retreat one should sit between six to eight hours a day, and between sitting sessions, practice walking meditation to move the body and energy, and further integrate meditation with activity. The duration of a retreat can vary according to one's internal needs, but a length of one, three, seven, ten or twenty-one days is particularly recommended.

Walking: Walking meditation is the first step in extending our meditative consciousness into daily life; it is meditation in action, or 'living' meditation. One can walk very slowly, quickly or just naturally. What counts is our internal concentration and ability to maintain the state we have reached during sitting meditation in activity. If one is unable to cultivate self-remembrance or abide in the inner state while walking, one should practice mindfulness of each step or conscious breathing. The deepest expression of walking meditation is an unconditional abidance in the state of pure subjectivity that transcends the polarities of sitting and walking, repose and action.

Breathing: A meditator has to know how to breathe. The way we breathe is a reflection of our consciousness, a direct manifestation of our physical, psychological and spiritual state of being. When we are lost in the mind and disconnected from inner peace and harmony, our breathing is shallow and limited to the chest. The more deeply we abide in our true nature, the deeper our breathing becomes. Correct breathing takes place from the lower belly and involves a complete exhalation.

To balance our breathing we must drop our existence into the depth of being and become one with the breath. Often a certain opening and healing of the diaphragm is necessary to unlock our breath, for this is the place in the body where we are most likely to unconsciously store tension, fear, anger, and power issues. When contracted, the diaphragm does not allow our belly to expand enough for us to inhale freely or exhale completely.

The first step in our work with the breath is usually the practice of conscious breathing through which we bring relaxed awareness to our body and sense of being. It is essential to do this in a natural and comfortable way, for if we are too self-conscious we will become tense. To bring true consciousness to the natural act of breathing, we surrender our awareness to the breath; we do not try to control it from the place of the observer. To transform our breathing we have to merge with the breath on the level of our consciousness and existence.

Eyes open or closed: It is a matter of preference whether we sit in meditation with our eyes open or closed. Since we tend to leak consciousness through the eyes and become distracted by visual signals from our surroundings, the most common approach is to keep the eyes closed. The advantage of having closed eyes is that we have more energy to focus inside. The disadvantage, especially for a beginner, is that we daydream or fall asleep more easily. Another possible drawback of meditating with closed eyes is that we can develop an addiction to various states of bliss or quietude and may begin to perceive the outer world as a threat to our own private peace. From this point of view we can say that to meditate with open eyes is on some level more 'real', and a positive safeguard against spiritual escapism.

Meditation with open eyes generates more alertness and enhances our ability to integrate our inner experience with the external world. But in the final analysis, closing the eyes for meditation is more logical, because our aim is to withdraw attention from the seen to the seer. Closing the eyes gives us more force to dive deeper inside and merge with the inner realm. If a meditator is unable to internalize his whole consciousness with his eyes open, he may become stuck on the surface of the now. In such a case it is best to close the eyes to generate more internal energy and establish the necessary depth of being. Alternating meditations with open and closed eyes can help maintain the balance between surrender to the inner state and the integration of that experience with consciousness of the outer world.

Ultimately, we should not restrict ourselves to a single approach, but remain flexible, adapting our practice to suit our present needs and natural tendencies. When we finally merge with the inner realm and begin to experience it as not separate from the outer realm, we realize that having the eyes open or closed actually makes no difference.

Directing attention: Our relative consciousness never ceases to grasp at objects, both external and internal. Due to this total instability, it is extremely difficult to experience real clarity and calm. The fundamental questions for a beginner in meditation, therefore, are how to cope with the commotion of the mind and where to direct attention.

The physical inactivity of sitting meditation can cause the mind to become even more disturbed and chaotic than usual. The mind cannot bear the stillness, and responds to it by compulsively populating the space of consciousness with endless thoughts. Any effort to control or repress this thinking only increases its intensity. Mind

cannot be conquered by mind. By developing one-pointed attention
we harness the mind's energy so that it can be channeled towards an
awakening to the non-referential state of being.

We can direct our attention in meditation in three ways: towards
the mind's activity, towards a single object of concentration, or
beyond both, towards our subjective essence. By directing our
attention towards the mind in vigilant self-observation we develop
disidentification, understanding and awareness; by paying one-
pointed attention to areas of our reality other than the mind, such as
breathing or bodily awareness, we develop concentration, calm and
mindfulness; by stepping directly out of the mind through the turning back of our attention to our true center, we radically transcend
concentration on mental phenomena in a sudden awakening to our
fundamental awareness.

The practice of watching the mind, one of the universal methods
of meditation, is the first step in transcending our habitual and unconscious identification with arising thoughts. Through this method we
strengthen the position of the observer, creating a stable counterforce
to the continuous stream of thoughts that invade our consciousness.
The observer is the aspect of the ego responsible for bringing integrity to the functioning of our mind and linking us with the essence of
our innate subjectivity. By watching arising thoughts yet remaining
uninvolved, we create a space in our intelligence from which we can
disidentify from our subconscious, instead of just thinking mechani-
cally. However, although this approach is beneficial, it cannot bring
us to the true state of meditation. It is a technique that serves only as
a preparation for becoming more conscious, and at some stage must
be transcended. Self-observation or detached watching cannot take
us beyond the mental realm, because the watcher himself is a faculty of the very mind he watches. It is only when the observer links
himself to the essence of awareness that he gains the necessary depth
and solidity to move out of the vicious cycle of thinking, identifying,
observing, disidentifying and thinking again.

In the approach to meditation that emphasizes the development of one-pointed attention, relative awareness is trained to constantly focus on an object external to the mind to keep it from being distracted and lost in thought. The practice of one-pointed attention is still a mental exertion confined to the mind, for attention is not awareness, but its functional expression.

To develop one-pointed attention we can initially practice conscious breathing, feeling how the belly rises and falls with each breath, or in a more advanced method, focus our attention on our inner space of abidance. Instead of working directly with the mind, we channel our attention towards conscious repose in being or the heart. Although we cannot fully pacify the mind in this way, we open enough space beyond it to experience a level of tranquility and immersion. By expanding into being, we become empowered to work with the mind in a much more efficient and conscious way.

While they are useful tools, watching the mind, cultivating mindfulness, or bypassing the mind by directing attention to areas of our existence other than awareness itself, do not allow us to reach true and abiding peace. To transcend the mind in a real way we have to illuminate it by giving birth to the center of awareness. A meditator who is spiritually mature should strive to awaken his essence beyond the mind from the very start, not paying *indirect* attention to an object of attention, but *direct* attention to its subject.

Indirect meditative techniques generate an energy of attentiveness that acts as an opposing force to the mechanical mind, but their utility is limited. Due to their external orientation, they do not uncover the inner essence, and therefore cannot result in awakening. In contrast, direct work with awareness is based on self-knowledge and the complementary practice of self-remembrance. Direct work with awareness involves the cultivation of the state of self-awareness, and eventually leads to a permanent presence beyond the mind.

When the energy of our mind turns towards the original source of attention, we enter the domain of consciousness without content.

The essence of the mind is not thought, but objectless attention, the core of our subjective existence. The birth of pure awareness allows us to shift out of the mind into the essential nature of our luminous presence, the entryway to the natural state of pure meditation. Unless we bring more consciousness to the mind and embrace it with the light of our presence, it cannot be transmuted into a force that is aligned with our spiritual awakening. The only way to pacify and transcend our mental agitation is to behold and embrace it from a level of existence deeper than the mind itself.

Pure meditation: Pure meditation is beyond the directing of attention to any particular area — it is an objectless state of being. Attention has to become absorbed in the depths of the now for the state of meditation to manifest; otherwise, it is the very thing that separates us from our positive absence. To embody the fullness of our abidance in the state of meditation we have to pass through the gate of pure subjectivity and submit our existence to the beyond. A meditator first moves beyond the mind by establishing his attention in the center of awareness, and then surrenders that attention by dwelling vertically in content-free awareness. Eventually, he surrenders beyond awareness by merging with being and actualizes the state of pure meditation, the natural absorption in existence.

Just sitting: The purest form of meditation practice is 'just sitting'. The most sublime aspiration of a meditator is just to be, just to sit. Just sitting is at once a practice and our natural state of abidance in the now, for though it must be actualized through effort, it is intrinsic to each moment of being. By cultivating the mode of just sitting we attune our existence to the natural repose of reality as it is. In just sitting it is not our body that sits, but our awareness; our attention is at rest, absorbed in the vertical plane of pure being.

We practice just sitting by continuously returning to the condition of 'sitting mind'. We grow in our consciousness, establish a flow of unbroken presence, and drop our awareness into the depths of reality. The practice of just sitting involves an element of transparent exertion through which the state of being can fully manifest and reach unconditional naturalness.

beyond the mind

A healthy attitude towards arising thoughts is essential to regain autonomy from the mind and awaken the state of meditation, for they are the main distraction in our effort to reach our deeper self. In meditation, we should neither indulge in thinking nor battle with the mind. Meditation is not an absence of thoughts, but a continuity of being undistracted by thoughts. As a thought arises, we neither accept nor reject it, for acceptance and rejection are energies linked to the mind, and therefore cannot take us beyond it. When we accept a thought, we fuel it with our involvement; when we reject a thought, we fuel it with our denial. The moment our me disengages from thinking, a thought cannot sustain itself and dissolves, for it has no energy of its own. We must, however, have a stable place beyond the mind to which we can anchor ourselves; otherwise, we will remain caught in a wheel of arising and disappearing thoughts towards which we must constantly cultivate our limited powers of non-identification.

In an unconscious person, consciousness recreates itself through psychological and phenomenal awareness. The mind cannot exist in emptiness. The moment it is faced with inactivity it generates boredom or falls asleep, but even then, it constantly dreams. No wonder it is so common to drift and daydream during meditation — the mind becomes stifled by stillness and seeks release through other outlets.

Although the cultivation of observation and the crystallization of attention are the essential means to go beyond the mechanical mind, they are not enough to transfigure the construct of our consciousness. Our consciousness has to become conscious of something other than thinking, other than observing, other than objectifying itself. We have to give it the ultimate object — its own subjectivity. In the same instant that we neither accept nor reject an arising thought, we must become aware of the pristine space that dwells at the root of the mind — awareness itself. The moment we pay total attention to our innate presence, the chain of thinking is broken and consciousness without content alone prevails.

Usually a beginner loses focus and by force of habit leaks his consciousness into thinking, objectifying his sense of me in the mind. However, whenever he returns, moment to moment, to the center of awareness and gradually anchors attention in pure subjectivity, the whole structure of his consciousness becomes centralized in being rather than thinking. By giving our consciousness the supreme object of our presence, we decondition it from pursuing external objects. As we gradually learn how to live through pure consciousness, our mind surrenders to its host, the ground of I am — the soul.

To stabilize the center of awareness does not mean that thinking stops entirely — a certain amount of thinking is a natural part of our human functioning. The correct relationship with thinking is established when our me becomes rooted in the essence beyond the mind. Here, the arising of thoughts is in harmony with our existence, the exalted consciousness of silence and presence. Thinking that takes place in an unbroken space of awareness is an exercise of clear intelligence, a positive expression of our meditative consciousness. While in the initial stages of practice we are engaged in a horizontal struggle between getting lost in the mind and returning to our presence, as our practice matures, the movement of thoughts no longer occurs outside of our essence, but is contained within pure awareness.

prior to the presence and absence of thought

To uncover the true nature of awareness demands a great deal of precision and sensitivity. For a beginner who is fully identified with the mind, a momentary gap in thinking is often translated as a meditative experience, for it is the closest thing to a feeling of peace he experiences. However, meditation is not grasping at the absence of thought, but abidance prior to both thought's presence and absence in the domain of being and non-perceptional consciousness.

Though the observer may contemplate the interval between thoughts in the futile hope of discovering the nature of thoughtlessness, he merely objectifies it as the seen. He perceives the non-existence of thoughts as a vacant space opening up in front of him instead of becoming vacant himself by watching nothing. To watch no-thing is awareness, wakefulness without a reference point.

The observer cannot capture consciousness unless he stops seeking it outside of his own existence. He must renounce his mental exertion and 'stand still' in awareness to discover his true nature — he must surrender to the very awareness from which he arises in order to obtain the supreme insight into his true self. Awareness is not found within the mind, for it is the background of both the thought and the thinker. It cannot be grasped by perception or reflection; to know it is to become it.

the multilayered mind in meditation

Meditators are often confused about the relationship between arising thoughts, the role of the observer, and their meditative state. We can be clear on this matter only when we understand the multilayered nature of our consciousness and how it coexists with the ground of I am. Before we can reach a balanced understanding of the relationship between thoughts and the inner state, we must become conscious of the various ways in which the mind operates during our meditation practice.

The mind is a living organism of intelligence that must maintain a complex relationship with the whole of our consciousness to retain its basic sanity. The capacity of the conscious mind to assist in meditation directly corresponds to the depth of our spiritual awakening. If we are totally lost in the mind it cannot possibly serve our evolution into the state of meditation. To empower the intelligence of the

mind so that it can become a transformative force in our consciousness, we must first realize our spiritual essence. Here, by 'essence'
we mean the state of pure awareness; but if a meditator has reached
a deeper awakening, 'essence' would actually signify the whole of
the inner state, and ultimately the soul. The relationship between the
essence of I am and intelligence is reciprocal. In our initial effort to
enter the state of meditation, intelligence supports the growth of our
consciousness and the awakening of the essence; through the actualized essence, intelligence gains the necessary power to integrate the
entire mind with the inner state.

Since it is the conscious mind that bridges our unconscious self
with our conscious abidance in the inner state, its role in the process
of awakening is of paramount importance. It is the mind aware of
itself that engenders the conscious sense of me — the observer — so
fundamental to our inner growth into being and understanding. If
the function of the observer is not activated, we cannot transcend our
subconscious reality and enter the state of meditation. Only when
this function has been fulfilled and our abidance in the inner realm
is fully realized can we begin to surrender and merge the observer
with universal consciousness.

To help us better understand the complex nature of the conscious mind and its evolving role in our meditation practice, we will
now describe the various ways it behaves in relation to both our
essence and our subconscious reality. It must be noted that until the
fifth stage, the meditator is still unawakened to his essence.

1. *The conscious mind lost in the subconscious, or the subcon-
    scious alone:* The basic condition of forgetfulness — attention
    is absent and one is lost in thought.

2. *The conscious mind coexisting with the subconscious:* One
    experiences a degree of presence within the mechanical activ-
    ity of the mind — thinking is divided between conscious and
    subconscious.

3. *The conscious mind aware of the subconscious:* One becomes mindful of mechanical thinking and the observer develops a sense of distance from the mind. However, unless one has awakened the center of awareness, and consciousness has been largely transformed, awareness of the subconscious does not put a stop to the momentum of the thinking mind. In spite of being aware of arising thoughts at times, a beginner still thinks constantly. Only when awareness has fully matured does the act of becoming conscious of the subconscious lead to the instantaneous cessation of thinking.

4. *The conscious mind alone:* One is fully present within the thinking process, yet unaware of the essence.

5. *The conscious mind aware of the essence coexisting with conscious thinking:* Awareness of the essence and conscious thinking occur simultaneously.

6. *The conscious mind aware of the essence coexisting with subconscious thinking:* The observer is connected to awareness of his essence while unfocused semi-conscious thinking takes place on the periphery of consciousness.

7. *The conscious mind aware of the essence becomes aware of the subconscious:* Similar to the third stage, but here the meditator already abides in awareness, so there is more power to drop thinking and surrender the mind.

8. *The conscious mind aware of the essence and consciously thinking fully surrenders to the essence:* While consciously thinking, one renounces all thinking and surrenders to the essence.

9. *The conscious mind aware of the essence alone:* One's intelligence abides in pure awareness and the mind stops. This state can occur on two levels: on the lower level, the observer is still separated from his essence and the ego remains the primary experiencer; on the higher level, the observer is merged with the inner state and his consciousness of I am becomes universal.

an open secret

A meditator can be said to have reached the mature state of meditation when he experiences any of the last five modes of consciousness. Although to be lost in the subconscious is a relatively negative experience, minimal subconscious movement is a natural part of the functioning of the human mind, and therefore acceptable, as long as one abides firmly in the inner state and is able to instantly return to conscious presence and surrender excessive thinking. Still, there is no excuse for indulging in thinking during meditation. When our mind surrenders and integrates with the inner state, thinking is minimal and occurs in slow motion, causing spaces to open between thoughts where silence can prevail. Even when thinking occurs, one should continue to dwell in unbroken unity with the state prior to thought.

the two-fold internalization of consciousness

Because our essence leaks into the state of forgetfulness when the mind is exteriorized, the withdrawal of consciousness is an absolute requirement to enter the state of meditation. The withdrawal of consciousness has both horizontal and vertical orientations: in the horizontal withdrawal, consciousness turns back to its non-dual presence of self-luminous I am; in the vertical withdrawal it is rerouted into the state of being, which counteracts the upwards movement of the mind and life force. The horizontal internalization is a function of self-attention; the vertical internalization, of our surrender to the inner state. Unless we realize the two-fold withdrawal of consciousness, we cannot become absorbed in the self.

Awakening to awareness through the horizontal withdrawal of the mind is our point of entry into the depth of the now. If one practices vertical surrender without first having obtained ones true presence, the mind will remain fundamentally fragmented and lack any continuity of intelligence and consciousness within the experience of being. Only the soul can enter the inner dimension. It is the unity of the horizontal and vertical internalizations that enables us to enter the inner reality and realize the wholeness of the soul.

75

meditation and boredom

Boredom is an interesting state of mind. It inspires us to act, but never allows us to rest in contentment. We get bored when there is nothing to do and when we lose interest in what we are doing. The deepest kind of boredom, however, is boredom with being. Due to the shallow nature of the human personality, to 'just be' is a tedious and dull experience. It is not the soul that is bored with being, but the mind, for the mind lives through movement and is unable to rest. The moment the mind stops being occupied or entertained it gets restless and irritated. The monotony of being is simply intolerable. The repetitiveness of each moment devoid of activity creates a feeling of stuckness that sends an immediate signal that it is time to 'do' something. This very unconscious mechanism is at the root of our fundamental resistance to being.

Some meditators believe that they do not get bored in meditation because they are having such a 'deep experience'. In reality, however, they have not yet begun to meditate. Unless one has passed through the experience of utter existential boredom, one has not entered true meditation. Boredom cannot be by-passed; it must be experienced fully before one can move beyond it. Ultimately, meditation can be said to have two sides: boredom and bliss. The degree to which we experience boredom or bliss reflects the depth of our absorption in reality.

The presence of boredom in meditation points to the fact that we are so dependent upon receiving constant stimuli from the world or our own mind, we feel frustrated by the non-happening of the now. Boredom, in its essence, is the pure suffering of existing as a separate consciousness. We confront the most acute sense of separateness when faced with inactivity, because action serves as the primary distraction to our claustrophobic self-consciousness. Boredom is actually the basic background of our human existence, but we only experience it directly in meditation, for here we are called to suspend our involvement with the phenomenal reality and renounce all reference points apart from being. In the space of just being, we confront our fundamental boredom, naked and alone.

The best way out of boredom is to recognize the profound value of being. However, as we cannot appreciate what we do not experience, an unconscious person who lacks any real experience of being has no way to relate to the positive essence of boredom. What the average meditator translates as 'being' is but the frail touch of each moment, a vague reverberation of the now. He has no inner space within which to connect to something deeper than his personality and link himself with the meaningfulness of existence beyond boredom. To move out of the boredom inherent to separate consciousness we must enter the realm of meditation. In sitting meditation, we channel the energy of the mind through the portal of inactivity into abidance in the inner state. When we reach a significant level of absorption and the mind surrenders, boredom begins to dissolve into the bliss of being.

To transcend boredom does not mean that one never gets bored anymore. Boredom is an indivisible part of meditation as long as one has not fully merged with the inner realm. To transform boredom is to awaken a profound sense of endurance within the experience of the impersonal void of each now. As boredom arises in each now, one surrenders within it. One has to accept and befriend boredom before it can be transmuted and absorbed by its source.

Our experience of boredom evolves as we come ever closer to our original absence and realize the emptiness of self. As our abidance in reality deepens, our sense of boredom becomes relaxed and transparent. It no longer creates restless energies and agitation, but reflects the absolute patience of existence.

It is a common experience that the moment a new layer of depth within the inner state is reached, the sense of boredom is temporarily suspended, for the observer feels tangible bliss as a result of having shifted beyond his previous state. However, as time goes by, the novelty of the experience wears off. No matter what depth the observer reaches, his initial fascination and excitement inevitably wane and he gets bored all over again. To go beyond boredom through the medium of the spiritual path is not to seek new states, but to resolve boredom's primal cause, our separateness. As we mature we realize that boredom cannot be overcome by intensifying our inner experience, for it is not a reflection of the lack of depth of our state, but of our inability to merge. Only when the observer surrenders and becomes one with the inner realm can boredom be dissolved, for he is not only the victim of boredom, but its cause. It is our disappearance into reality that ultimately takes us beyond boredom, for it liberates us from the very one who is subject to both boredom and its absence.

meditation: the means and the goal

Meditation is a gradual path based on sudden awakening. Each moment of meditation points to reality, but the complete realization of that reality is the outcome of a gradual process. This seeming paradox needs to be grasped in order for us to comprehend the true meaning of a practice that itself transcends the dualities of path and goal, effort and effortlessness, doing and being. Meditation is both the means and the goal, for though it has its roots in the perfection of pure being, it must unfold in time before it can reflect this perfection in our actual experience.

If we see meditation only as a means to an end our meditation is not pure, because we are using it to achieve goals that are external to the immediate. The very spirit of meditation is based on surrender to the now. However, if we perceive meditation solely as an end in itself we lose our connection to the whole process of transformation and inner evolution.

Meditation is the goal in and of itself, for its very nature is abidance in the now; it is also the means to reach that which, though of the now, is far beyond our initial realization of the now. The now is indeed the ground of pure subjectivity upon which we abide, but our relative ability to access it does not guarantee that we have reached its true depth — our *present* experience of the now may be shallow. To fully realize the dimension of the now we must go through the process of expansion and awakening until we can merge with the realm of pure subjectivity. Ultimately, we can see meditation as a practice in which the goal and the means are fully intertwined. As the goal, meditation reflects our fundamental union with the reality of the now; as the means, it signifies the process of reaching its fathomless depths.

the gateless gate

Although meditation is the inner gate out of illusion, from the viewpoint of higher truth there is no gate to pass through and nowhere to go. Meditation is the gateless gate to the natural state of our abidance in the universal now. To penetrate the dimension of meditation is to realize the mystery of this gateless gate, to merge one's true existence with the supreme beyond.

being and understanding

Being is beyond understanding, but without understanding we cannot transcend the plane of becoming. Despite its fundamental simplicity, we must contemplate the dimension of meditation deeply to fully comprehend its intangible nature. No matter how gratifying our experience in meditation is, there are important questions to ask as we enter this new space: How can we penetrate the unseen depths of the inner realm? How are we to grasp the subtle reality beyond the mind? What is the true state of meditation and how can we differentiate it from the maze of meditative experiences we pass through? Is the inner state the same as the one who experiences it? Is the knower of the inner realm external to the place in which he abides? Who am I and where am I within the state of meditation? What is this great void of the cosmic beyond upon which we dwell when submerged in meditation? What levels of inner depth does our consciousness traverse in our progression towards surrender? How can we actualize the complete state of meditation? How can we merge with the universal self? We can unravel many questions about the multifaceted reality of meditation through the mind, but the ultimate answers lie in pure being and non-conceptual understanding.

self-knowledge and meditation

Meditation is an act of being, whereas self-knowledge is an act of knowing. Two mutually supporting aspects of the inner path, meditation and self-knowledge are indivisible from one another. Self-knowledge is required to penetrate to the essence of meditation, and meditation brings stability and depth to the knowledge of our true self. Meditation without self-knowledge is utterly impotent, dull and mechanical; one cannot enter meditation's true core. Self-knowledge without meditation is shallow and leaves us trapped on the exterior of the inner state, disconnected from the beyond.

The secret of self-knowledge lies in the existential leap from objectivity to subjectivity — from living on the periphery of the mind to realizing the heart of I am — the ultimate centering act of consciousness. Meditation is the practice of staying in the presence of that self-knowledge. As we dwell upon the knowledge of I am, by the law of spiritual gravity, the vertical pull of the now reveals ever more depth in the experience of the self. This depth is itself beyond self-knowledge, for it is the very source of both self and knowledge.

It is quite common for those who follow the path of self-enquiry to reject the practice of meditation. Even if their enquiry does yield positive results, they frequently become stagnated on the path. This is due to their inability to both stabilize and deepen that which they have awakened. Then there are seekers who do practice meditation, but not self-enquiry. Due to their lack of conscious intention to gain self-knowledge, their practice remains rooted in ignorance, powerless to yield true awakening.

Unfortunately, in some traditions, due to the misperception that 'no-self' is the opposite of self, the belief in no-self is used as an excuse to reject the practice of self-enquiry. The confusion here stems from a lack of understanding about the difference between the individual and universal dimensions of the self. The term no-self, in its correct definition, does not signify a negation of the individual self;

rather, it denotes the non-abiding, empty nature of the universal self. Self-enquiry is a tool used to awaken the essence of the soul, not the universal self, which is realized through our surrender and absorption in the beyond. To negate the individual self is foolish, for without its presence, neither self nor no-self can be realized. Here we can see how a simple concept employed without imagination can sabotage the positive movement towards awakening to pure subjectivity.

Traditionally, self-enquiry is applied either to expose the illusory nature of ego or to realize the universal self. Though this approach may be fruitful in the sense that it can open one to the inner realm, it leads to fundamentally false conclusions because it bypasses the essence of the enquirer himself. Self-enquiry practiced correctly points beyond false individuality and identification with universality to the personal essence of the soul's consciousness, the knowledge of I am.

As essential as it is, no amount of self-knowledge can bring us to the kind of depth that is reached through meditation, which exists on a much deeper plane than the consciousness of awareness that characterizes self-inquiry. True meditation is a condition of pure surrender through which our sense of I am merges with the universal state of oneness.

two levels of pure subjectivity

In our explanation of the inner realm we draw a clear distinction between two basic strata of pure subjectivity: the first is the subjectivity of the soul, the knower and witness of the inner state; the second is not an entity, a personal essence or an individual knower, but the dimension of being, the unmanifested ground of existence. The *one* who abides in the state of meditation is the pure subjectivity of the individual soul, and the dimension in which the soul abides, is the pure subjectivity of universal I am. Over the course of our inner evolution this distinction becomes more and more transparent as these two levels of subjectivity progressively merge into one, undivided reality.

absolute objectivity

In the discipline of hard science, the term 'subjective experience' generally denotes an experience that is relative in nature, and therefore cannot be objectively described or confirmed. In contrast, the term 'objective experience' signifies an occurrence that is factually verifiable, and as such, independent of our individual experiences or opinions. The 'subjective observer' is therefore seen as an impediment to empirical analysis. However, in the science of spirituality, the subjective essence is understood to lie far deeper than the relative subjectivity of the mind and personality. Our true subjectivity is in fact absolutely 'objective' because it reflects the eternal light of universal I am.

Despite the fact that in the language of meditation and consciousness the term 'objective' usually points to something external to I am, we should not assume that the reality of objects and appearances is in existential opposition to pure subjectivity. This is true only in the case of an unconscious person in whom the light of subjectivity is lost in ignorant identification with phenomenal existence. When pure subjectivity is fully realized it transcends the polarity of inner and outer, containing them both in the space of all-pervasive oneness. Ultimately, there is only one reality — nothing exists outside of all-that-is.

attention and letting go

There are two fundamental aspects of meditation: centering and absorption. In meditation we must maintain the correct balance between alertness and calm, concentration and letting go. Through centering we gain a stable sense of self and presence; through absorption we move into the depth of being. We cannot reach a state of true absorption prior to centering our consciousness. By establishing ourselves in pure awareness, we move beyond the gross level of the fragmented mind and give birth to a real center from which we can begin to surrender.

In our meditation practice we must first establish the necessary level of concentration, and then solidify our attention. Although the term concentration implies a gathering of energy towards our center, in practice, concentration is more outwardly oriented than attention. Attention is closer to the essence of awareness than concentration — in its purest form it is self-attentive. Concentration is the ability to focus the mind and energy, attention is one-pointed awareness; concentration enables us to temporarily put the mechanical mind on hold, attention allows us to go beyond it. Through concentration we drop our forgetfulness, through attention we abide in remembrance; concentration brings us to the present, attention bridges us with our essence.

However, in our effort to enter the state of meditation, attention by itself is insufficient. Although it enables us to abide in the present and links us with pure awareness, attention cannot enter the dimension of the now. Attention dwells only on the surface of meditation. The real depth of meditation is reached through absorption, which we access by letting go of attention. Letting go is the surrender to the depth of the now that opens the soul to the gravitational force of the beyond.

The condition of not-letting-go is the unconscious exercise of self-control through which we sustain our sense of separate existence as human beings. Because we exist in a perpetual state of tension and self-holding, we need to spend a long time in meditation before we are able to let go into an existential state of ease and become absorbed in the simplicity of being.

Excessive concentration and self-control, and their opposites, inattentiveness and lethargy, are the most common impediments in the practice of meditation. We need to maintain a precise equilibrium between attention and letting go. If we do not generate enough attention, our attempts to let go will lead to daydreaming or sleep; if we are too alert, we create strain and become overly self-conscious.

The ability to preserve the proper balance between awareness and surrender in our practice reflects our relative effort and cooperation in activating the natural state of meditation. In the natural state, no effort is needed, because one abides beyond the polarity of attention and letting go. The natural state is a state beyond the mind's fluctuating energies in which attention and letting go both become immersed in the void of pure being.

meditation: the passage to the beyond

On its surface, meditation is a time of peace and quiet during which the mind is put at rest. True meditation, however, is far beyond any experience of psychological relaxation or calm. There is nothing wrong with feeling blissful or enjoying inner peace, but meditation is much more than that. To recognize the sacredness of meditation we have to meet the metaphysical depths of the inner dimension. The purest motivation to meditate transcends the search for personal satisfaction, pleasure, or even peace; it is the deep desire to enter our original home and move from illusion into reality. To enter the inner realm and dwell in the pure subjectivity of being is to regain our true life, to find our roots in the source of creation.

In the initial stages of our meditation practice we come face-to-face with the unconscious mind and our disjointed state of being. Since we are moving out of suffering and forgetfulness during this period, we can consider it a 'negative' phase in our evolution. But when we become more integrated inside and gain entry into the inner realm, we begin the 'positive' phase of practice based on internal expansion. To support this expansion, we literally 'sit' in the inner realm and, by the divine law, gradually merge with the beyond in a process that continues until the state of complete oneness is reached. Even after realizing oneness, the movement into the inner realm does not stop, for the beyond is infinite and thus there is no end to its revelation.

the bottomless depth of meditation

Meditation has two functions: to enable us to expand into our true self, which is soul-realization, and to support our expansion into the beyond, which is self-realization. There is no end to either expansion. Even after the soul is realized she continues to grow into an increasingly higher condition of her eternal identity. The very nature of existence is movement. Nothing can stop, for to stop is to regress, and in the context of spiritual evolution, to die.

Before the transcendental state is fully realized and our individuality merges in samadhi, a meditator journeys through many different layers of pure being, each containing enough depth to bestow an unconditional sense of gratification. Although settling our existence down into the state of absolute rest is not an easy task, as we grow within the inner realm, there is more and more pure contentment. Only when we have gone through the whole process of expansion, however, can we experience the ultimate contentment, the infinite bliss of absence.

the art of non-doing

If we look carefully, we can see that everything in existence is in motion, besotted with the will to become. This is particularly true for human consciousness. The human mind has become a reflection, even a caricature, of universal movement. While to be endowed with active intelligence is natural and positive, when we become subjugated by our own compulsive thinking, we lose our connection to the basic goodness of being and the silence essential to our spiritual sanity.

We cannot experience reality outside of the individual consciousness that constitutes our unique angle of perception. Our mind is the only tool we have to recognize existence; but at the very same time, the mind is the veil that separates us from reality as it is. Rooted in interpretation rather than direct perception, the mind creates a virtual world of its own that is alienated from the whole of reality as it is. To apperceive existence in its true form, we must transcend our unconscious tendency to ceaselessly think about, label and interpret all that appears in our field of cognition. Only a still mind can see and reflect reality from a place of non-modified lucidity. The foundation of meditation is the condition of non-doing — the complete stillness of consciousness within the state of being.

divine passivity

The state of non-doing is the most profound experience for a human being, for it occurs only in the context of oneness with existence. It is an experience of unity, freedom and bliss. This extraordinary unity of consciousness and inactivity is not inertia, but supreme repose in the divine. It is 'divine passivity', the ultimate state of rootedness in the source and mystery of creation. To arrive at this divine inaction, the will of our individuality has to merge in loving union with the will of the beloved.

the dynamics of non-doing

Non-doing represents a tremendously vibrant and dynamic condition of being. It is a state of continuously letting go into the mystery of the now in which the presence and absence of the soul merge into an indescribable amalgam of pure existence; personal and impersonal meet and unite in the realm beyond effort and effortlessness.

Non-doing is a state of letting go whereby the will to be is surrendered into the abyss of universal emptiness, the timeless space of the now. Through our relative surrender, the gravitation of the beyond pulls our soul into the inner ocean of pure rest so that we can move into a place of absolute peace.

Non-doing by its very nature is beyond activity and inactivity. It is none other than reality itself — the unborn base of all-that-is. Non-doing embraces both motion and stillness, containing all manifested existence within its transcendent non-abidance. When the soul merges with the primordial essence of non-activity, her existence is transported into the beyond to embody the perfection of being. It is from the dimensionless space of pure being that all of creation is seen as uncreated, all change as unchanged.

What are the practical means to achieve the state of non-doing? From a place of clear presence, one cultivates the art of surrender. The success of this effortless effort does not hinge solely on our intention to let go, but also on the transmutation of our mind and transformation of our energy. Our awareness and our energy body have to open up and shift into the inner realm — our sense of existence needs to move beyond the created reality and relative, time-bound consciousness. Since this transformation takes place on the subtle plane, beyond the control of the conscious mind, the only thing we can do is cooperate through the continuous practice of letting go in a space of patience, endurance and submission to the beyond. Ultimately, the complete opening to the realm of pure being is the result of deliverance coming from the depths of the absolute reality into which we surrender.

dropping the doer

The ego can do many things, but it simply cannot meditate. Pure meditation is not a form of doing, but a condition of being beyond the exercise of any method. A meditator who relies on any method of meditation cannot cross into the vertical reality of the now, for the mind can only operate in the horizontal dimension of space and time. To open the space of pure meditation, the 'doer' must yield to being.

We should not, however, attempt to drop the doer prematurely. Since the fully mature state of meditation cannot be achieved until we complete the inner path, we need the support of the doer as we go through the process of establishing the condition of non-doing. This may appear illogical, but there is a very simple explanation: individual effort is performed within the sphere of the subtle ego, an *extension* of the mind that serves as a conscious link between the subconscious self and the inner state.

The ego assists us in two ways in the practice of meditation: it helps to awaken the inner state, and it learns how to surrender itself in order to merge with that state. To comprehend this more clearly, we must recognize that the ego is not an independent entity, but a vehicle of the soul. While the false ego only serves the mind's agenda, the mature, conscious ego is an intelligent representation of the soul in her human personality. It is the conscious ego that becomes present in the mind and overrides the subconscious ego lost in daydreaming, the conscious ego that lets go into the inner state.

In the process of merging with the inner state, the ego does not disappear entirely, rather its motives and purpose change. Prior to its surrender, the ego performs the role of subject, believing itself to be the host of our consciousness. But as awakening grows roots within our existence, the ego gradually moves to the periphery of our identity where it remains as a purely functional expression of the soul. It continues to support the deepening of the inner state, but its presence grows progressively more transparent and silent; it ceases to control the process of meditation and begins to humbly assist it.

Our final aspiration, therefore, is not to eliminate the ego, but to transform it into an instrument of inner awakening. In the complete absence of ego no meditation can take place, for the soul requires its energy and intelligence to open the inner state. Only when it has fulfilled its purpose can the ego be fully surrendered to the silence of pure being.

One of the principal tasks of the doer is to check the quality of meditation and gently balance the energies of doing and non-doing. The relationship between the doer and the state of non-doing actually runs parallel to that of attention and letting go. The activation of attention is a function of the doer, whereas letting go is the surrender of the doer into the ego-free space of non-doing. The doer is on both sides of the equation, for even though he surrenders, the surrender itself is on some level an act of will. After recognizing an absence of mindfulness, the doer, or 'checker', makes the decision to concentrate; or, having verified that there is a sufficient amount of presence, the checker introduces the intention of letting go into being. The wisdom of meditation calls for a precise balance between utilizing the ego and dropping it — they should in fact be a simultaneous occurrence.

By letting go, the ego drops itself, and an immediate opening into the state of pure meditation occurs. As time goes by, however, the ego reappears, assessing the state or wandering off into daydreams; hence, in the next instant, the ego has to repeat the act of activating attention or surrendering. This dance of checking, becoming present and letting go takes place within an effortless, natural flow of intelligence. As our awakening deepens, the interplay between the checker and the inner state gradually merges into one movement, a movement of the now. In due time, the ego dissolves into the inner dimension to such an extent that it ceases to possess the power to assert its separate existence. Naturally, the functions of checking and cognizing still operate at times, but without the presence of an individual agent. The power of recognition and intelligence is owned by *no one* — intelligence moves in the impersonal awareness of pure reality.

the state of effortlessness

The state of effortlessness is the natural condition of being, the ego-free dimension of pure meditation. If effort on the path is not eventually dropped, it is an indication that we have either not awakened to our true self, or are unable to merge with the depth of reality. The evolution into effortlessness is a natural process based on a gradual fusion of the individual with the universal.

Although there are many levels of effortlessness, the essence of the natural state is always the fundamental experience of just being. Hence, as long as we recognize the core of I am and being, we have relative access to the effortless state of pure meditation, even in the initial stages of our practice. As our practice gradually deepens and our state becomes more integrated, the natural state of being dissolves all need for exertion. We can finally rest, free of our relative self, in the fullness and emptiness of primordial consciousness.

beyond meditation

We use meditation as a medicine to heal the disease of ignorance. When its curative function as a remedy has been fulfilled, both the disease and the medicine should be forgotten. To 'practice' meditation past the point of our recovery from ignorance defeats its entire purpose — to be.

One should not remain forever dependent on meditation as a means to reach further expansion. Unless we go beyond meditation and become one with the inner realm, there will always be a split between the act of meditation and our continual abidance in the now. Only through the power of surrender to the now can we transcend the dichotomy of doing and being and see meditation as not existing apart from reality as it is.

Although meditation points directly to the heart of the now, the *practice* of meditation beclouds the perfection of being. The very need for exertion that practice implies reconfirms our split from the whole. To reach completion, we need to arrive at a point in our evolution where all effort can be dropped and absorbed by reality. To go beyond meditation is to dissolve practice in the exalted realization of the natural state.

beyond practice

Although meditation is the means and the goal, meditation as 'practice' represents only the means. Correct practice does carry the seed of the essence, but the full realization of the essence eliminates any need for practice. Hence, dropping practice is a natural outcome of completing the inner path.

There are two extreme views regarding the subject of practice: one claims that there is no need for practice at all, as one can reach self-realization directly, the other maintains that not only is practice necessary, but that there can be no end to it, for even after enlightenment one still needs to meditate in order to perfect the inner state. Neither of these views reflects the whole truth. It may be true that one can experience awakening without meditation, but one can never arrive at complete self-realization in this way. As for the belief in the need for never-ending cultivation, it is a false conviction based on confusion over the difference between partial awakening and complete realization. Partial awakening does indeed demand the continuation of practice for the sake of the stabilization, integration, and deepening of the states to which one has awakened. Complete enlightenment, however, by definition, eliminates the need for any additional practice. The state beyond practice does exist, and represents the essence of freedom.

In some cases, the decision to drop practice reflects one's inner potential and the desire of the soul; in others, it is resistance coming from the mind. Unfortunately, meditators generally lack sufficient knowledge of the inner realm to sense the difference. They either give up their practice prematurely or insist on continuing with it when it is no longer relevant. As an example, one should not stop cultivating self-remembrance prior to stabilizing awareness, or continue practice with being when the absolute state is already established and integrated. Prior to reaching complete enlightenment, the decision to drop a specific practice should be based on a clear view of one's potential and the expansiveness of one's spiritual aspirations. As we progress, we pass through many different levels of the relative states beyond practice. At these signposts of inner expansion, we can simply relax, enjoying what we have attained. As time goes by, however, we consciously dive back into the adventure of the inner work, responding to the call for further evolution. A true seeker never gives up the inner work before becoming unconditionally free.

sudden and gradual enlightenment

As long as the science of enlightenment has existed there has been disagreement between different traditions as to whether self-realization is the outcome of a sudden awakening or a gradual process. There is no confusion though, if we are able to see this issue from a higher perspective. Awakening is always sudden, for it is a breakthrough in our experience of reality. Complete enlightenment, however, cannot happen suddenly — the chasm between ignorance and self-realization is simply too wide to cross in a single instant. A gigantic leap of this sort would defy the laws of nature, consciousness and energy.

We need to understand that enlightenment is not a mere shift in perception and consciousness. It is an existential metamorphosis on all levels that radically transforms the frequency of our energy system and the delicate balance of our brain and subtle bodies. A sudden and complete enlightenment that bypassed all intermediate stages of awakening would undoubtedly result in a mental and emotional breakdown, or even physical death. The body and mind require time to adjust to the dramatic change in our energy and sense of identity that the radical transfiguration of enlightenment engenders.

The generally accepted models of sudden and gradual enlightenment are based on the false assumption that ignorance and enlightenment are strict opposites, having no intermediate reality. However, the matter is much more complex and fluid, for there are many transitional stages between forgetfulness and awakening. One can be more or less ignorant, just as one can be more or less awakened.

Awakening is sudden by nature, but rarely instantaneously complete. A post-awakening period of cultivation of the state that has been awakened is almost always necessary for the sake of its stabilization and integration. Only when a particular awakening has matured into relative completion can one then initiate the process that leads to the subsequent awakening. In this way, one journeys step by step towards becoming more whole and complete. The concept of gradual enlightenment is valid provided we accept that it is a gradual process composed of sudden awakenings. It is gradual in the sense that one's inner state progressively expands as one awakening follows another in tandem with the cultivation of the inner state as a whole.

Cultivation is both the polishing and perfecting of an already awakened state, and preparation for the awakening to follow. However, although necessary to assure the ensuing awakening, cultivation is never its complete cause. The correlation between cultivation and awakening is in fact extremely subtle: awakening is never the direct result of our effort, yet without our effort, no awakening can take place. Through cultivation we prepare our existence for the influence of the higher intelligence that alone can shift our consciousness to a more elevated state of light.

In the earthly dimension, it is most often a human guide who initiates the inner awakening of a seeker. This initiation takes the form of an energetic transmission of the states beyond the mind, and requires the medium of a self-realized being who embodies the awakened reality. To make himself as receptive as possible, the seeker has to prepare for the initiation through practice. He must bring his energy and consciousness as close as he can to the verge of the state that is to be awakened so that he can be reached by the transmission. A transmission of this type is not the simple transference of a state. It is the planting of a seed of higher consciousness that, in order to result in complete awakening, must be nurtured through cultivation into maturity. Whether realization happens spontaneously or through grace, the principles of sudden awakening and gradual cultivation apply.

the natural state

The natural state of meditation is the true goal of all meditators. Beyond the polarities of inner and outer, activity and non-activity, thinking and non-thinking, doing and being, the natural state is unaffected, unconditional immersion in reality. Through the realization of this state we move completely into the dimension of pure subjectivity, the domain of the self. We continue to exist *in* the world, but are no longer *of* the world; our essence is rooted in the beyond. By the power of our expansion into the realm of pure being we return to our original state, yet still maintain a life on earth. This secret domain of immaculate peace is the abiding place of all beings who have yielded their existence to the eternal light of I am.

non-being

Non-being is the deepest experience of meditation. It is not the opposite of being, but the absence of the checker within the state of pure being. That which we perceive as 'being' in fact exists only in reference to an experiencer. Without a knower, there is no one to relate to being as something to dwell upon, no one to be. When the knower merges with being, he is no longer external to where he abides — he disappears into existence.

Non-being is an experience without an experiencer, knowledge without a knower, freedom without anyone being free. It is the state in which the division between the inner state and the observer is dissolved into one reality. This supreme experience-non-experience of reality can be revealed only to *no one*. In the absence of oneself, the universal self is all-that-is.

the state of bliss

It is a common error to cling to superficially blissful experiences in meditation. Most so-called meditative experiences are external to our real nature and possess no existential value. The mind, lacking in true depth, is totally captivated by stimulating experiences and desperately strives to relive them. However, because these experiences are not anchored in the essence of pure subjectivity, the experiencer is separated from the experience. The illusive bliss that a beginner sometimes accidentally accesses can never become permanent, for it is still confined to the mind. A meditator must guard himself against addiction to blissful experiences for they can easily divert his attention from the real work of diving into the trans-experiential dimension of pure being.

There is an unspoken law of meditation that before one can enter the state of real bliss one has to pass the gate of neutrality, absorbing and integrating the essence of unqualified emptiness: disidentification from experiencing, non-evaluation of experiences, non-doing of being, non-dwelling upon phenomena and non-abidance upon the beyond. To enter reality, a meditator has to establish himself in a state beyond pleasant or unpleasant, blissful or boring. He has to be unconcerned with that which he is experiencing to truly become one with it. Only then is he granted the impersonal bliss of existence.

A neutral quality experienced in meditation shows that one abides in reality, for one has moved beyond the mind; yet it also indicates that the experiencer is still separated from the space of his abidance. Neutrality can be said to be the closest experience to reality for a separate experiencer; beyond it, the experiencer is no more. The moment the gap between the experiencer and the inner realm is bridged by his absorption, the true nature of reality divulges itself as pure bliss. We are not speaking of the kind of bliss that one can relate to, or get used to and become bored with, for it is not experienced through our presence, but through our absence. In the absence of a meditator, the hidden depth of meditation opens as the homogeneous consciousness of divine absorption. Once we have crossed over the neutral dimension of meditation, we begin to disappear into reality and merge with the supreme bliss of the self. The bliss of meditation is innate to the divine realm of the source — it is uncaused, unoriginated, unbecome — it just is. To taste the timeless bliss of being through the consciousness of the soul is to merge with the unborn heart of the beloved.

realm of the inner state

The inner state is a reality in and of itself — a landscape of consciousness and being, the space of our inner abidance in the now, the existential bridge between the soul and the plane of universal I am. We can see the inner state as the gateway to the beyond, and also the natural condition of being known as the state of meditation. To meditate is to dwell within the inner state, and to abide in the inner state is to be in the state of meditation. The depth, stability, richness, expansiveness and strength of our inner state determine our ultimate relationship with the absolute reality.

There are three aspects of the inner state — awareness, being and heart. Through the complete realization of each and all of these aspects, we create a solid ground of unbroken abidance beyond the mind wherein and whereby we can awaken our soul and transcend the dimension of illusion. Each aspect of the inner state represents a different mode of expansion in our journey towards wholeness. To enter the plane beyond the mind with wisdom and a higher purpose, we must understand the multifaceted nature of the inner state and the interlinked practices of awakening, cultivation, stabilization and integration.

consciousness

Consciousness is the brilliance of the supreme self illuminating the whole of existence with the radiance of knowing from within and beyond all forms of life. It is the mysterious power of cognition that constitutes the essence of creation, the very substance that makes the evolution of intelligence possible. Consciousness is the light of recognition without which reality would vanish into naught.

Although consciousness is the foundation of creation, within the context of ignorance it relates only to the reality external to the self. 'Worldly' consciousness, un-aware of its fundamental nature, is actually a dream-like state of forgetfulness. The pseudo-awareness of an unconscious person is impossible to differentiate from its external expression, the mind. His minimal presence is sufficient only to fuel phenomenal consciousness and ego, not to solidify a true sense of identity. A sense of me based on the mind cannot create stability of self. The tragedy of the human is that he is not a being at all, but a chaotic flux of subconscious thought. Only by giving birth to pure awareness can one awaken from this painful and fragmented state and enter the stream of conscious evolution.

the awakening of awareness

The average human being, regardless of his intellectual capacity, is far from conscious. It is not mental acuity or the ability to solve complex problems that makes us conscious, but the light of I am. Artificial intelligence can perform highly intelligent functions, yet itself has no consciousness. A mind that is not grounded in clear presence lacks any true center to which it could refer its thinking processes. Unless we realize the unchanging background of all thoughts, we cannot meet our own existence, our inborn presence beyond thinking. Awakening to the state of presence is beyond any relative experience of becoming more and more aware of something external; it is a profound existential shift to objectless awareness.

The light of attention is the foundation of each act of perception and cognition, and can either be dispersed in the semi-conscious activities of the mind or focused in a one-pointed way upon itself. Ordinarily, we center our attention either through objects external to the mind or within the activity of the mind, as in conscious thinking. In order to channel our awareness in the service of self-knowledge, we must shift our attention from object to subject. When attention becomes aware of itself, it gives rise to the state of self-attention, or pure-attention. To be *just attentive* without any kind of object is awareness. Awakening to this pristine consciousness, we experience the miracle of regaining our true center.

the location of the state of presence

The assertion that the location of pure awareness can be pinpointed is commonly refuted by the argument that consciousness is 'every-where': if consciousness is all-pervasive, it cannot have any bodily point of reference. However, this reasoning is flawed, for it con-fuses the universality of consciousness with the individuation of its manifestation. The state of pure awareness that we experience in our human form is an individualized expression of universal conscious-ness and does indeed have a dwelling place within the human body. Psychosomatic awareness runs throughout the whole body, but con-scious attention is generated exclusively in the brain. Thus, the state of presence is awakened and experienced in the headspace.

The actual center of awareness is located in the middle of the brain, but the expansiveness and distribution of its energy are deter-mined by one's level of awakening. In the initial stages of practice the state of presence is usually recognized towards the back of the head when the eyes are open, and in the whole space of the head when the eyes are closed. One feels awareness more at the back of the head when the eyes are open due to the polarization of attention — aware-ness of the outer versus awareness of awareness. This is sometimes referred to as the 'double arrow' phenomenon, in which attention points out and in simultaneously, causing an intensified withdrawal of energy inwards. In the process of stabilization and integration, the state of presence matures and expands until it is gradually felt more as a spacious field of awareness that is both inside and outside the head. The fully awakened state of presence transcends the dichotomy between remembrance of our essence and recognition of our surroundings, encompassing both our pure subjectivity and the outer field of perception as one reality.

Many seekers confuse awareness with the heart or being aspects of the inner state. Because the states of heart and being are naturally cognized by awareness, they can be easily misidentified as that which makes their recognition possible. We can feel the heart and being through awareness, but awareness as such flows from a different place. It is not unlike the reflection of the moon in the lake being mistaken for the moon itself. The light of awareness can be experienced through a variety of different energetic states, or even as a general sense of body consciousness; but to feel pure awareness, we need to direct our attention to the area from which it originates — the headspace.

the energetic experience of the state of presence

The experience of consciousness, unlike all other relative energy experiences, is inimitable, for the experience is none other than the experiencer himself. The state of presence appears to be an 'object' of experience, since it can be verified by the checking intelligence, but it actually constitutes the identity of the experiencing subject. In all other types of energy experiences the subject is external to the object of experience. Only in the realm of I am does the subject not precede the object of experience in the flow of cognition, for here the subject is the experience. Thus the state of awareness can be called 'self-experience' — it is how I am knows it is I am. Consciousness does not need an intermediary to know that it exists and is conscious; it illuminates itself with the light of pure knowing intrinsic to its original form.

The process of giving birth to the state of pure awareness is rooted in the practice of centering the mechanical mind into a single area of self-attention. The state of self-attention, however, is not the final goal, but a transitional phase between forgetfulness and pure awareness. The experience of self-attention is more horizontal in nature than the state of pure awareness, the result of attention being pulled back upon itself. Pure awareness manifests when attention incorporates an element of being and begins to abide in the vertical reality. This more natural state of awareness has no center of attention; it is a spacious field of open luminosity. Our task, having solidified attention to the point of constant presence, is to diffuse that presence by means of surrender. The cultivation of presence moves beyond self-remembrance into a practice of de-centralizing awareness through which the state of self-attention is transformed into a condition of expansive restfulness and non-focalized abidance within the space of pure subjectivity.

The quality of the energetic experience of the state of presence depends on the level of its maturation and expansion. Initially, due to the need for internal focus and self-remembrance, the energy of awareness is more concentrated, and if practice is unskillful, it can be uncomfortable and tense at times. In the cultivation of awareness we do need to crystallize attention in order to transcend the mind, but we must very carefully balance concentration with relaxation to avoid *over*-crystallizing it, which would hinder our ability to achieve the natural state of presence.

Objectless awareness is the meeting place between the horizontal and vertical planes of existence — the here and the now. Through its natural evolution and integration, the state of presence eventually develops the qualities of clarity and bright vividness with respect to the horizontal dimension, and serene, effortless absorption with respect to the vertical. It is still experienced in and around the head, but in a transparent way, merged with the infinite vastness of reality.

Some souls experience the state of presence as bliss, others as more neutral and ordinary; but what is most critical is that we realize the essence of awareness not merely as an energetic state, but as the awakened consciousness of the soul. The living core of pure awareness is the sense of I am through which we meet the original light of our subjective existence.

the essence of individual consciousness

The fact that awareness is awakened does not mean that it is automatically realized as the essence of the soul's consciousness. Too immature to meet his true self, the average seeker recognizes only the energetic aspect of the state of presence, missing its deeper significance. To recognize only the energetic dimension of awareness is a limited realization, not a real awakening, for the heart of awakening is the meeting with our pure subjectivity. Practice with awareness that is not based on the knowledge of I am is merely mechanical and cannot be considered true self-remembrance.

Although the essence of awareness represents the center of our identity in the mind, the state of presence is often understood and experienced as impersonal. This is due to the fact that when one shifts from the habitual sense of me in the mind to the state of pure awareness, one moves from a personal to a comparatively impersonal experience of oneself. Additionally, because seekers are often strongly influenced by notions of the impersonality of consciousness, they tend to interpret their experience of awareness through the lens of this conditioning. The correct interpretation of pure awareness is not based on any particular belief or philosophy, but on an existential shift of identity. It is true that the state of presence is impersonal from the standpoint of our personality, since its existence is not derived from thoughts, subconscious impressions, memories or self-image; but it is very personal from the standpoint of the soul, because it constitutes the core of her identity in awareness. It is personal in a superior sense, as it embodies the light of pure subjectivity.

It must be clearly understood that pure awareness is made of the impersonal light of universal consciousness, while the state of presence is an individualization of that impersonal energy. It is similar to the space inside our home: though belonging to the vast universe, it temporarily becomes personalized by the unique flavor we give it. It is only because we are so identified with the egoic sense of self that we tend to translate the experience of I am in an impersonal way. Unless we are able to meet the light of I am within our deep silence, we will never be able to truly understand the secret of awakening.

to embody the light of I am

There are three possible errors in how we relate to pure awareness. The first is to objectify it as external to our sense of me; we experience awareness either as the 'background' of our existence, or the internal space in which we abide. The second is to perceive only its impersonal aspect; we feel as if there is nobody experiencing awareness, or that awareness itself is 'nobody'. The third is to over-personalize it by identifying I am with me; we experience awareness not as amness, but rather as I-ness — the state becomes tainted with excessive self-consciousness. Here we experience awareness as personal because we are on the wrong 'side', so to speak — it is personal from the standpoint of me, not the soul.

To correctly relate to the state of presence is in fact to stop relating to it at all — it is to become it. Ultimately, the ability to embody the light of I am is a function of our ongoing evolution into transcendence and soul-realization. By gradually merging our existence with pure awareness we become that ancient light of I am, the natural state of impersonal individuality, free of self-denial and self-reference. Then and only then can our true subjectivity be realized as who and what we are in our timeless purity.

the witness and witnessing

In some traditions the essence of awareness is referred to as the 'witness', or witnessing consciousness. 'Witness', however, is not the most appropriate term, since it has dualistic connotations, implying an act of witnessing that is horizontally separate from that which is witnessed. However, since it has already been assimilated into the language of spirituality, we would like to explain the meaning that the term 'witness' should convey.

To begin with, it is essential not to confuse the witness with the observer. The witness belongs to the soul and the observer belongs to the mind. The observer can emulate witnessing, acting as a detached intelligence by observing without getting involved; but the false sense of witnessing here is not based on our real presence — it merely reflects how the ego 'feels' itself as it attempts to remain disidentified. Such pseudo-witnessing is an experience entirely confined to the mind.

When awareness is unawakened and not present as the base-consciousness, the observer can only witness from his sense of me. The center of true witnessing is not me but I am. Pure awareness witnesses by virtue of being naturally distinct and uninvolved, not because it is disidentified. The true witness does not observe.

Awareness needs relative consciousness — mind and ego — in order to observe that which is first witnessed from the much deeper place of our essence. Observation is active, witnessing is passive. Observation is continuously recreated through the will of the mind, witnessing is a steady stream of unchanging consciousness. To be in the state of witnessing is to exist behind everything arising in the field of cognition — perceptions, thoughts and feelings — as an immobile background of unconditional presence.

cultivation of the state of presence

What we gain through recognizing our essence for the first time is a new insight into the nature of awareness, not the state of awareness itself. Although a beginner can access the state, the unconscious tendencies of the mechanical mind prevent him from abiding in his awareness with any real continuity; hence the need to cultivate the state of presence with the sole objective of stabilization.

Cultivation is a time of concentrated effort dedicated to the further awakening, strengthening and stabilization of awareness. During the cultivation period, the main difficulties in holding onto the state of presence, apart from general forgetfulness, are energetic in nature. The state is feeble and unstable and one is unable to maintain steady inner focus. The uncultivated brain simply cannot contain the high frequency of pure awareness with any clarity, strength and consistency. As a result, one quickly becomes tired or agitated during practice. These struggles are natural in the work with awareness. One simply needs to be patient as different aspects of our existence and consciousness realign themselves so that the dimensional leap into a constant state of presence can occur.

As we have made clear, the state of presence is cultivated through the horizontal pulling back of attention from object to subject, from seen to seer. The consciousness of an ignorant person is exteriorized from the headspace, leaking its light into the outer reality through the eyes and other sensory gates. Mental consciousness still operates in the head, but it has no energetic presence or stable sense of identity, for the elusive subject is fully identified with material and psychological objects. For this reason, to gain inner stability and internalize one's consciousness, one must practice self-remembrance and merge attention with its source. Through this practice, the state of pure awareness matures, steadily growing in strength and continuity until a clear state of presence is established.

The entire process of cultivation is based on the very natural effort of returning to oneself through the practice of self-remembrance in both meditation and activity. As one progresses, abiding in the state of presence becomes increasingly spontaneous and natural. There is still a need for effort, but it gradually loses its rigid quality, becoming more subtle and transparent. This type of natural engagement with presence characterizes the most developed stage of cultivation prior to stabilization.

unskillful self-remembrance

The main hindrance in the cultivation of the state of presence is unskillful self-remembrance, which most often results from not having clearly met the essence of awareness. A seeker ignorantly chooses a point of focus within the headspace that bears no relation to the essence of consciousness, and rather than cultivating mindfulness of his true subjectivity, he objectifies the space inside his head, or specific areas within this space, in order to have something to which he can affix his concentration. This kind of artificial practice has nothing to do with real self-remembrance. Due to its unnatural character, it is not only spiritually useless, but can create stress and strain within the headspace.

Another common error in the practice of self-remembrance is to confuse the sense of me with the sense of I am. This point is not sufficiently clarified on the classical path of self-enquiry, which does not differentiate between the sense of me and the essence of consciousness. The sense of me is the axle of our conscious mind and ego-structure, not the center of consciousness. The center of consciousness is I am, not me. To distinguish between the experiences of me and I am, we must be able to differentiate between our fundamental consciousness and our secondary sense of individuality.

Me exists between I am and the mind as the mediating sense of identity that links the soul and the human. During thinking, it is not I am, but me, that enters the mind to become the thinker. Me is the sense of I am reflected in intelligence, the consciousness of oneself. I am is the consciousness of awareness prior to and underneath our sense of me. I am is impersonal in the sense that it is beyond self-referral, while me is personal, for its very essence is self-reference. Me becomes more impersonal by surrendering to I am; I am becomes more personal as it is illuminated through me.

For me to assist the awakening of awareness, it must realize its own essence beyond the mind. However, me cannot reach solidity if I am has not been awakened, for its existence has no stable ground upon which to base its continuance. Our pure me is founded upon I am, and as such, precedes the self-image created by the ego-me — it is direct, instantaneous and independent from thought. The evolution of I am and me are mutually supporting: I am awakens through me, and pure me awakens through the birth of I am.

In experiential terms, me and I am also differ in their energetic and spatial character. Though close to each other in the headspace, conscious me is experienced in the frontal lobe of the brain, and pure awareness in its central area. If a practitioner focuses his concentration in the front of the head it indicates that he mistakenly cultivates a stable sense of me, not pure awareness. In order to abide in I am, one must internalize one's concentration and withdraw attention to a deeper space within the head.

stabilization of the state of presence

It is our observation that many seekers on the spiritual scene lack any concept of stabilization. We frequently come across those who cannot understand why, in spite of having temporarily moved to a deeper state of consciousness, they have entirely lost their awakened state. Most often their bewilderment is due to the fact that they cling to a simplistic paradigm of sudden enlightenment. They perceive enlightenment to be an instantaneous and total transformation when in truth, complete enlightenment is the result of a long and arduous inner journey.

To stabilize the state of presence is to permanently establish one's previously fluctuating awareness. Prior to stabilization, the state of presence is activated and maintained through the practice of self-remembrance. In more advanced stages of cultivation, it increasingly manifests of its own accord and maintains itself independently of me. Once the state has been stabilized, the practice of self-remembrance can be dropped; awareness is permanently and unconditionally present. It can no longer be lost, for it has become indivisible from our true identity.

Although stabilization is the fruit of cultivation, cultivation is not its direct cause. Stabilization is ultimately an occurrence based on grace. Grace, the force that can stabilize any state, awaits its materialization in the plan of each soul's blueprint. The role of the practitioner during cultivation is to bring himself to the highest possible level of inner maturity so that grace can enter and the relatively unpredictable event of stabilization can take place. The stabilization of the state of presence denotes a major breakthrough in our evolution, signifying that we can finally begin our true journey into the inner state from a place of awakened consciousness and integral identity.

integration of the state of presence

The integration of the state of presence is the post-stabilization ripening, refinement and final expansion of its energy into a natural condition of pure awareness. It is a critical step in our inner journey towards the attainment of the state of pure subjectivity as our natural state.

Integration is not the result of personal effort, but the consequence of an organic maturation within the already stabilized state. Cultivation of awareness does not necessarily enhance integration. In fact, inept cultivation can actually impede the integration process. Unless the personal will relaxes within the state of presence, a practitioner will habitually maintain an unnecessary level of concentration that prevents awareness from reaching its natural condition of spacious luminosity.

To support the integration process, we should simply rest in conscious abidance within awareness. Sitting meditation is one of the most effective means to further the integration of awareness, as well as other states, for it is here that the natural deepening and alignment of energy takes place. The process of integration requires a certain amount of time and patience, and must be completed before one aspires to undertake the next step along the path.

stabilization of recognition

In most cases, the stabilization and even energetic integration of the state of presence does not result in complete continuity of conscious abidance in awareness. Although the state may be energetically established, our sense of I am remains unintegrated with the consciousness and intelligence recognizing it. Until we stabilize the *recognition* of presence, the state remains fractured and cannot serve as a vehicle for the transformation of the mind.

That which forgets and remembers the state of presence is not our intelligence, but its very subject, me. When me is integrated with I am, it is able to participate in both presence and thinking, being and doing. Because it cannot completely renounce its involvement in the mind, me needs to learn how to maintain conscious recognition of awareness while intelligence is actively engaged. It must unite with the center of awareness so that an unbroken continuity of recognition can manifest.

After the initial awakening of the state of presence, me has the incentive of stabilization to inspire its self-remembrance. However, once the state has been stabilized, me must strive for a new goal — the merging of me with I am. This requires a higher form of self-remembrance: the constant recognition of awareness. Every time that me remembers the state of presence, it not only arrests the subconscious flow of the mind, but also intensifies the quality of awareness itself. The state of presence is magnified by the very fact that me is recognizing it; two forces of consciousness meet to engender a single holistic experience of self. Though I am is independent of me, true awareness must encompass me in order to reach its highest transformative potential and become whole.

integration of intelligence

Constant recognition of awareness cannot be reached unless our intelligence has been profoundly transformed. Instead of getting lost in the mental reality, intelligence must channel its power of cognition into constant illumination of the integral silence of I am. If our intelligence has not been aligned with I am, it is the mind, not the soul that is the experiencer of presence, since awareness has not yet become the actual subject. Intelligence, the cognizing link between me and I am, is therefore unable to register the existential shift of identity from ego to pure presence and remains identified with the psychological self. In order to transcend our subconscious self and integrate me with presence through the stabilization of recognition, self-remembrance must continue, but now on the level of consciousness and intelligence.

For intelligence to support the stabilization of recognition, true understanding must be born within the mind. The mind must see through its own illusory nature and deeply appreciate the tremendous value of pure presence. Only once we have matured into the profound understanding that we in fact *are* the consciousness of awareness can we renounce the subconscious, awaken true sincerity, and surrender to what is real. Each moment that we are lost in thinking, we are lost to the light of awareness, the foundation of our spiritual integrity. This is simply unacceptable for one who honors the silent truth of consciousness. An integrated intelligence is characterized by maximal silence and minimal thinking. The moment silence begins to rule the internal space of the mind, intelligence can be said to have integrated with pure awareness.

living the state of presence

The awakening of awareness is not only a great blessing, but a great responsibility. Very few seekers are actually able to see its profound value. After an initial period of fascination, their interest usually wanes. Such is the case of a seeker who has been initiated into the energetic aspect of the state of presence, but remains unawakened on the level of consciousness. Although he has access to a state beyond the mind, his experience is an energetic phenomenon external to his true subjectivity. It is the existential awakening that signifies real illumination, for it transforms the very consciousness of the soul.

Living the state of presence reflects the integrity of our consciousness and the dignity of our intelligence. From our true presence we derive inner stability, strength and natural contentment. We no longer allow ourselves to be lost in the dull state of unconsciousness and the misery of forgetfulness. By the power of continuous abidance in pure awareness we surrender the mechanical mind and serve, with our very existence, the light of I am.

awareness and ego

We awaken the state of presence to transcend our superficial personality. Unfortunately, however, there is a danger that awakening awareness can actually reinforce our ego-consciousness. Awakened awareness frees us from unconsciousness, but also empowers the ego sense of identity by giving it the center of presence. Even though the state of presence is our essence beyond the mind, when the awakening of awareness is not linked with a simultaneous awakening of the soul, the ego automatically claims the state as its own center of self-reference.

An ignorant ego may try to exploit the energy of awareness for selfish purposes rather than channel it towards its own spiritual awakening and transformation. We can take as an example a martial arts adept who cultivates a high concentration of awareness with the sole intention of defeating his opponents. In more extreme cases, concentrated awareness can even be directed to exercise mind control over others.

If impure, the ego will automatically link itself to our lower nature and subconscious tendencies. An ego that is insensitive, arrogant and greedy does not see the spiritual path as a bridge to oneness, love and transcendence, but as an arena in which it can expand its sense of self-importance. Unless we reach an essential level of purity, our ego will be tempted to abuse the power it gains through spiritual expansion.

After awareness is awakened, it is crucial that we surrender into being and the heart, and in so doing, dissolve the mind's tendency towards excessive self-consciousness. A seeker has to have the wisdom and humility to understand, deep in his heart, that the only legitimate reason to awaken pure awareness is to create a stable connection to I am in the mind to which the false me based on self-image can be surrendered. We must clearly see that the one who walks the spiritual path is not the ego but the soul. All the ego can do to serve the soul's awakening is align itself with her evolution and surrender its existence to her higher light.

Unfortunately, we cannot avoid crystallizing the ego in our work with awareness. Only a solidified sense of me can counteract the constant activity of the mechanical mind, which is actually a subconscious aspect of ego that has no real center or ability to focus attention. In order to gather its dispersed and restless energies for the sake of becoming conscious, me must develop one-pointedness and self-attention. Though there is some risk involved, the crystallization of the ego does not bring harmful results if one has a competent teacher, true sincerity, and purity of intention. It is no more than a tool we use to penetrate our separate existence so we can further merge it with awareness and being, and poses no real threat if we are true to our evolution and higher purpose.

conscious awareness

Even though we sometimes use 'awareness' and 'consciousness' interchangeably, from a deeper perspective, they are not the same. The word 'aware' comes from 'wary', a condition of being cautious, as in 'beware'. The word 'conscious' comes from the Latin 'conscius', which means 'knowing inwardly'. We can understand from the etymology of these terms that to be aware is more relative in nature than to be conscious, which refers to a state of pure knowing. One may lose awareness and remain conscious, but one cannot remain aware after losing consciousness. Mindfulness is an expression of awareness, not consciousness. To pay attention, to be vigilant or watchful — these are functions of awareness. To be conscious means that one is awake, that one knows one exists. It is only because we are conscious that we can be aware.

Ultimately, to be conscious is simply a deeper experience than that of being aware, because it points more directly to the level of our intelligence and sense of subjective existence. To be conscious indicates that intelligence and sensitivity of self are also engaged in the act of perception. To be aware is more functional; awareness is connected to the clarity and discipline of recognition.

An ordinary person is only conscious by the virtue of having a sense of me linked to the waking state. To be conscious one requires at least *some* presence, otherwise consciousness simply melts down into subconsciousness. However, as we evolve and awaken to our deeper identity, what it means to us to be conscious expands to include the realization of our essential I-amness. To be truly conscious is to embody the light of the soul.

Our understanding of what it means to be aware evolves in a similar way to that of being conscious. Awareness can be said to be an expression of consciousness. It is the light of I am channeled through me to illuminate creation with recognition. In the state of forgetfulness, the faculty of awareness is limited to the mind and disconnected from the essence of I am. Awareness is unaware of consciousness. Only upon awakening can awareness recollect its source.

Consciousness belongs to the soul, awareness to me. In the human dimension, consciousness needs awareness in order to awaken. Awareness is like a mirror in which consciousness is reflected back on itself so that it can recognize its essential nature. Consciousness without awareness is like a flower in a dark room that exudes a scent (a sense of amness), but cannot be seen (beheld as I am). Awareness is the radiance of consciousness; consciousness is the substance of awareness. Consciousness realizes itself by being brought to light through awareness, and awareness awakens by becoming stabilized in the essence of consciousness. For awareness to actualize its pristine nature of spacious clarity, it must surrender to consciousness so that consciousness itself will fill it up with the primordial knowledge of I am.

awareness and being

In order to solidify awareness in a natural way, it is essential to incorporate an element of being even prior to the stabilization of the state of presence. The energy of being is first added by relaxing the awareness in the head and vertically dwelling within that space. Gradually, as awareness become more stable, we allow our energy to drop below the head into an overall experience of being. To prevent losing our awareness in the headspace, however, we must maintain a gentle level of concentration and self-remembrance. At this stage, attention should be divided horizontally between outer involvement and inner self-remembrance while in activity, and vertically between resting in being and experiencing presence in the head in the non-activity of sitting meditation.

As we incorporate the energy of being in our work with aware-ness, we must be very careful not to allow the state of presence to become depleted. A seeker who relaxes deeply into being, but whose soul is not awakened, may lose his 'enlightened' relationship with awareness and cease to consciously abide in it. If we put too much emphasis on surrender in our practice before the state of presence is fully mature, awareness can actually get 'lost' in being; both our existential and energetic connection to the state degenerate. For this reason, it is essential that the proper balance between awareness and being be maintained.

Ultimately, one must embrace the simultaneous recognition of awareness and being as a unified space of awareness-being reality. Once awareness is fully established and integrated with being, we move beyond self-remembrance — awareness and being merge into one self-cognizing state of pure subjectivity.

being

Now we shall speak about the foundation of all — being. All creation is contained within the dimensionless sphere of primordial absence, the original void that constitutes the ground of being. Being is indeed the secret of existence and the unseen source of creation.

Although being is not an active principle, in its absence, not even the slightest movement in existence can take place. Without being, nothing can be and nothing can become. This infinite space of immobile reality upon which all universes dwell cannot be fathomed by the mind or the senses, yet it is the very womb of creation, the bottomless depth of universal I am.

to be

What does it truly mean to be? Although 'being' is one of the most commonly used and seemingly uncomplicated terms in the language of spirituality, very few truly understand its profound significance. Being is far more than non-involvement or passive abidance in the moment. It is the timeless beyond itself, the inmost sphere of pure existence that contains the totality of creation.

Being is found beneath the flow of time; it is the very source of this moment. It exists beyond the three-dimensional world of perception, beyond mind and consciousness. It is the black hole of existence through which creation manifests, the primordial emptiness from which consciousness arises in the instantaneousness of each now. It is only through the grace of being that we can transcend our separate self and realize oneness.

To experience being, one has to surrender vertically into the inner plane of rest. Unlike ordinary relaxation, which is experienced by the mind and body, being is felt through the inner body of the soul. If the energy body of being is not awakened, one is at most capable of experiencing a weak and insignificant connection to the now, and only in rare moments of complete restfulness and ease. But when one is open to the gravity of the now, being links the soul with the unmanifested reality of the source.

Through awareness we become present beyond the mind, but we cannot merge. It is being that enables us to achieve true absorption in reality. To be is to dwell within the now — and the now is the portal leading to the dimension of pure being, the place within time through which we are transported into the timeless.

where am I?

The question, 'Where am I?', though generally overlooked, is no less important than the primal question, 'Who am I?'. To gain clarity as to where we actually are, we need to enter the dimension of our abidance in the non-perceptual ground of all-that-is. The question 'Who am I?', points to the soul; the question 'Where am I?', to being, the primordial source from which the soul manifests. The vastness of the unfathomable depths within which we are who we are can only be discovered through our existential surrender into the void of the beyond.

the secret dimension of the now

Being is the very essence of the vertical dimension of the now. But when and where is the now? The abode of the now bears no relation to phenomenal existence; it lies beyond all spatial and temporal points of reference. Though here is now, the now is not *here*; it cannot be found in space, time or consciousness. The now can only be discovered by diving into the source of creation. To enter the now is not a matter of mental contemplation or enquiry, but a function of meditation and surrender.

What we commonly call the present moment is not of the now, but of the past — it is the now ever-receding from the observer. Ordinary consciousness can only relate to the now through the observer's recognition of the immediate past; the checking intelligence requires temporal distance from any experience in order to

119

register it. We call this passing now the present moment, yet it is already behind us. An unawakened human cannot actually experience the immediate. His highest expression of mindfulness is awareness of the immediate past. He does not know the now.

To enter the dimension of the now, and to experience the now in the now, we need to move beyond the inherent duality of experience and experiencer. Our consciousness has to enter the vertical dimension of the source and become one with the now as it manifests from beyond the now, as the now, in each now of creation. The experiencer of time must merge with the root of time in order to establish himself in the state prior to time so that he can witness the now before it becomes the present moment.

Being is the connective space between consciousness and the now through which consciousness surrenders to, and progressively fuses with the source. In the natural state of being, consciousness is inseparable from both the now and its source. The ultimate observer of the now knows the now through his own absence within the presence of the unmanifested.

That which enters the domain of the now is our very soul, within which lies the inborn knowledge of the timeless. To know the now is to dwell within the now, to purely experience the taste of being that arises from our unity with the universal source. To embody the now, our existence has to be absorbed into the vertical plane of reality — the supreme depth of being.

the vertical reality

How can we know the vertical reality while locked in the world of appearances? Until we awaken our pure subjectivity and enter the realm of objectless existence we simply cannot. Since it is through consciousness that we recognize the phenomenal world, to know prior to the known we first need to turn consciousness back upon itself — we need to withdraw our sense of identity from the horizontal plane of time, space and mind by awakening pure awareness.

The moment consciousness becomes self-conscious, the original knowledge of I am is recollected and we meet the primordial point of reality through which we can discover our abiding place within the vertical reality of the now.

From whence does the sense of I am originate? Upon what does consciousness dwell? It is often assumed that because consciousness is the original source of all creation, it does not require a dwelling place within existence. However, even though consciousness is the source of creation, it is not the source of itself; consciousness manifests out of the original now, which is prior to it.

Unless we gain a degree of mastery over the art of letting go, we will never access the source of consciousness. To let go is to release our whole existence into the vertical dimension and descend with the pull of gravity into the secret space of the bottomless now. Though unseen and intangible, only by the grace of the vertical reality does creation have a place within which to abide.

surrender into being

Being exists beyond polarities, but if we relate it to the time-dimension, we could say that its opposite is becoming. From the viewpoint of our human reality, being and becoming are seen as opposites, for we are unable to integrate them into our existence as one. Becoming occurs within the reality of space, time and consciousness, whereas being is the fundamental ground of pure isness upon which the movement of creation takes place. In reality, the soul participates in both of these dimensions, and is therefore subject to both being and becoming. She in fact bridges them with her own existence. In the natural state, there is a precise equilibrium between her essence, which abides in being, and her human aspect, which is constantly becoming. When attention is fully identified with objects, the soul gets lost in becoming and surfaces out of being. Excessive involvement in the outer world exteriorizes our consciousness from the now, disconnecting us from our ancient abidance in the source.

Most creatures are naturally, though unconsciously, connected to being, but humans have become uprooted from its sacred ground. The very make-up of the horizontally inclined mind and its mission to serve the personal will are in conflict with the nature of surrender. When the movement of the mind overpowers our internal calm and stillness, we lose our intrinsic connection to the inner plane and are pulled away from the now; we defy the gravitational pull of being by fueling the outward movement of our energy and consciousness. The only way to reactivate our lost quality of being is through the conscious practice of surrender in meditation. In meditation we open to reality by pacifying the activity of the mind, maintaining our presence, and continuously letting go. In the very simple act of sitting in the now, a natural opening and deepening of being takes place, allowing us to return to the state of inner rest. Meditation is none other than the timeless act of sitting in being.

Our experience of being is deepened in meditation, but not by any active effort on our part. In meditation we do not *do* anything to reach being, rather we *undo* all that opposes the non-activity of the absolute. It is the natural pull of the gravity of the now, not our relative exertion, which makes the absorption into being possible. Although our intention to surrender can be seen as the deepest expression of our free will, in truth we can do nothing but get out of the way. The more we try to do anything, the more we disturb the natural process of surrender. Initially, we do not sit in surrender itself, but sit in being with the intention to surrender, as all elements contrary to surrender — energetic resistance, mechanical thinking, and excessive self-consciousness — gradually loosen their grip. In time, the power of the now pulls us into the condition of pure rest so that we can embody the state of surrender. By yielding to the emptiness of being, the soul moves into the dimension of repose and stillness.

As we have mentioned, being should not be confused with common relaxation. Relaxation points to *who* is abiding, whereas being points to *where* we abide. The experience of being is far beyond any ordinary experience of restfulness — it is an entirely new dimension of abidance in reality. Being is the absolute unconditional repose of existence as it is. One cannot truly relax within the confines of one-self, since the separate self by nature exists in a condition of primal tension. For a human to reach the supreme relaxation of being, he must merge with the beyond.

the body of being

Although an ontological dimension beyond our individuality, being is still reached through the soul. As she grows into the now, an infinitesimal portion of universal being is transferred to the soul's existence, awakening her identity so that she can actualize her com-plete energy body. Through this inner expansion, the soul develops a new body, the body of being.

On the macro-scale, the self has the absolute as its body of being, but on the micro-scale, the soul, who is a microcosm of the self, must be endowed with a body of being in order to experience her wholeness. The expansion of the soul into the beyond can occur only through the being aspect of the inner state, for it constitutes the very root of her identity and the space of her abidance in the now.

When the soul is unawakened, the experience of being is trans-lated as a state of rest in the beyond. When the soul is realized, the state of being is integrated with a sense of being oneself — we no lon-ger differentiate between who we are and where we abide. Although being is ever beyond our individual self, we merge with it in the transparent meeting space where the body of the soul and the ocean of the now intersect. Only here, where individual and universal are dissolved into one indistinguishable whole, can the realization of oneness take place.

the energetic experience of being

The state of being transcends ordinary 'experience' because it cannot be objectified. It does not exist apart from the experiencing subject. However, even though the dimension of being is beyond human

123

experience, it may still be experienced by the soul in the mystery of her surrender. The soul experiences being not through thought, emotion or perception, but through the merging of her own existence with the pure subjectivity of the now.

Because being is an energetic dimension, the experience of being naturally takes place on the energy level. The energy of being is characterized by tranquility, calmness, stillness, relaxation, ease, peace and a blissful sense of inner repose. Since to be is to rest within the non-abiding void of the now, it is the flavor of rest that predominates. Though beyond us, being lets us anchor our sense of I am in its absolute stillness. To experience the bliss of being is to be received by the beyond.

the mind and being

It is not that the mind experiences rest through being, but that rest is experienced *beneath* the mind as the foundation of our existence prior to the arising of awareness and thought. The state of being does not require the complete surrender of the mind for its actualization, because it is independent of consciousness. The full realization of being requires only partial surrender of consciousness, but total surrender *under* consciousness.

We can say that the state of being is at once dependent on, and independent of the mind's attitude. Initially, it is through the surrender of the mind that we are able to relax into being, but when it is fully established, being is completely autonomous from the mind. Ultimately, through the evolution into transcendence that takes place beyond our awakening of the inner state, consciousness and the mind surrender so totally that the soul herself can merge with being and reach absorption in the beyond.

the body and being

Although the nature of being is non-abidance, through her surrender a human soul can actually abide in that non-abidance and realize

124

being as her original abode. It is true that the universal dimension of being has no point of reference in the manifested reality, yet this unseen realm is experienced as individualized in relation to our physical reality and personal angle of perception. The dimension of being itself has no spatial location, but we do experience it within our human form in a specific way. Although being points to the intangible beyond, its energy naturally penetrates the physical and subtle bodies. The feeling can be likened to that of being submerged in a warm ocean with closed eyes; what one feels is not the whole ocean, but the contact between the body and the water where the sensation of the ocean's presence radiates beyond the skin, around the body.

The energy center of the body, the hara, is located in the lower belly, so the energy of being is initially registered in and around the lower part of the torso as a descending sense of gravity and a feeling of heaviness from the weight of inertia. When we surrender into being, energy naturally gravitates towards this area, centering our vital force and anchoring our body in stillness. However, the experiential location of being varies depending on the level and character of one's inner awakening. For instance, a person who has activated the heart center will experience the energy of being not only around the belly, but also around the chest; the experience may even begin in the heart since energy will naturally be drawn there. Or, if awareness has already been awakened and integrated with being, the experience of being will also include the headspace. The more the three aspects of the inner state merge, the more any distinction between them dissolves into one homogenous field of being.

Those at the beginning of their work with being are generally unable to connect to the being of the beyond, and feel its energy exclusively in the body. Bodily awareness is often the only channel through which a connection to the now can be made for those who live in the mind. Due to its transcendental nature, an extraordinary maturity is required to realize being as the inner home of the soul.

Although vertical absorption brings about a certain horizontal expansion of the field of being, we should not focus on the horizontal experience. We do not verify our experience of being by checking the quality of energy states around the body as they may or may not be related to being. It is only by assessing our vertical expansion that we can truly gauge its depth. We may feel a horizontal expansion of energy beyond the body, or an auric field surrounding us, but we must not be concerned with these types of relative energies — they are only by-products of meditation. Rather, we should focus on how profoundly we dwell vertically within the now.

cultivation of being

Since the work with awareness takes place on the horizontal plane, it can be easily completed in activity. To reach the necessary depth and stability of being, however, we must cultivate it in sitting meditation. Unless we sit still, the energy of being has no chance to fully drop into the depth of the now.

Initially, the work with being requires the temporary suspension of one's horizontal involvement. As time goes by, we introduce our practice with being into everyday life as well; but until a significant depth of being has been established through sitting meditation, practice in activity is no more than a conscious effort to relax and cannot take root.

To cultivate being, we patiently sit in the now, perfecting the art of letting go. Sitting and letting go — letting go of everything that is not of pure rest. In due time, as our energy becomes increasingly absorbed in the dimension of the now, we experience the unconditional, natural state of being.

the depth of being

That which prevents the merging of the soul with the ground of being is the seductive pull of the vital force, which naturally emanates outwards towards creation. When we sit in meditation, we are situated between two opposing forces — one pulling us towards creation, the other towards the uncreated. In order to counteract the outward movement of energy and consciousness and merge with

126

being, we must surrender. Letting go into the gravity of the now, we gradually transcend the fluctuations of mind and energy and become rooted in inner stillness.

The process of growing into the depth of being naturally takes time and requires a great deal of patience, for we must completely transform our relationship with existence by allowing our consciousness to surrender to the source. How deeply we can submerge ourselves in being directly reflects the energetic purity and restfulness of our state, as well as the existential quality of our inner absorption. The more we move beyond our relative energies, the more we experience the unchanging, immaculate quality of being. When we reach the final depth of being, we embody the inner solidity and unbroken stillness of the beyond.

the absolute state

The ultimate experience of being is the absolute state, in which the soul fully transcends the fluctuations of her abidance in the now and enters the unoriginated, unbecome, unmanifested ground of reality — the absolute. The absolute is the primordial void that contains totality, the foundation of the never-ending expansion of creation, the living depth of absence. Everything dwells upon the absolute; all manifests from it at the beginning of creation and all returns to it at the end of time. The absolute state is not the absolute itself, but the meeting between the soul and the absolute.

To be able to distinguish the absolute state from a deep experience of being we must understand that they represent entirely different dimensions of realization. Their difference cannot be measured by degrees of depth. The absolute state actually signifies a quantum leap in the depth of being, beyond depth itself. Prior to reaching the absolute state, being is experienced on the side of creation; after, on the side of the uncreated. The significance of this statement needs to be contemplated deeply.

Let us imagine an intermediate space that lies between the original void and the reality of creation. Such a space does indeed exist, for there must be a bridge between the radically polarized dimensions of absence and presence. This mysterious 'in-between' space can either be approached from the side of the source or from the side of manifested existence: the absolute pulls the soul from within, the soul surrenders to it from without. When the soul surrenders to the gravity of the original void, she is absorbed into being from the side of creation. Still, she has not yet moved to the abode of the absolute. To cross the invisible border that separates the dimensions of presence and absence is to experience death while living. Those who have crossed over to the abode of the unborn have the rare privilege of becoming immersed in that which is beyond both life and death — the supreme source.

In the absolute state, all relative instability of energy within the experience of being is transcended and we attain the ultimate experience of pure rest. Though empty and immobile, the absolute state has the extraordinary strength and power of the absolute itself. Just as pure awareness is the zero point of consciousness and the now is the zero point of pure awareness, the absolute is the zero point of the now. The absolute has no attributes but one — it *is*. The original isness of the absolute is the sacred container of all existence.

entering the absolute

How does one enter the absolute? How is it possible to move beyond all relative experiences of being and pass through the gate of unconditional stillness? Only when we have expanded the frontier of our surrender to its final limits can we dive into the inner ocean of the now and relinquish the pull of the vital force, letting go of everything that holds us to the will of self.

To move our sense of I am beneath consciousness and the life force is ultimately not a function of effort. Our willingness to let go is an essential element of our passage into the absolute, but the final shift is a function of grace. We make ourselves available to the pull of the absolute by very precisely tuning our existence to the supreme

being

stillness of pure rest, and the absolute itself opens the door for the soul to enter. Through the practice of dropping our will, we fall with the force of gravity to the place where presence touches the realm of absence, and upon reaching this final limit of letting go, a power from the beyond receives us into the domain of immaculate rest.

To assist us in the practice of letting go into the absolute we can employ the practice of surrendering with the exhalation. We fall with the out-breath into the gap of pure being, which opens up for a short moment at the end of the exhalation, then rest in that space before inhaling. In this gap lies the secret passage to the other side of the now; it is precisely here that our energy can momentarily return to the condition of pure rest. Prior to opening to the absolute, our consciousness cannot stay in this gap for more than an instant, for it immediately feels suffocated by its own inactivity. Consciousness cannot free itself from its inherent will to act until it becomes absorbed into the dimension of absence. When the inner gate to pure rest opens up, we catch a second breath — a breath of eternity not taken by the lungs, but by the consciousness of pure freedom. The shift to the absolute state is an implosion of energy that sucks our being into the supreme repose that awaits us beyond the now.

stabilization of the absolute state

As with the state of presence, the principle of stabilization also applies to the absolute state. The shift to the absolute indicates that we can access the state, but only when our energy is properly aligned. Due to our inability to rest in the beyond with constancy, we can consider the unstabilized state as still belonging to the coming and going of experiences, a phenomenon not inherent to our true nature. Before stabilization, the absolute state is not yet the real foundation of our existence.

Stabilization in the absolute is the flowering of our continuous dedication to surrender and unbroken abidance within the state of pure rest. We have to become inert like a stone. Maximum vertical inertia combined with the drawing-down of gravity from the source intensifies the inner pull to its limit so that our energy can gradually settle down into the bottom of being. When our being reaches the necessary degree of maturation and inner expansion and fully merges with the absolute, the state finally stabilizes and becomes the natural base of our existence. At all times we are contained within the pure perfection of the groundless ground of total life.

integration of the absolute state

Before the absolute state is fully refined, there are still subtle energetic oscillations within the quality of our inner abidance. The integration of the state involves polishing the condition of pure rest until maximal transparency is attained and the state is thereby rendered natural and complete. It is an organic process that we support with the practice of deep breathing in sitting meditation, and by consciously surrendering to the state at all times.

Once integrated, the absolute state reflects the perfection of our abidance in the supreme absence of the beyond. Although not the final goal of our evolution, the integration of the absolute state lays a tremendously significant foundation for our future attainment of wholeness, representing the solid ground of reality from which the soul draws the power she needs for her expansion into universal intelligence.

How deeply the absolute state is ultimately realized is determined by the strength of awareness and being with which the soul enters the beyond. If awareness and being are fully empowered, the soul has the necessary force to penetrate the innermost core of absence; otherwise, the absolute will be experienced in a more shallow way, as a plane of emptiness or tranquility. We call the highest realization of the absolute the 'diamond mountain', since it embodies the qualities of infinite strength, solidity, clarity and depth.

heart

The heart is the sun of creation — the ultimate magnificence, compassion and love of the god state. The heart reveals divine beauty, tenderness, prayer and devotion to us. Truly, without the heart there is no reason to live, for in the heart resides the light of our original divinity, our ultimate link with the love and grace of the creator. It is only in the heart that we can find the true meaning of our existence.

The heart holds the timeless memory of our transcendental origin and the knowledge of our final destiny. Through the heart we meet the essence of our soul, and through the heart we return to the abode of the beloved. It is the heart that makes our humanity sacred and bridges us with eternity. To open the heart, our existential center, is the key to our psychological sanity in the human dimension and our spiritual awakening as the soul.

the heart

Although we naturally feel the heart to be the most personal facet of our existence, its multilayered reality includes an impersonal aspect as well; it is both the core of the soul's identity and the energetic realm of her abidance in the divine. As a 'state', the heart is similar to awareness in that it represents both a dimension within the impersonal energy of the inner state as well as the essence of I am. However, there is a difference between the sense of I am in the heart and the sense of I am in awareness: I am in the heart is even more personal, more primordial, for it signifies the original light of our identity, whereas I am in awareness is an expression arising out of that light. Through I am in awareness, the soul expands her self-identity from the heart to the mind — she awakens her center within the dimension of thought. But it is within the heart that the fundamental nature of the soul's existence dwells.

the awakening of the heart

Sometimes we speak about awakening *to* the heart, and sometimes about the awakening *of* the heart. There is a difference. In speaking about awakening to the heart we point to the realization of the absolute heart of existence and the eternal heart of the soul; the awakening of the heart signifies the opening of the human heart. Since the human heart connects the mind to the soul, its awakening is one of the most important steps in our evolution. By awakening the heart, we gain access to the ancient knowledge of our true self and enter the realm of the creator, the beloved parent of our soul.

Most humans try to protect their emotional vulnerability by building walls of insensitivity around their hearts. These shields may shelter us from hurt, but they also separate us from our inner beauty, tenderness and capacity to love. We cannot begin the journey into the heart unless we first dissolve the armor of resistance and self-protection encasing it that we ourselves have constructed.

Even though the spiritual heart lies beyond personality, the first stage of its opening is emotional in nature. We need to bring the forgotten heart of the child that we were once upon a time, and still are deep inside, into the present. We need to surrender to our inner sensitivity and open to the heart's purity. Only by humbly returning to our innocence in prayerful devotion to our divine essence can we truly reconnect to the truth of the heart.

Surrendering to the heart, we open up the dam of our sadness. We must fully experience the inner pain that we have never stopped pushing away, and embrace it with love and forgiveness, allowing tears of grief and longing to flow from the hidden recesses of our being. These tears cleanse our heart, purify our mind and open us up to a loving communion with the divine.

the energetic experience of the heart

The energetic opening of the heart is not itself a complete awakening, but represents a shift into the heart that brings profound change to the quality of our existence. Energy moves to the heart center, inundating it with a gentleness and sensitivity that gradually dissolves inner wounds and blocked energies born of fear, pain and the very knot of separate self.

The spiritual heart, located in the center of the chest, is where we find the energetic portal to the dimension of the soul and the divine. Initially, when working with the heart, one may feel an expansive warmth and tenderness in this area. The more it opens, the more the heart's energy radiates both inwards, towards its own center, and outwards, to circulate around the chest. One increasingly experiences the heart as a field of pure feeling, softness and love.

After the energetic shift into the heart is complete, the state of the heart is rendered permanent and can be considered stabilized. However, we do not put much emphasis on the idea of stabilization in the work with the heart because the journey into the heart never ends. Upon stabilization, the heart simply opens to a new, more universal evolution and expansion into the divine.

A seeker who has shifted into the heart but not yet stabilized the state often experiences a contraction of the heart when identified with negative thought patterns and emotions. However, for someone already established in the state, the heart will never lose its energetic openness; thoughts and emotions of a lower nature may close the human and existential dimensions of the heart, but never the energetic one. Psychological confusion and mental agitation affect the emotional aspect of the heart because the mind and the heart are interconnected, but they cannot touch its spiritual depth.

In one who is unconscious and lacks the presence of awareness, the mind continuously eclipses the reality of the heart. Even if sensitive and compassionate, he cannot experience the heart with any consistency due to his fragmented consciousness. In fact, the heart of a loving but unconscious person is almost always closed, for to be unconscious is to have no soul. There can be no real love if there is no clarity of awareness and continuity of presence. Only a conscious person can surrender his mind-based intelligence to the silent depths of the heart.

As an energetic state, the heart shares the qualities of impersonality with the other aspects of the inner state, and along with them, constitutes the environment of our internal abidance in reality. The energetic awakening of the heart creates the ground for further inner expansion, but the actual conversion of our existence into a higher state of light and love requires a much deeper awakening and further purification.

the enlightenment of the heart

Far more profound than the energetic opening of the heart center, the enlightenment of the heart enables us to contact its living depth and realize our pure subjectivity, the intrinsic knowledge of I am. The enlightenment of the heart is comprised of two aspects: the awakening of the soul and the purification of intention. Because we elaborate on the awakening of the soul in great detail further on, we shall confine our discussion here to the purification of intention.

To undergo inner transformation it is not enough merely to be 'in touch' with the heart; the purification of intention requires that the mind submit to the heart. The negativity of the mind can only be purified when the core of its identity yields to the truth of the soul. If the mind is not aligned with the soul, it can endanger the awakening of our higher self, for its subconscious tendencies are not based on the principle of light. Only when the mind's intelligence awakens to the higher purpose of our existence and gives up its egotistical self-infatuation can it finally surrender to the soul.

The purification of intention is the coming together of our human intelligence with the truth of the heart, a process that takes place deep within the soul's consciousness. It does not bring about the complete transformation of the mind, but it is a significant turning point. The triumph of our higher nature over our subconscious tendencies ushers in a new era of our evolution — the mind finally begins to serve the heart. Prior to the purification of intention, the mind and heart pull in opposite directions, but the enlightenment of the heart liberates us to honor that which is in harmony with the truth of higher wisdom.

the layers of the heart

The outermost layer of the heart is directly tied to the human personality through the emotional body. For this reason, the first essential step in our human expansion into the heart is to shift from living through thought to living through feelings. Feelings are simply closer to reality than thoughts, because they touch that part of us which is existentially more real and more intimate with the soul.

Outer impressions are digested by the mind and, once assimilated, reside there as memories, creating a virtual reality through which our emotions are filtered when we think about our relationship to the world. Most humans experience the heart only when a deep feeling provoked by the external reality is channeled through the emotional body. When we are moved through an intense encounter, we are not experiencing the heart itself, but its response to emotional stimuli. We may feel joy in our heart when we are in love, or compassion when we encounter deep suffering, but these feelings are external to the reality of the heart itself. As long as it is lost in the phenomenal reality, the heart cannot recognize its own subjectivity.

To be connected to one's feelings is in itself very meaningful, but when our consciousness is ruled by lower intelligence, our feelings can easily be channeled in the wrong direction. We can take as an example people who are brainwashed to feel their heart when experiencing patriotism or religious fervor. They might even be ready to die for an imaginary idea that deeply affects their emotions. This type of heart opening has no connection to the wisdom of the soul. Unfortunately, the deep emotions of most humans are usually no more than unconscious impulses triggered by unintelligent messages generated by the collective mind.

Though still linked to the emotional body, the next level of depth within the heart is where we experience the heart itself. We may feel a deep sense of sadness or happiness in the heart unrelated to anything in particular. The emotions are still engaged, but they are flowing towards the heart center, identified more with the heart's essence than any psychological content. Previously, all of our emotions were directed outward; now they begin to move inwards towards our pure subjectivity.

A tragedy such as the death of someone we truly love can take us back to the lonely reality of the heart in which we experience the pure quality of existential suffering. If we only have access to the first layer of the heart, we will identify solely with the event that moved it. But if we are able to connect to the heart in a more profound way, we will experience it in its subjective purity. Significant moments like these can push us deep into the personal dimension of the heart. The more we are in touch with our heart at these times, the more we may question our relationship with the world and, disillusioned with our reality, dwell in existential emptiness. Times like these when we are able to feel and experience our existence in the primal space of aloneness are actually precious opportunities to realize the mystery of being oneself and encounter the light of pure subjectivity.

And so, layer by layer, we move from thought to feeling, and from a place of deep feeling, become conscious of our primal bond to the heart. In due course we come to a pristine experience of the heart, beyond any dependence on external influences to help us feel. At last we can meet the knower behind all feelings — our very soul.

The soul exists between the emotional body of the human and the inner dominion of the beloved. She either travels a trajectory outwards towards the world through human emotions, or inwards through the heart and her own existence to the divine. The divine dimension is the final depth of the heart — the eternal source of all hearts, the absolute love from which the heart of me emerges.

the essence of love

The word 'love' is grossly misused and misinterpreted by the sentimental human psychology. It is a term not only worn-out and commercialized in society, but in religion and spirituality as well. What does it truly mean to love? What is love?

The essence of love is the heart as it is. Love does not have wants, for it reflects the pure perfection of divine wholeness. It is not a commodity, nor a means to satisfy our inexhaustible emotional needs. Love is a limitless space that contains all-that-is beyond any subject-object relationship. Unless we realize the state of oneness and dissolve the illusory separation between ourselves and existence, there is no way that we can know true love. As love is the nature of the self, only through unity with the self can we merge with the natural state of love.

the center of feeling

Despite the excessive development of the mind that makes most humans so abysmally out of touch with their feelings, the fact remains that it is how we feel that matters to us the most. How we feel determines the very meaningfulness of our existence. The heart is the center of feeling *and* the center of perception. Whether we are conscious of it or not, all that we experience is registered and interpreted in the heart. Most people simply do not feel what their heart feels; they feel what their mind 'feels'. Their actions and responses are not rooted in the knowing of the heart, for their connection to the heart is blocked. To go beyond our superficial psychology and contact the truth of the soul, we must consciously open to our deepest feelings so that our experience of reality reflects the living wisdom of the heart.

the wisdom of the heart

Because the heart's deep wisdom originates from the soul, our higher being, it operates in a different way than the intelligence of the mind. The wisdom of the heart is not based on methodical reasoning or the analysis of events, but on the direct discernment of right from wrong. The decision-making process within the heart relies on intuition, feeling and pure knowing. We should be careful, however, not to make impulsive decisions based on overpowering feelings in the name of listening to the heart. Spontaneous emotional reactions do not necessarily have anything to do with the wisdom of the heart. Unless we are awakened and purified, our instinctive emotional responses are most likely tied to our lower nature and disconnected from our spiritual heart.

Higher wisdom is born of the integration of the intelligence of the mind with the sensitivity of the heart. To access the heart's inherent wisdom, we must see its clear reflection in the mirror of the mind's intelligence. The mind has to tune into and decode the inner voice of the soul, and with discrimination and understanding, articulate the heart's guidance.

the gate to the divine

Although the spiritual heart is felt in the body, its unmanifested essence resides in the inner realm. One side of the heart points to creation where human reality reigns; the other, to the unborn side of the heart where the creator resides. In order to enter the divine realm, we need to melt the boundaries between our individual heart and the universal heart. Only by becoming drunk with the divine, and in that intoxication forgetting oneself, can one merge with the beloved.

No one who is locked in the prison of self can bask in the glow of the inner sun of creation. Through our surrender into the final depth of our individual heart we become submerged in the ocean of the universal heart where our eternal parent awaits us. Finally we realize that the true heart is not contained within our individuality — it is the totality of existence, the divine realm itself.

the horizontal expansion of the heart

Through being we experience non-separation; through the heart we realize oneness. If the pull of being overrides the energy of the heart, the soul is alienated from the reality of creation; hence, the pull towards the source must be balanced with a horizontal expansion of the heart. The unity of being and heart enables us to experience a perfect equilibrium between the horizontal and vertical dimensions.

If the heart is not awakened, the gravity of the now pulls the soul into the beyond through the gateway of being, bypassing the heart. But if the heart is open, the gravity of being does not draw any energy away from the heart center; being and heart are experienced as one. The balanced combination of their energies gives rise to a double, yet unified expansion into the beyond. Being actually becomes the vehicle that transports the soul into the divine realm. The fruit of this dual expansion is the directionless state of all-embracing presence — the realization of everythingness. It is only due to our ignorance that we need to awaken each aspect of the inner state separately in order to realize them as one reality. From a higher perspective, the absolute and the divine are indivisible.

abiding in the heart

The most meaningful experience of the heart is natural absorption within its depth. To be absorbed in the heart is to merge with the heart. When we merely *feel* the heart, our separate self is still too distinct — our very presence makes absorption impossible. Only through conscious surrender can we reach the degree of absence necessary to become one with the divine. By the simple act of sitting and letting go into the unity of being and the heart we grow roots into the divine dimension. The heart absorbs our separate self into the presence of the soul and her absence in the supreme beyond. We disappear into the heart and reappear in the state of wholeness.

the inner state awakened

The birth of the complete inner state within our existence is the basis for our evolution towards wholeness. From this foundation we go beyond the mind and enter the realm of the soul. In the fully actualized inner state, awareness, being and heart create one holistic experience of our abidance in reality.

Without the vital knowledge of the integral reality of the inner dimension, it is virtually impossible to understand the awakening process. Seekers who do not possess a holistic vision of the inner state cannot progress in a clear way, for even if they do experience a certain level of awakening, they cannot identify what they still lack inside for their completion. How can one attempt to reach completion if one does not know what it means to become whole? Before we can fully awaken to the dimension beyond the mind, we must understand how its various aspects interconnect. This clarity liberates us, opening the door to our true evolution.

not soul, not self

An essential point that requires demystification is whether the inner state represents the universal self or the individual soul. In truth, it is neither the soul nor the self, but the dimension within which they meet. The inner state is the internal environment where the soul abides and awakens as well as her portal to transcendence; it is the soul's existential extension into the realm of the self. However, until the state of transcendence is realized, the inner state functions less as an entryway and more as a connective space between the soul and the beyond. Only when the dimension of absence is reached in its final depth does the inner state become a wide open gate to the supreme self.

The inner state transports us to the beyond, but it is not the beyond itself. When the soul awakens, the inner state becomes one with her individual subjectivity, but continues to serve as her portal to universal subjectivity. As the soul progressively merges with the realm of absence, the boundaries between the inner state and the beyond become more and more transparent until they finally dissolve into the ultimate reality.

the union of identity and abidance

The experience of the inner state has both a personal and impersonal quality. The sense of I am inherent to the states of presence and the heart is of the soul, and the impersonal void of being is of the self. If the soul is unawakened, the inner state serves only as the place of her abidance in the universal reality — it is not filled with the presence of her individual essence. When she awakens, however, the soul transmutes the energy of the inner state into the light of her true identity. Through the integration and unification of her I amness and beingness, the soul at once awakens and transcends herself in the realization of oneness with the beyond.

a unique vision of completion

Everyone needs the complete inner state in order to become whole, but the extent to which each aspect is awakened depends upon the make-up of the soul and her unique potential. Not everyone is destined to achieve exactly the same state. Our spiritual potential, level of consciousness, and blueprint determine the quality of the final state we need to realize. For example, not everybody has the capacity to reach the absolute state — in fact, it is neither required nor desired by all souls. To arrive at a clear vision of our own completion, we need to receive guidance from a competent teacher, or to intuitively recognize the singular flavor of our inner evolution.

integration of the inner state

The energetic quality of the inner state reflects the dynamics between its three constituent aspects: awareness, being and heart. Depending on their past evolution and spiritual constitution, seekers will have a natural predisposition towards one of these aspects, and greater difficulty awakening others. Some are more open to the dimension of being, others to awareness or the heart. The fact that one experiences problems awakening one aspect of the inner state over the others is certainly no excuse to remain incomplete; it is simply a positive indicator of the areas that need to be given more attention in order to awaken the inner state as a whole.

Once each aspect of the inner state is completely awakened, we are ready to enter the phase of integration. The integration of the inner state refers to the post-awakening unification of awareness, being and heart. Just as each aspect has to integrate within itself, it is also necessary that they integrate with each other. Prior to integration there can still be friction within the inner state; one may have excessively crystallized awareness and find it hard to surrender into being, or if one's energy is pulled disproportionately into being, difficulties may arise in merging being with heart or awareness. There are many possible scenarios of discord between the three aspects. In all cases, awareness, being and heart need to be brought into balance with each other so that they can be transformed into a single organism of I am. The more they are integrated, the less there is any division between their energies. Through the process of integration, awareness, being and heart gradually dissolve and expand into each other, giving rise to one field of pure transparency — the natural state.

abiding in the inner state

Through the birth of the inner state we gain tremendous stability inside; we reach a permanent ground of awareness-being-heart that cannot be touched by the ever-changing reality of the world. Besides opening us to the inner realm, the establishment of this state readies the soul for the essential processes of purification and healing that were impossible to engage in fully before she dwelled stably beyond the mind. When we are totally identified with our psychosomatic existence, there is simply no space within which real transformation can occur.

142

The inner state is more than just the static foundation of our inner peace and comfort; it is a dynamic reality of continuous growth towards the soul's transcendence of earthly consciousness. Having awakened the inner state, we are no longer ruled by lower intelligence and can finally begin our true life, guided by the intrinsic wisdom and purpose of the inner realm.

realm of the soul

The soul is another name for our true self, the heart of our individual existence. Unlike the personality, the soul exists independently of the mind; she is by nature free of the incessant fluctuations of our mental and emotional states. She is made from the radiance of consciousness and pure intelligence and, in her essence, is in a timeless state of unity with universal being and love. She exists to serve the never-ending evolution of light and understanding as she expands towards the fathomless depth and mystery of the god state. Although individual and unique, the soul remains eternally one with the impersonal movement of universal intelligence — she is a single angle of perception through which the beloved beholds the consciousness of creation.

The awakening of the soul is the most significant step in our evolution towards the realization of oneness, wholeness and completion. Prior to her awakening, the soul finds herself imprisoned in the plane of lower intelligence and exists merely as her personality. She is limited to her ego, locked in the subconscious reality of the mind. The light of her presence has been lost in the shadow cast by her human self. To awaken her true nature, the soul must transcend her forgetfulness and realize her essence of I am. Through the vehicle of me, she gives birth to her ancient identity of pure subjectivity and actualizes her divine individuality at last.

from ego to soul

We are not who we appear to be, and we appear to be who we are not. In truth, human beings are not individuals, but endless copies of the collective mind. Immersed in total illusion, we live like sleepwalkers, oblivious to our true self. We have sacrificed our original beauty, strength and freedom for a false existence created by the mind.

The term 'ego' denotes the self-limiting aspect of the soul's identity which, prior to her awakening, functions exclusively through the personality. The ego, however, needs to be seen not only as an aspect of ignorance, but also as a positive stage of evolution in which consciousness becomes self-aware for the first time. The essence of ego is its sense of me, the foundation of the conscious mind. In forgetfulness, this sense of me is fully identified with the mental reality. However, once awakened, this very me bridges our unconscious self with the consciousness of the soul.

One of the most dramatic occurrences in human evolution is the shift of identity from ego to pure me, in which the soul moves out of complete self-forgetfulness and into increasingly higher states of self-remembrance. So ordinary yet so profound, the culmination of this inner journey of remembrance is the event of becoming oneself. To be a true individual is to be who one is in the ultimate sense of the term, to awaken the light of our soul-identity whose seed lies dormant within our most secret existence.

the evolution of consciousness

What makes us human is the ability to know that we exist. Our mind, aware of its own activities, constructs a subjective sense of 'I' to whom all its acts refer. The development of this self-consciousness in humans is certainly a positive evolutionary step, for it raises our awareness above that of all the other species that inhabit our planet. And yet, despite its significance, this step from the unconsciousness of the animal kingdom to the consciousness of human kind, does not signify a true awakening. Human beings are still more unconscious than conscious. They are in fact only semi-conscious, for their consciousness is limited to the mind and alienated from the self. Although the mind manifests from the self, the self is not recognized by the mind.

imprisoned in the mind

At humanity's present stage of development, individuals have no stable existence or sustained center within; their identity remains exclusively based on ego. This is why most seekers are not able to answer the simple question, 'Who am I?'. Their ego may have sufficient sense of self to ask this question, but not to answer it.

The stage of evolution in which we recognize the sense of me is the first step in coming to know our true self. However, the sense of me created by the mind, which constitutes the core of our ego-identity, is but a shadow of the real me. We only begin to discover who we really are when we give birth to our presence beyond the mind. A human being unable to affirm his existence as 'I am therefore I am' is not at all conscious.

the ego

The human ego is a mental agent that possesses a sense of me based on self-referral. Although all creatures share the sense of me, there is a significant difference between the me of a highly evolved animal, such as a cat, and that of a human being. A cat does indeed have a sense of me, and its whole organism serves the 'love to be' of that particular me. However, the cat's sense of me does not have the clarity and strength of the human ego. It has an unfocused, dreamlike quality — more automatic, reactive and instinctive. We refer to this as 'subconscious me'. The sense of me of a human ego is far more sophisticated and complex, having the capacity for a higher level of both concentration and abstraction. It can maintain a continuity of focus during thinking and even think about itself. The self-reflective faculty of the human ego utilizes not only thoughts, but also a wide spectrum of emotions, in order to project its image — out to the world to gain approval or manipulate its environment, and in towards itself to maintain psychological integrity and a positive self-image. But no matter how sophisticated it is and how strong its sense of individuality, the irony of the ego is that it remains fundamentally ignorant of its own essence.

Mind and ego represent two sides of the same consciousness: the mind is the flow of thoughts, and the ego is the mechanism of self-reference within this flow. The ego must be recreated moment to moment through self-referral. For an unconscious person, a gap in self-referral is experienced as a moment of blankness or of being 'spaced-out'. Without the mind to fill this gap, he has no means to confirm his own existence.

While entrenched in its pseudo-identity, the ego serves as a shallow substitute for the soul. By compulsively clinging to its self-image, it deceives itself into believing it is real. It seeks love and acceptance just to feel that it exists. Yet in spite of all its desperate efforts to escape its own emptiness, the ego will never reach true solidity until it transcends itself by awakening to the light of the soul.

the shadow of the soul

In the state of ignorance, the ego exists as a false I created by the mind claiming to be our true self. It masks the soul, concealing her real essence, and uses the light of I am to generate its own sense of me. Although linked to the dimension of pure subjectivity, the ego's sense of me is but a pale reflection of our real self. For the soul to own her me and liberate it from the mind, she must awaken.

The relationship between the ego and the soul can be likened to that of a minister and a king. The minister, our ego, serves the king, our soul, but the king owns the kingdom, our existence. The minister becomes dangerous the moment he begins to behave as if he were the rightful ruler. This usually happens when the king is still a child and does not yet have the maturity to administer his inherited power. In due time, however, the king becomes ready to claim his supremacy and puts the minister in his proper, subservient place. The situation with the soul is similar; she is initially too immature to rule the ego. In most humans the soul resembles a baby totally unaware of itself. For the sake of our spiritual sanity, it is imperative that the soul awaken to her own existence and gain the maturity to assume the governing position within our consciousness.

the role of the ego

The majority of spiritual traditions make the error of denying the ego any positive role, reducing it to a mere barrier to freedom and liberation, or even negating its reality entirely. However, to negate the ego is pure hypocrisy, for it is the ego itself that is doing the negation.

As we have pointed out, simplistic negation of the ego is spiritually dangerous, and any teaching that fails to perceive the ego as essential to understanding and consciousness is out of touch with reality. The ego cannot simply be negated; its energies must be embraced and redirected so that they may ultimately serve as fuel for our awakening. It is not the ego itself that is false, but its ignorance, unconsciousness, and illusory separation from the soul.

The proper function of the ego is to bridge the subconscious self with awakened consciousness. By internalizing the energies of consciousness, the ego begins to support the soul's awakening to the realm of pure subjectivity. Having reached this relative spiritual maturity, it can now direct its energy towards positive enquiry into the nature of self. It questions its own existence and seeks transmutation into a higher me, the me of the soul. It is when the ego reaches its highest power of attention, intelligence and sensitivity that the realization of I am takes place.

The ego also plays an important role in protecting our relatively separate existence. The human being, regardless of his spiritual awakening, still remains bound by the laws of empirical reality. Even a self-realized being needs to have a 'minimum ego' to survive on the physical plane. This minimum, or *natural* ego, operates not as an expression of ignorance, but as an extension of the enlightened reality, a function of intelligence that serves the soul, free of self-image or any sense of separation.

Before we can dissolve the ego, we must accept its presence and submit it to our higher wisdom. For someone who has just entered the inner path, the dissolution of ego is not the proper aspiration. Instead, one should bring more acceptance, wisdom, understanding and purity into how the ego functions in the mind so as to align it with the will and light of the soul.

the multidimensional self

To comprehend the interconnection between soul and ego, we must take into account our multidimensional existence. Our sense of identity is composed of many layers that express themselves simultaneously on multiple levels: body and mind, thought and emotion, intuition and intelligence, ego and soul. The ego and the soul are the two main dimensions of our subjective reality necessary for our complete human experience. The human is the vehicle of the soul, and the ego is the self-consciousness of the human. In the hierarchy of the subjective reality, the ego has a much lower position than the soul, serving merely as her link to the phenomenal world. Unlike the soul, the ego is not a part of eternity.

the ego and self-enquiry

Self-enquiry can be described as the ego's existential effort to reveal our eternal self hidden beneath the layers of our human personality. Self-enquiry, the awakening question of our true identity, links the intelligence that seeks its true identity to the awakened answer, the soul herself. Because it points beyond the mind, self-enquiry must transcend mental effort in order to illuminate the direct experience of our essential self.

The main point of confusion on the path of self-enquiry relates to the false assumption that through the power of enquiry we can instantaneously access the ever-present self that remains unrealized only due to ignorance. The reality is that our true self cannot be recognized prior to first being awakened and actualized. Self-enquiry is not limited to seeking and seeing who we are in the present now; it actually opens the space of intelligence and being within which the soul can finally remember and awaken her timeless essence.

the ego seeking the soul

How can the ego assist in the awakening of I am if the soul is not yet consciously present? The ego cannot manifest the soul, nor can it perform the act of awakening. Its function is to align the mind with the quest of the soul so that she can realize her innate potential. On the conscious level, the ego initiates the inner search, but in reality, the spiritual quest is the command of the soul. Even before she is awakened, the soul instinctively begins to search for her true identity by enquiring into the essence of pure subjectivity through the medium of her ego's intelligence. Although stimulated by the ego, awakening itself takes place beyond its bounds — it is a radical movement of perception and being from the mind to pure subjectivity. True awakening happens within the soul's consciousness.

Despite its positive contribution to the awakening process, there exists a danger that after the birth of our pure subjectivity, the ego will claim I am as an experience it *itself* is having; it will see I am as an object and itself as the subject, thus thwarting the realization of the soul. Hence, after awakening, the ego must submit itself to I am so that the soul can become our real center. Only when our identity shifts from ego to I am can the soul embody our true subjectivity as the host of our existence.

the soul becomes I am

When the ego finally forfeits its false sovereignty, the soul can fully awaken to her subjectivity and become I am. A seed dies by initiating the birth of a tree, yet in a mysterious way, it becomes that tree's future life. Similarly, the mind's sense of me serves the awakening of the soul only to ultimately sacrifice itself for the emergence of the real I. In this way, its energy is not nullified, but transformed into the life of the soul. Although the ego begins the journey, it is the soul that completes it. The seeker becomes the sought.

who am I?

Self-enquiry is the internalization of consciousness through the medium of the mind. Properly applied, self-enquiry can bring us to the threshold of pure subjectivity, but it lacks the power to awaken the whole experience of the soul. Through self-enquiry we may recognize our essence, but to become our complete self, we must evolve and expand within this essence beyond enquiry.

The traditional aim of self-enquiry is not to awaken the soul, but to realize her absence, either through identification with the all-pervasive self-of-all or the negation of the personal self. As we attempt to transcend our personality through self-enquiry we should take care not to negate our soul as well. Our aspiration to merge with totality should not lead us into self-denial. If our self-enquiry results in identification with the universal self, we suffer a case of mistaken identity, having confused our relative subject with the absolute subjectivity.

For self-enquiry to reveal our true identity, we must be free of both ego-based perceptions of reality and strictly impersonal interpretations of enlightenment. We must dwell neither in a void of negative absence derived from the negation of our personal self, nor an illusion of omnipresence derived from identification with universal I am. True self-enquiry points to the essence of our individual existence, the heart of me.

The soul is not the universal self, and never will be. Her very creation implies a level of individuation. In the realization of the self we reach unity with the supreme reality; we do not become that reality. The state of unity is a plane rich in diversity that contains infinite individual angles of perception, all existing within the unified whole.

the light of I am

To enquire into the truth of our existence is to investigate the very fabric from which consciousness is made — the light of I am. How do we know that we exist? How do we experience the sense of being alive as distinct from our psychosomatic reality? Isn't it through the innate knowledge of I am, the essence of creation? I am is the radiance of the heart of the beloved through which all beings can become conscious of their existence. The whole spiritual path points to the task of regaining this sacred knowledge. To seek our true self is to yield to the luminosity of the heart in which the silent confirmation of our existence is eternally present as: I am that I am.

the essence of me

A tremendous maturity is needed to meet the essence of me within oneself. This maturity cannot be gained from the world, because the world has always conspired against the truth of me by fostering our addiction to the reality of objects. Unconsciousness strives to maintain itself as the status quo by keeping us disconnected from our essence. It is not by chance that so few individuals desire awakening, and even fewer actually reach it.

Many seekers pursue the path to enlightenment, but most are merely grasping at goals that have no connection to the essence of me. Rare are those who can experience bliss just by being alone and savoring the taste of I am. Those who truly seek the essence of me are fond of solitude and silence, for in those spaces they can feel their me more deeply. One has to have a natural inclination towards deep intimacy with one's innermost existence. Awakening to the essence of me is a profoundly personal realization, a true love affair with self.

awakening to me

The axis around which our individual consciousness revolves is our innate sense of me. We could not function within our human identity without the inborn knowledge of me that is present behind all of our experiences and psychological states. Who is the observer within us so intrinsic to our existence and understanding? Beyond his observational role, the observer possesses a sense of identity unrelated to any of the functions he performs in the mind. The observer observes from his sense of me, not as a watcher or thinker, but as a pure reflection of the soul's being in the mirror of human consciousness. However, when we are unconscious, our me, although partially present, has no stability within the chaotic flux of the mind. The complete presence and solidity of our sense of me can only come through the awakening of awareness. An awakened me has a clear identity distinct from the movement of thought. Because it dwells in awareness, it gains the natural constancy of subjective presence. In our higher consciousness, awareness and me become one: awareness is the 'amness' of me, and me is the 'I-ness' of awareness. Me is no longer separate in the soul who is integrated and whole.

Because me represents the individual awareness of the soul, awakening to me is a prerequisite for the awakening of the soul. Before the soul can awaken as the soul, she must awaken as me. Although me and the soul both represent our true identity, the soul is closer to the source, and me is closer to creation. The soul is our original I am, and me is her personal expression. To be realized, me must unite with the soul, who in turn must awaken through me.

Me is a more active principle than the soul, bringing the element of luminosity into her consciousness without which she could not realize herself. Without me, the soul lies eternally dormant in her unmanifested essence. I am is the original state, the samadhi of reality, and me is the radiance of clarity and intelligence. I am is the absorbing consciousness, and me is the awakening consciousness. When me finally merges with I am and awareness becomes absorbed in consciousness, the original awakened-absorbed-consciousness is met as the timeless ground of creation.

the evolution of me

Me begins the complex journey from the state of forgetfulness to complete realization by enquiring into the essence of consciousness and supporting the awakening of awareness. Next, me assists the stabilization of awareness through the practice of self-remembrance. Me then reaches its own stability through its conscious abidance in, and relative merging with, I am.

Initially, me supports our transformation by solidifying its own essence. As we continue to evolve, however, me becomes more oriented towards its own dissolution into the inner realm. After the three aspects of the inner state have been fully awakened, me expands in a holistic manner to realize itself as transparent me. Me then surrenders itself in the realization of the transcendental state by identifying with the vertical absorption of awareness. Finally, me realizes itself fully through the samadhi of me and merges with the consciousness of the soul in the realm of absence.

the dimensions of me

Out of the creator manifests the soul; out of the soul manifests me; out of me manifests the observer, our conscious ego, the thinking center of the mind. The observer, being a function of the mind, does not have a constant presence, but arises only when needed to serve as a conscious link between pure me and arising thoughts. Only pure me has real continuity and substance, for it is unconditionally present. Through the awakening of pure me, we transcend the instability of personality and solidify our fragmented self into our true identity. Me is divine in its essence, the face of the soul in creation. The supreme cause wills that it manifest as the singular consciousness of our sacred individuality.

the seat of the soul

For a human being lost in unconsciousness, the only trace of light is preserved in the heart. Prior to her awakening, this is where the essence of the soul resides. We can meet our me through awareness, being or intelligence, but it is in the heart that we encounter the deepest, most intimate core of who we truly are. Unless we meet the soul in the depth of the heart, the essence of our true self cannot be actualized. The heart's essence is indeed the seed of our future self.

meeting oneself

We do not need to reach far for what we seek. It is so immediate, so direct. One has to embrace the mind, becoming calm and clear, and in the purity of that silent presence, relax deeply into oneself. This is the only way out of despair, the only way to leave the tragic reality of the lost soul behind. Nothing is more urgent than meeting oneself — it must happen right now.

soul-realization

Our evolutionary mission is to transform the tiny spark of purity and longing in our heart into complete awakening. However, because our capacity to realize the soul is fundamentally limited by our fragmented consciousness identification with the personality, our efforts have to be supported by the grace of the beyond. The realization of the soul is part of the divine plan, and anyone who serves it will receive assistance from the whole of existence.

the body of the soul: the union of personal and impersonal

The dimension beyond the mind can be understood either as a state we are in or as our subjective existence; it can be seen from the viewpoint of the inner state or the soul. In other words, the soul is the I am of the inner state, and the inner state is the internal space within which I am dwells. We can relate to our inner condition either as our identity or our internal environment.

It is the evolutionary level of intelligence that inhabits the inner state that determines whether its experience is translated as personal or impersonal. A seeker in touch with the light of pure subjectivity will recognize the sense of I am inherent to the inner state, while one unawakened to the soul will experience the state beyond the mind as an external, objectified space of abidance. Without the consciousness of I am to illuminate it, the inner state is no more than an empty shell.

We can look at each aspect of the inner state and see how the factors of maturity and conditioning can influence how we interpret our experience. For instance, a translation of the state of presence as purely impersonal indicates that we are still identified with the observing intelligence, not the light of I am. An interpretation of awareness as personal indicates that we have the ability to embody it as our pure subjectivity, but are unable to dissolve into it due to our self-consciousness. Ultimately, the state of awareness experienced in its fullness by a mature soul reflects both the personal quality of I am and the impersonal quality of the inner state.

In a similar way, the heart can be felt either as the essence of the soul, or as a field of energy. For those who subscribe to traditions that deny the existence of the soul, the experience of the heart will naturally be impersonal. On the other hand, for those on the path of devotion, the heart will be felt as purely personal. The complete experience of the heart bridges the personal and the impersonal by uniting the essence of I am with its abidance in the beyond.

The situation with the being quality of the inner state is somewhat different, for being does not constitute the soul's identity. Although the soul actualizes herself within being, being is essentially beyond any individualized energy. Being is the I am of the supreme reality, not the I am of the soul. However, as the soul merges into being, she integrates it with her sense of I am and transmutes it into her own body of pure subjectivity.

When we speak about the need to embody the inner state as a personal experience, we mean that it is personal to the soul, not to the ego. If the experience of the inner state is personalized by the ego, the soul over-identifies with the sense of me and cannot realize herself or merge with the beyond; she remains stuck in self-consciousness. In contrast, if the experience of the inner state is too impersonal, the soul is bypassed; her essence is either absent or unintegrated. A perfect balance should exist between the personal and impersonal aspects of the inner state, by the power of which the soul can be realized and our false individuality absorbed.

We draw a distinction between the inner state and the soul only for the sake of clarity, not to indicate any inner split. As our path unfolds towards its true purpose and we become more whole and integrated inside, the division between the inner state and I am gradually dissolves. At the end of the awakening process, the inner state becomes the very body of the soul, no longer distinct from her essence. Upon completion, impersonal and personal — the inner state and the sense of I am — are realized as one.

the levels of soul-awakening

To be human does not necessarily mean that we have a soul-identity, and to have awakened our soul-identity does not necessarily mean that our soul is realized. Although endowed with human nature from birth, a child needs to grow up in order to become a mature human being. Similarly, even though we all have a soul identity from the beginning of our creation, we need to reach a certain level of evolution before we can recognize and realize it completely. The awakening of the soul is a slow and gradual process. It differs for each individual, but always involves a long inner journey.

Although the awakening of the soul requires the inner state as its foundation, the presence of the inner state does not guarantee soul-realization. Soul-realization arises from a far more subtle and personal level of our existence, the primordial essence of I am. Ultimately, this awakening occurs on both energetic and existential levels. The energetic awakening is experienced as an inner expansion of our soul-body, and the existential awakening as the illumination of our consciousness. It is the existential illumination that gives soul-realization its true meaning and profundity.

The first step in the process of soul-awakening is the recognition of the essence of I am in the mind. Through this awakening, the mind begins to relate not only to its own content and ego, but to the soul as well. However, because awareness represents only a part of the soul's identity, the full realization of the soul requires further evolution. In our journey into the soul, we must expand beyond the realization of I am in awareness to its realization in the heart, for the heart constitutes the innermost core of our subjective identity. Similar to awareness, the heart does not contain the complete soul, but it is closer to the essence of our divine subjectivity. For the soul to awaken yet further, I am in the mind and I am in the heart must merge and become one. This unification enables us to experience the soul in a much more holistic and complete way, and becomes the foundation for the realization of her future wholeness.

transparent me

The first stage of soul-realization, transparent me, signifies the integration of the soul with the inner state. Through her circular expansion within herself, our me fully illuminates itself from within its essence and imbues the inner state with its complete presence. The soul transforms the energy of the inner state into the consciousness of her own existence — she begins to own the inner state as her body of I am. The attainment of transparent me can be seen as the first step in transcending the division between the inner state and the soul. No longer does the soul only *dwell* in the inner state, she becomes its embodying consciousness.

Transparent me contains the seed of wholeness due to its holistic nature; however, a large gap exists between one's initial entry into the dimension of transparent me and its complete realization. Frequently, a seeker may shift into the state of transparent me, yet remain unable to grasp its true essence. As with the awakening of awareness or the heart, transparent me can be realized either purely on the energetic level, or in combination with an existential awakening. A purely energetic experience of transparent me is the evolutionary equivalent of the state of no-mind or the state of oneness, not the state of pure subjectivity. When the maturity and sensitivity to meet transparent me as I am are lacking, one simply has to grow further into this profound realization in order to fully embody the soul.

Transparent me manifests from the uniting of oneself with the environment of the inner state. It is a state of existence in which all the centers of me and the inner state merge into an all-embracing field of I am, grounded in who we are, yet simultaneously fused with the beyond. In this state, the circulation of energy is directionless and the soul abides in the all-pervasive space of universal existence. This particular realization points directly to our pure subjectivity in its uncrystallized and non-self-referential condition of non-abidance. It is called 'transparent' because there is no longer any center of me as such; one's energy has reached the purest condition of translucency.

Transparent me describes a state of relative equilibrium between horizontal and vertical expansion. Because it has not reached the final depth of vertical absorption, it is not a condition of complete surrender; it can be said to exist *between* relative pure-consciousness and the absolute reality. Only when the soul crosses over into the realm of absence does she finally move beyond self-consciousness into the realm of samadhi to actualize her eternal self.

transcendental me

The soul represents a unique, individualized angle of perception, but she is impersonal and universal in her essence. Until the link with personality is completely severed, the pure existence of the soul remains intertwined with the ego self-consciousness. When she reaches the state of transcendence and the samadhi of me, the soul retains her identity, but her ego-essence of self-reference is dissolved. In this new state of being, the experiencer merges universally with reality and *no one* remains at the center of experiencing. There is no one, yet this no one is none other than our true self.

Transcendental me is rooted in the dimension of the eternal whole, beyond earthly and human existence. In this state of identity, one moves fully into the realm of non-being to become one with universal I am. In the space of transcendence, the soul meets herself in a completely new way; she no longer knows herself through her presence, but through her absence.

The soul cannot be fully realized prior to transcendence, for her me is still bound by the consciousness of the earth. As she moves through ever more transparent layers of oneness, shedding her human personality and dissolving into the realm of absence, she becomes freer to expand into her ultimate self. Upon transcendence, the gravitational movement of the soul's surrender ceases, and its pure power is harnessed to finally awaken her complete presence.

to become a divine being

To fully realize the soul is to reclaim one's essential self, to become a divine being once again. Although a divine being retains a level of individuality and maintains a unique existence, he is free of both self-consciousness and a relative sense of me. He has dissolved into existence, but continues to exist as an inimitable manifestation of the undivided whole. A divine being is one with universal evolution. Endowed with the soul's body of pure light and consciousness, he serves the never-ending expansion of truth, love and understanding.

the blueprint of the soul

Our destiny is encoded in an evolutionary blueprint that reflects the purpose of our existence and the plan for our completion. The soul exists to fulfill her destiny in time. What happens on earth impacts the whole cosmos, and what happens in the cosmos impacts the totality of universal evolution. Exactly how existence expands into the mystery of the supreme reality is determined by the thoughts, choices and actions of all beings existing within its space. Although our blueprint predetermines our destiny, by exercising our free will we can either accelerate or slow the realization of our evolutionary goal. Each one of us is responsible for the direction of our intention towards truth and enlightenment. The noblest way we can serve the universal light is by yielding to our own evolution. This is our highest duty, and anyone who is conscious must honor it.

the unique destiny of each soul

Each soul is unique, but as long as she identifies with the collective mind she has no true individuality. True individuality has to be awakened; it cannot be created by the mind. As hard as the ego may try, it simply cannot succeed in being original; and nothing is more unoriginal than two egos competing for originality.

The soul is unique because she is herself, not because she tries to become someone or something else. She has the inimitable flavor of pure subjectivity and a distinct place within the totality of existence. There is certainly a general connection between the destinies of all souls, that is, the global blueprint. Within this universal destiny, however, innumerable variants reflect the individual make-up and characteristics of each soul.

Every soul needs to awaken and realize the state of oneness, but the path to awakening will differ from soul to soul. The blueprint of one soul may reveal that she can reach completion solely through the heart, while that of another may indicate the need to reach the final depth of the absolute. For some, living in the world is necessary to reach completion; for others, renunciation is the only way. There is not just one, uniform path to enlightenment for all individuals. Each soul needs to expand the frontiers of her illumination in accordance with her unique spiritual destiny.

The destiny of our soul is essentially expressed in two ways: through the vision of our final completion and the nature of our evolutionary path. The vision of the soul's completion is determined by our singular blueprint, which reveals what specific elements we require in order to become whole. The nature of our particular evolutionary path is the manner in which the soul needs to reach that completion. The unlimited diversity of blueprints points to the truth that each soul has an exclusive place in the ecosystem of universal evolution and wholeness.

It is the consciousness of the supreme reality that has created our ultimate destiny. Our blueprint holds the plan of our evolution and the predestined vision of completion that reveals how our countless cycles of incarnations will end. It is an existential representation of who we are in our ultimate potential, our unfolded future now.

remembering our future self

We can perceive the model of existence as descending from the highest reality to the over-soul; then to the soul, pure me, conscious me, and subconscious me; and finally, down to the unconscious. However, in this dimension, the evolution of intelligence is based on the principle of ascension from unconsciousness to subconsciousness; subconsciousness to consciousness; consciousness to the soul; and finally, from the soul to the universal source.

It is a common misconception that to remember our original self is to bring into the present who we have always been. A seeker who unimaginatively follows the idea of self-remembrance may in fact falsely believe that he has already existed prior to this cycle of time as

165

his perfect soul, which only by some inexplicable misfortune became lost in forgetfulness. In reality, however, prior to becoming lost in the dimension of ignorance, we did not exist at all. Indeed, forgetfulness is our very beginning. The task of the great remembrance is to give birth to our soul for the first time. What we remember is our destiny, the exalted realization of our divine potential. The soul is not our forgotten past, but our ultimate future.

the soul — lost, dormant or active

The dormant soul can remain inactive for many lifetimes before she finally becomes ready to awaken. Only in rare cases of evolutionary deformity does the soul never awaken. When she becomes permanently stagnated in her evolution, or serves the lower intelligence of darkness over the course of many lifetimes, an irreversible corruption of intelligence can occur that results in her total annihilation. She becomes extinct — lost forever. Like a seed failing to germinate after many seasons, she finally disintegrates.

Because the soul cannot remain dormant indefinitely, if she does not consciously enter the stream of evolution, she will at some point exhaust the force-potential to awaken bestowed upon her at her creation. Each soul has only a limited number of lifetimes in which to become activated before she withers away and dies. If the soul is lost like this, one's individuality is erased and its essence of I am dissolves back into the source of creation. It is not a punishment; it is as if one had never existed. Unless our sense of me solidifies through the birth of I am, our continuance within the whole is not guaranteed.

The soul can only enter our conscious reality once activated. That she is 'active' does not signify that she is awakened, but that she exists in an intermediate condition; she has not yet become herself, but has moved out of her dormancy and can develop a living relationship with the personality. Present on a subtle level beneath our ordinary sense of me as the inner call, she begins to communicate with our ego identity in order to align our surface consciousness with the truth of I am. In this way, the soul guides our personal intelligence towards awakening through the media of intuition, feeling and inner knowing.

the wisdom of the soul

Spiritual intuition resides beyond the conscious mind, deep in the recesses of our inner being. The wisdom of the soul is not generated by the mind, it flows from her evolutionary instincts and spiritual sensitivity. It is through these faculties of higher knowing that she accesses the knowledge of her evolutionary blueprint encrypted in the memory of her timeless essence.

How can the soul unfold her destiny prior to her awakening? As we have previously described, the essence of the soul never becomes a part of ignorance, but timelessly abides in the place of her origin. Endowed with the intrinsic knowledge of our blueprint, our essence bridges the unawakened soul with her future realization. However, only when this knowledge is remembered and reflected in her human intelligence, and the spiritual intention and commitment to her evolution are awakened, can the soul begin her inner journey in a conscious way.

Seekers often try to avoid the challenge of seeking their inimitable destiny by identifying with traditional visions of enlightenment. They blindly believe that the general blueprint of evolution outlined by their tradition of choice directly corresponds to their own unique destiny. Sometimes this is true — their identification may indeed be in harmony with their soul's blueprint. But if they follow a path of evolution that is misaligned with their destiny, they can become disillusioned and stagnate. However, if a seeker is sincere, the soul's wisdom will steer him in the right direction sooner or later by creating life circumstances that trigger awakening, such as encounters with important books, teachings or masters. Seeing life from the perspective of many cycles of incarnations, the wisdom of the soul always directs us towards the inevitable fulfillment of our evolutionary blueprint. The soul is like a river that sooner or later must reach the ocean. Such is the divine law.

to have a soul or to be the soul

To be inspired and led by the soul's wisdom does not mean that one *is* the soul. Unless one becomes the soul and the soul becomes oneself, our conscious intelligence will remain existentially split from our fundamental identity. When the soul is active, one can be said to have a soul; only when the soul is awakened does one become the soul. To have a soul means that although our sense of me is still based on the mind, our higher being communicates its presence through the layers of our personality. To be the soul means that we have actualized our higher identity and that our conscious mind has become the intelligence of our eternal self.

In the plane of ignorance, the soul is not an actual entity; it is merely an embryo of our ultimate self. The soul must be realized to become our conscious reality. Only through her awakening does the soul become whole and replace our artificial sense of me with the higher consciousness of I am.

karma and blueprint

'Blueprint' should not be confused with fate, or karma. They are related, but not the same. Blueprint is the plan for the soul's destiny; karma is the law of cause and effect that rules the dimension of time and creates the relative material that the soul uses for the realization of her blueprint.

Karma is created by our thoughts and actions, external circumstances, and the influence of the collective karma. Karma can be positive, negative or neutral — it supports, impedes or has no significant effect on our evolution. As it is part of the time-space dimension, its effect cannot be bypassed until the soul reaches liberation. After transcendence, the law of karma still impacts the human, but it no longer binds the soul.

If we have a positive karmic connection to a particular tradition of enlightenment or a specific spiritual guide, the soul will use this association for her growth. But if we are pulled by a karmic connection that is not beneficial, like an attraction to a teacher who cannot help us, it is a case of negative karma. Positive karma aligns us with the blueprint of our evolution and helps us reach our evolutionary goals without having to face unnecessary obstacles; it can be understood as the force of purpose that links our existence on earth with the evolutionary intent of our blueprint. Negative karma ties us to all the tendencies generated by our past actions that pull us down towards our lower nature and unconsciousness.

Karma is not a fixed law of justice and causality that determines the course of our life or governs our future in an absolute sense. Its effect depends largely on the level of our consciousness. The more unconscious we are, the more we are conditioned by the karmic construct of our internal and external realities. As we grow more conscious, purify our intention and awaken our soul, an ever-widening space is created for our intelligence to operate within our karmic reality — we can gradually transform the negative karma that blocks our expansion into the light. The matrix of karma does not exist as external to self; it is intrinsic to the make-up of the subconscious reality that conditions our desires, perceptions and intelligence. Thus, to positively alter our karmic reality, we must transform and purify our own mind.

the goal of wholeness

The presence of existential suffering and discontent naturally point to the incompleteness of the soul — she cannot rest until she actualizes her blueprint. For the soul, lack of wholeness *is* suffering. Suffering can be viewed as a condition of existential insufficiency that reflects the gap between our ignorant and awakened self.

Although the final character of wholeness varies from one soul to another, it is nonetheless founded on the same universal qualities: human completion, abidance beyond the mind, soul-realization, transcendence and unity with the divine. To become whole is to reach complete autonomy from the external reality and be a light unto oneself — an immaculate microcosm of universal perfection.

realm of the human

Although most humans experience their consciousness as a distinct and autonomous reality, from a higher standpoint it is only a relative, temporary expression of the soul on the earth plane. Still, before the human can initiate the process of his own awakening and dissolution, he must reach a level of completion within his earthly existence. Only from a place of relative completion and maturity can we realize that our human life is not an abiding reality, but a transitory stage in our eternal growth towards higher consciousness and transcendence of the earth plane.

the human personality

The drama of our evolution begins when the soul enters the plane of time, takes human form, and forgets her eternal essence. The soul needs the medium of the human in order to enter physical reality, but the moment she becomes limited to her human consciousness she is sucked down into the dimension of ignorance. The unique predicament of the human is that he is at once the force that obscures the soul's essence and the very apparatus through which she awakens.

In his ignorance and alienation from the soul, the human exists in existential aloneness in the realm of ego, as if abandoned. Only by realizing the true purpose behind his creation from within his human existence can he return to the realm of soul. Before the soul can awaken, the human must awaken. And so we can see that human life has two aims: completion within the personal dimension and the awakening of the soul.

The need for personal completion is mandated by the soul's blueprint — it is necessary in order to fulfill her earthly destiny. The soul's evolution begins within the framework of her human personality and runs parallel to her human awakening. Through human longing the soul awakens; through human completion the soul is freed; through human surrender the soul transcends.

the structure of the personal self

The physical, mental and emotional bodies are the outer shells of the soul, and represent the human personality. While we remain in an ignorant state these bodies have a relatively autonomous existence, operating without any conscious connection to the soul. The human personality is actually a microcosm of the collective mind channeled through an individual stream of experience and memory, a hologram of personal identity. Since he does not possess I am, the human borrows his sense of identity from the soul in order to create a unified sense of self from this scattered flow of psychological elements. It is this reflection of I am in the mind that we translate as our sense of me, or ego. Although our human identity is devoid of any real substance while we are unawakened to the soul, there is still a definite wisdom, continuity and purposefulness in our psychological existence. Our countless incarnations are linked together by a thread of evolutionary continuance.

the force of desire

That which fuels our actions in the world is the force of desire. The three bodies of personality — physical, emotional and mental — are conditioned to seek satisfaction through their interaction with the world. The physical body seeks pleasure, comfort and fulfillment through the medium of the senses. The emotional body seeks gratification through affection, love, attention, acceptance, and recognition. The mental body derives pleasure by accumulating knowledge and understanding, and by growing in intelligence. These three bodies are fully intertwined, each affecting the performance of the other. Beautiful music or stunning scenery experienced through the sensory gates of the physical body creates excitement and pleasure in the emotional body, and is then registered as a positive thought in the mental body. The mind and emotions can never be fully separated; what we feel and what we think are always intertwined. Some humans live more through their emotions; others, more through the mind. But we all feel what we think and think what we feel.

We live because we desire to live. We have been drawn to the earth because this is where we hope to fulfill our countless desires. The inability to reach satisfaction in this reality is caused by the illusory nature of these desires, which promise so much, yet rarely bring fulfillment. Some desires are perfectly natural and in alignment with our growth, but most are generated by the greed of the mind and its perpetual state of dissatisfaction. The force of desire should not rule us blindly, for what we desire, we shall become. To live intelligently, we need to understand the nature of our desires and the potential consequences of their fulfillment. A human being should channel the energy of desire with a discrimination that is in harmony with the deeper wisdom and purpose of evolution.

the complexity of the human being

As human beings, we are clearly not able to handle the amount of self-consciousness originally allotted to us by evolution. We have become unnaturally disconnected from both the wisdom of the earth and the higher purpose of our evolution. Our spirit simply cannot catch up with the disproportionate development of our brain. An overdeveloped mind that is disconnected from its spiritual essence is at great risk of misusing its mental power for selfish and exploitive purposes, and destroying its environment and itself in the process. Our intelligence is a gift that allows us to function efficiently in the world, but with this gift comes great responsibility. The intelligence of the mind has to be transformed so that its power will serve our spiritual evolution, expanding beyond territorial instincts and the primal need for survival.

Our psychological well-being is based on a delicate balance between the movement of thinking and the stillness of silence. The moment thinking overrides silence, our consciousness becomes unnaturally agitated, and the resulting friction creates states of neurosis and depression.

The human being is the only creature that suffers because of his own mind. The overactive mind undermines our basic sanity, the sanity of silence. No wonder there is so much suffering all around us. The only way to transcend this fundamental disturbance is to become more conscious, transform the mind, and gain a deeper spiritual perspective.

the art of living

The chief characteristic of human existence is a discord between the natural desire to reach peace, harmony and love, and an inability to overcome the obstacles that stand in the way of their fulfillment. One of the solutions that various spiritual traditions offer to resolve this problem is the renunciation of the world. Relative renunciation is a valid option, but only for those who are comparatively mature, both in their spiritual and worldly existence. We enter the earth-plane not only to transcend it, but also to experience it fully. Although no true satisfaction can be found in the realm of illusion, to seek happiness is an integral part of our human life. To renounce and withdraw completely from the world is not the way, since we have chosen to be here, and anyway cannot escape. To exist as a human personality is a challenge that we must face from a place of wisdom, clarity, humility and acceptance. If we do not pass through certain experiences and embrace the lessons they teach us, we will never become whole. Living in the world, we need to grow on two levels: psychological and spiritual. To master the art of living we must learn how to participate fully in human life while maintaining a relaxed detachment from the world and growing inwardly into the realm of the self.

free will

Thinkers have long been engaged in academic discussions over the question of free will. However, the existence of free will can neither be affirmed nor negated through linear logic or philosophical argument. Only by going beyond the mind and getting in touch with deeper layers of consciousness can we discover the power of free will that is inherent to our spirit and intelligence.

Beyond the issue of the presence or absence of free will lies the far more important matter of its accessibility. The ability to access free will and its potency is determined by the level of one's evolution. Because most humans are locked in the subconscious realm, which is completely conditioned, they are cut off from the power of free will. Free will is a characteristic of higher intelligence and cannot operate within the mechanical mind. It can only operate when it refers to pure subjectivity and therefore cannot fully emerge until the soul awakens. As we get more in touch with the light of I am and the soul's purpose, we begin to mature into the ability to access a will no longer determined by our reactive consciousness, but by the infinite will of the divine.

The mind merely imagines that it has the freedom to choose, while in truth, all of its choices are pre-determined by a combination of karma and subconscious tendencies. It is only from the place of awakened free will that we can begin to serve our highest good and initiate the process of growing into the light of the self.

purification and healing

The human personality is no more than the totality of its past experiences. It actually cannot move into the present — it can only circulate within the prison of its own history. That which blocks the positive movement of personality is the presence of negative impressions, emotional wounds, energetic blocks and psychological dysfunction. For most human beings it is essential to go through the processes of cleansing and healing in order to come closer to the experience of love, joy and peace. Indeed, even without spiritual awakening, the personality has the potential to reach a certain, if limited, degree of balance and harmony.

Awakening represents a positive movement towards a higher state of being and understanding; purification is the liberating cleansing of the mind. Although the processes of purification and healing are indivisible from our evolution, for a person who has not yet entered the inner path they occur only within the sphere of personality. However, for someone who has already reached a level of inner awakening, purification and healing, while still associated with the personality, take place within the realm of the soul. It is essential to understand that even with inner awakening, expansion beyond the mind is not sufficient to reach complete emancipation. Until the mind has become pure and the heart is healed, the burdens of our past will not allow the soul to achieve true freedom.

the weight of the past

The past manifests in our present as the force that shapes our thoughts, emotions and perceptions. Despite our unchanging essence, as dynamic beings endlessly engaged in the process of becoming, we are the result of both the individual and collective unfoldment of time. The concept of freedom from the past should not be viewed in a simplistic way, for the evolution of intelligence is rooted in all the past stages of its progressive understanding. Our present is created not only by our individual past, but also by the past of the whole of humanity and all other species inhabiting the planet. We are all interconnected. The notion that one can and should entirely disconnect from the past is a fallacy. The past should not be rejected, but outgrown and transcended, so that the power of the now can fully manifest the truth of the present.

Freedom from the past on the personal level refers mainly to those elements of our past that are not aligned with our present — all that pulls us away from the now with the dead weight of limited ideas, conditioned behaviors, negative emotions and memories. Everyone carries a heavy load from the past that cannot easily be dropped. Only by awakening the soul can one initiate the process of releasing oneself from this burdensome yoke and dissolve all that stands in the way of the creativity, wisdom and freedom of the now.

subconscious tendencies

All of our past impressions, as well as the information of our past actions, thoughts and emotional responses, are permanently stored beneath the level of the conscious mind in the unconscious. The subconscious mind is like a computer endlessly processing the material that enters our consciousness from the unconscious in order to protect our delicate inner balance and sanity. However, the subconscious mind is not able to process incoming negative experiences and thought forms to the extent that they are fully transformed and healed. Consequently, over time, countless unresolved thoughts, emotions, and impressions form energetic nodes that lock parts of our psyche into the negative past. This is the common origin of psychological difficulties, neuroses, and even mental illness.

A human being has countless subconscious tendencies that disturb his peace and ability to function in a positive way. Some of the most deep-seated are fear, anger, attachment, greed, envy, pride, self-centeredness, arrogance, self-pity, insecurity, lack of self-worth and self-victimization. We call these subconscious tendencies negative because they are not in harmony with the peace, kindness, and balance that are both natural and essential to our well-being.

Because it actually rules the life of the personality, we must bring more consciousness and understanding into the subconscious in order to understand how it operates. By using a very sensitive type of mindfulness we can get in touch with this subtle area and become aware of various psychological patterns and habitual behaviors. We can also begin to see how our subconscious tendencies are connected either to an imbalance in our relationship with the world or to ourselves.

working with the subconscious mind

Work with the subconscious can only begin under the condition that we become conscious and present to our true self. Prior to the awakening of consciousness, we cannot deal with our subconscious reality constructively, for we have no integral identity upon which to base the inner work. There is simply no space within the subconscious reality for intelligence to counteract the automatic and unconscious functioning of the mind. The mind cannot be transformed by the mind, only by the one who exists beyond it.

We can divide the work with the subconscious into three basic stages: first, we go beyond the mind by awakening pure awareness and the inner state; next, we embrace and transform the mind from the position of the soul; and finally, we surrender the purified mind so it can merge with our higher self.

It is not our intention to delve too deeply into the psychological intricacies of the mind, but rather to portray a general picture of the essential work with the subconscious. The following nine steps represent the basic process of how to relate to and transform the mind. This model as a whole is relevant only for those who have the potential to awaken awareness. For others, practice should be limited to work with mindfulness and non-identification.

1. Awakening to I am
2. Non-identification with mind
3. Awareness of mind
4. Awareness of emotions
5. Acceptance
6. Understanding
7. Embracing negativity
8. Intention to change
9. Surrender

Awakening to I am: Since we cannot effectively work with the mind unless we are able to step out of it, we must first awaken to our real center. In order for this awakening to occur, we need not yet be concerned with the transformation or pacification of the mind. Such is the liberating power of self-knowledge and sudden awakening. The mind, with all its countless problems, can indeed be bypassed through the internalization of consciousness. Through the awakening to I am, one can move to a place within oneself that is unaffected by the coming and going of thoughts. The I am that we refer to here relates primarily to pure awareness, although in a larger sense it connotes the entire inner state and the soul.

Non-identification with mind: Although after the awakening of I am one can dwell in a reality beyond thought, the bonds of our identification with the mind still have to be severed. The mind has many different ways of holding our attention and keeping us confined to its territory. This explains the confusion of many seekers who cannot understand why, in spite of their initial awakening, they remain so strongly identified with their mental self. This situation is natural, however, because regardless of whether or not we are awakened, the mind is an integral part of our multidimensional reality.

The mind does not exist in opposition to our true self. Creating distance from the mind is simply a necessary intervention that makes the process of reclaiming our true autonomy possible. By exercising non-identification with the mind we learn how to regain control over our compulsive attraction to thoughts. Non-identification allows us to transcend the split between the freedom of I am and our defenselessness against the pull of the subconscious, thus empowering the soul's independence from the mind.

Awareness of mind: Although through non-identification we can move away from the mind, its negativity remains unresolved. Therefore, the work that follows non-identification initiates a movement of turning back towards the mind in order to face its reality directly.

Awareness of mind is a directionless seeing of arising thoughts. We do not judge the mind's content, nor attempt to analyze or understand it. We just watch the mind with a choiceless yet attentive awareness. This transitional phase of our work between disidentification and understanding is essential to bring more consciousness into the mind and develop the quality of detached observation. By practicing awareness of mind we learn how to maintain distance from thought and gradually begin to understand the nature of our mental reality.

Awareness of emotions: Many meditators experience that it is much easier to distance themselves from their mind than their feelings. This is natural, for every human being is more identified with emotion than thought. Since our experience of reality is primarily based on feelings, the emotional body is existentially much closer to us than the mind. Unless they are linked with feelings, thoughts are emotionally neutral and therefore easier to observe.

Practicing awareness of emotions is similar to practicing awareness of mind. However, in awareness of emotions one has to be more sensitive, and often more firm, in order to maintain a space of non-identification. What makes the work with emotions more difficult is the fact that to be aware of them does not necessarily make them disappear. A thought cannot sustain itself longer than a moment if we do not fuel it with our attention, but deep emotions, such as sadness, have a continuity that is independent of our conscious involvement. Emotions are present on the energetic level and, unless shallow, cannot be dissolved through observation. In our practice we should maintain a calm, uninvolved consciousness within the presence of emotions. At times, deep breathing combined with surrender to the inner state can discharge and relax disturbing emotions, creating a space within which the weight of our being can become more pronounced than the emotional body thereby supplanting our habitual identification with arising emotions.

Acceptance: The next step in our work with the mind is acceptance. In this practice we begin to see the mind as it is without any particular desire to change it. We do not take the mind too seriously, but relate to it with gentleness and a sense of curiosity. We let the mind be as it is, and in this act we relax. The moment we relax, the grip of the mind loosens, for without our involvement it has no one to control. Acceptance is not psychological abnegation or indifference. It is a profound affirmation of the mind as an indivisible part of who we are.

One of the pitfalls in the work with the mind is aiming for perfection. Psychological sanity is not based on having a flawless mind, but on being at ease with its imperfections. In truth, the mind can never reach perfection. What it can achieve is relative harmony, purity and wisdom. In the very act of accepting the mind, we can actually transform a large portion of its unconscious energy into an open space of well-being.

Embracing negativity: The acceptance we apply to deal with negativity is characterized by an absence of struggle. The mind has to be seen as a part of our existence that needs not only to be accepted, but also embraced with love and forgiveness. It is not the enemy, but an aspect of our identity that has been corrupted by the dust of negative impressions gathered along our journey through time. We tend to view the mind horizontally as something that exists in front of the observer, but to embrace the mind is to see it as contained within the soul's body. By embracing the mind with the light of I am, one creates an environment of non-violent transformation and healing.

Understanding: Having embraced its negativity, the next positive movement towards the mind is our attempt to understand it. That which we do not understand will naturally rule us. For example, if we do not recognize that the root of our envy is our own sense of deficiency, there is no real way to transform it. The role of understanding is to illuminate the mind with a non-judgmental consciousness that sees through and beyond the causal forces that create our thoughts and subconscious tendencies.

The term 'understanding' as it is used here should not be seen to suggest an excessively psychological approach that is overly self-analytical and introspective. We can easily become mired if we delve too deeply into the complexities of the mind. Rather, we require a gentle yet penetrating understanding that will help us to gain clarity about the mind's nature and mechanisms, as well as the psychological roots of our thoughts and emotions.

Intention to change: Cultivating the intention to change is the next step in the transformation of the negative tendencies of the mind. Non-identification and awareness of mind, accepting and embracing the mind's negativity, and seeking to understand the mind, are all strategies that gradually saturate it with the higher consciousness of the soul. It is upon this foundation that we can finally begin to align the mind with the soul's intelligence. Our sincere intention to change is the ground of our real transformation.

Most often we cannot do anything about our disturbing state of mind. When all other relative means prove insufficient, we find our deepest power in the strength of our intention. The intention to change is more than an honorable wish or intellectual gesture we make while moving on with the rest of our lives; it is an act by which we can actually alter the past.

Surrender: Transcendence of the mind does not occur through negation, control or repression, but through transformation and surrender. Only a mind that has reached a high level of maturity, wisdom and purity can be renounced. Surrender of the mind, unlike non-identification, is a vertical release that signifies our true absorption in reality. It is the final stage in the intricate process of moving beyond the mind.

cutting through ego-image

Cutting through the lower tendencies of the ego is an essential part of the spiritual path and a critical step in the process of purification. The core of all negative ego tendencies is an obsessive attachment to one's own image that is based on self-concern and a total fixation on how one is seen by others. Suffering a permanent inferiority complex, the ego constantly checks itself and fashions its performance for the eyes of other people to try and confirm its self-worth. The less it trusts itself, the more it tries to prove itself.

As we have already pointed out, preoccupation with ego-image can even slink into high levels of spiritual realization. An example is a seeker who competes with others on the path in an effort to surpass their states of attainment; he feeds his pride and craving for recognition from his spiritual environment rather than nourishing his inner self. The way the ego operates is truly embarrassing. Its exceedingly immature inclinations are so deeply rooted in the human psyche that their removal presents a lifetime challenge.

To deal with the addiction to one's ego-image appropriately, one must apply discriminative wisdom and bring real understanding into the workings of the mind. Without humility, honesty and purity, one cannot drop egomania. Going beyond the ego-image is primarily a function of our spiritual awakening, and indeed a flowering of true understanding.

the purification of the mind

Although our lower tendencies are undeniably the cause of our suffering and ignorance, not all negative reactions — for instance, justified anger or fear — are expressions of an impure mind. Many such automatic emotional responses are in fact perfectly natural. One actually

185

cannot function in the complex reality of the earth-plane without 'negative' emotions, for they very often safeguard our survival and reflect the need of the moment. However, negative emotions that originate from our lower nature and express our basic impurity do not serve the necessity of the now, as they are entirely conditioned by our past ignorance.

How does the mind become cleansed? Because of its unknown nature, purification is often believed to be a function of grace. This is true provided we take grace to be an organic process intrinsic to evolution rather than a miraculous event. Purification occurs naturally, in accordance with our evolutionary timing, karma, destiny and blueprint. Grace is eternally present in the heart of the soul, and progressively manifests as we mature to the point of transformation. As the amount of light increases in our being, all that is not of the light gradually dissolves.

So while our cooperation is the most critical condition for purification, it does not in itself result in complete purification. Rather, it is a preparation for higher energies and consciousness to enter our being. What supports our cleansing the most is having an open heart that can bridge our human psyche with the plane of the soul and serve as a portal to the grace of the divine. Since our unconscious has been formed by countless previous births, only higher intelligence, the aspect of universal consciousness that links our evolutionary now with our future self, can transform the totality of our past. The force of universal intelligence, which is based on the wisdom and grace of the creator, naturally responds to the sincerity of our intention to seek purity and freedom, and manifests the necessary assistance.

healing the heart

Healing is another aspect of purification. Whereas cleansing is a transformative process that occurs in the mind, healing is experienced solely in the heart. Over the course of the infinite past, we have accumulated an enormous burden of suffering and traumatic experiences that manifest as emotional wounds in our subtle bodies. Because life on earth is an existential struggle on all levels, the experience of emotional hurt is universal. However, it is not the experience of pain itself, but our inability to heal and transform it that scars us.

Instead of learning from our lessons, we ignorantly presume that we are victims of circumstance or blame the merciless nature of life for our misery. When we feel that we have been treated unfairly by others we respond with self-pity and resentment. The experience of being hurt renders us fearful, vulnerable and helpless. Our healthy relationship with ourselves is compromised and our positive perception of life dims. We develop anger, animosity, distrust and bitterness towards the world and others, and damage our primal connection with the reality of love, tenderness, beauty and openness.

Because unhealed emotions stand in the way of our positive expansion, it is essential to let go of past wounds and courageously face our unresolved issues. As much as possible we need to bring all that blocks our positive experience of life to the threshold of the conscious mind. To do this, we must be introspective, conscious and sensitive. When we become more aware of what needs to be healed, we can consciously initiate healing in the heart. The function of the mind is only to recognize what needs to be healed and direct awareness to those areas. Ultimately, the heart heals itself. Its incredible capacity for self-healing is activated the moment we embrace the denied aspects of our past self with the light of love, consciousness and understanding.

spiritual awakening: the foundation of transformation

As we have made clear in our discussion about the subconscious mind, the transformation of personality cannot be achieved through psychological means alone. Therapeutic models can help us become conscious of what needs to be changed, but do not actually provide the means to make any changes. On the whole, psychological therapies are based on the false assumption that we can be transformed by manipulating the subconscious, or by becoming more conscious of the unconscious. They fail because they give too much power to the past. By overemphasizing our personal history, they perpetuate our dependence on it rather than freeing us from it. For example, by delving too deeply into childhood issues we can actually reactivate memories that are no longer relevant to our present identity. If we put too much energy into the past we resurrect it and make it stronger and more real than the present.

It is certainly important to address past issues, but only productive if we are empowered by the now. The strength and autonomy we derive from abiding in the inner state enable us to face our inherent tendencies in a new way. In truth, we are both dependent on the past and independent from it. Psychological therapies believe in the former, traditions of enlightenment in the latter. Only by combining these two viewpoints can we gain a balanced perspective on our human evolution. We must see that by sensitively incorporating psychological work into our expansion beyond the mind, we can create a positive, holistic base for our growth into awakening and completion.

The more deeply we enter the realm of awakening, the more power we can generate for the transformation of our personality. It is indeed the inner self that governs transformation. The light of the soul gradually envelops the shadow of personality, transmuting and merging it into her wholeness. The same energy that created the mind eventually returns to the integral consciousness of our original I am.

the human and the soul

The soul can enter the earth only through the human form and can remember who she is only within her human consciousness. The dormant soul needs the human to realize herself, but the moment she awakens she is faced with the fundamental discord between her human nature and her eternal essence. The human is of the past; the soul is of the now and the future. Only when the human has arrived at an essential degree of maturity, purity and understanding can he be aligned with the soul and become ready to surrender.

human purity and the soul

The human can never reach the transparent purity of the soul, as it is not the nature of the personality to embody perfection. On some level, the personality will always reflect the imperfections of the time dimension to which it is subject. For this reason, sages of the past who wished to bypass the imperfect quality of personality renounced both the mind and the world. If we choose to live in the world, however, we must accept that perfect harmony can never be attained on the human level; at most we can achieve a minimum of discord and a maximum of peace and purity. To become pure and real, a human must come as close as he possibly can to the soul. When the process of purification is complete, the relationship between the human and the soul reaches its optimum transparency and the true purpose of the human is realized — to reflect and serve the soul on earth.

surrender to the soul

It is our destiny that upon completion our human aspect must surrender to the soul. From the point of this surrender onwards it is no longer the human, but the soul, who is 'in charge' of living on earth. When the human personality moves from its false center to the periphery of the soul's existence, true subjectivity is awakened.

realm of the human

The human returns that which he took from the soul many eons ago — the knowledge of I am — and gives up all of the identities he accumulated over the course of time.

We cannot realize the state of surrender without first undergoing a deep purification that enables our human aspect to fuse with the soul. From this union emerges the unified energy of a whole human being — one who has gone beyond personality, yet continues to expand on earth, as well as on the inner plane.

serving the soul

After his surrender, the role of the human is to yield to the transcendent will of the soul. He does not merely submit to a reality deeper than himself; he serves his own highest good, for the will of the soul is one with our supreme wisdom and the evolution of universal intelligence.

We serve the soul by supporting her expansion into light, not by constantly striving to reach higher spiritual goals. The soul has no goals, she has a purpose: she exists to totally experience each now. The soul lives in emptiness, beyond the mind, her will merged with the will of the whole. Her existence is not based on psychological continuity, but on the wisdom of the now. Spontaneous inspiration coming from her higher being and universal I am is the source of all her actions. She continuously evolves, not because she consciously desires to do so, but because it is her nature to grow. If the soul were to halt in her evolution, she would delay the universal expansion of which she is an indivisible manifestation.

A human who has surrendered to the soul still has a personality and carries human memories, but does not have a crystallized sense of false identity. Unified in all aspects with his higher being, he is no longer human in an ordinary sense: his existence belongs to the soul. From the viewpoint of integral consciousness, only one being exists within us — the one who owns the knowledge of I am, the soul.

the human being

At this point we can perhaps begin to understand what it means to be a human being. As psychosomatic creatures restricted to ego-consciousness, most humans have neither soul nor being — they are body and mind alone. Just to be born human does not make one a *being*. A true person is an awakened soul actualized on the earth-plane as a human being.

We can see the complete human being both as a human who has surrendered to the soul, and a soul who has transcended, embraced and integrated her human manifestation within herself. One does not become a human being merely by belonging to mankind. To become a human being, one must fulfill the exalted goal of evolution — the awakening of the soul — our true purpose for living in the dimension of forgetfulness.

human completion

In the holistic vision of enlightenment, human completion is integral. Holistic enlightenment incorporates human completion as a new dimension within the expansion into the state of transcendence. In order to be truly whole, the soul needs to be able to express herself as a whole human being. The completion of the human makes this possible.

psychological completion

Psychological completion is not just the work of one lifetime, but of countless incarnations. As most humans seem unable to assimilate their experiences in a constructive way, they must go through the same life-lessons over and over again in order to reach maturity and understanding. Threatened by our spiritual progress, lower intelligence feeds on our evolutionary stagnation. The unconscious repetition of our lessons is the very essence of the dimension of forgetfulness.

Most humans' concept of happiness and joy is highly unintelligent. Having no connection to their higher nature, they seek satisfaction and fulfillment in the impermanent, robotically following collective impulses. On our journey towards completion, we must break free from unconscious living. We must bring true wisdom into our perception of life by becoming conscious of our human nature, and of those areas of our personality which are still fragmented and incomplete. We must also learn from our experiences, and recognize what we still need to experience. In this way we assist the noble movement towards the very reason for our creation — the realization of light, truth and love. To be truly whole, we must arrive at a full experience of our human existence that consists of mental and emotional maturity, the fulfillment of our major desires and our completion in the world.

the fulfillment of major desires

Since it is our unresolved desires that cause us to enter the earth-plane, their fulfillment is essential for our human completion. However, we cannot succeed in this mission if we remain the victim of our desires. We need to see that our relationship to the world is no more than a sophisticated matrix of desire that we mistakenly believe to be our life. Unless we gain a higher perspective, we will compulsively generate desire upon desire in an attempt to infuse meaning into our existence and, as a result, will become caught in a vicious cycle of existential unfulfillment.

Although desires are a natural force of life and their actualization often has a constructive purpose, they become destructive if they rule us. We must be able to discern which desires steer us towards a more rich and meaningful life, and which burden us with a sense of disappointment, frustration and depression. Only those desires through which we can grow are real and relevant to our evolution. Because all other desires are created by the mind, they are intrinsically false and must be renounced. Still, we do not need to fulfill all desires, even if they are relevant and justified. We must primarily address the major, root desires that express the original cause of our birth in the body, for it is these desires that bind us to the earth. Root desires can be linked to many spheres of life, such as romantic fulfillment, family relationships, financial security, creativity, and spiritual and philosophical understanding. If we do not satisfy our root desires, our karmic bonds will keep us chained to the plane of illusion.

Not all root desires are necessarily based on the wisdom of the soul. Some are just obsessive fascinations that have crystallized in our subconscious mind. However, even these may need to be addressed in order to free our mind. For example, a person who is fixated on public recognition will not be able to rest until he gains the admiration of others. Similarly, a sexually repressed anchorite whose root-desire for physical communion is left unexpressed will be controlled by this desire and may stagnate on the path. Unless properly understood, our desires become hooks of lower consciousness that keep us from advancing in our evolution.

completion in the world

The spiritual path should not be perceived as a way to escape the world. The human in us has to become fulfilled through a total experience of life in order to reach completion. Many seekers are actually driven by their fear of life, not a deep longing for awakening. To succeed on the path, however, we need to be well-grounded in the world and free of fear. Otherwise, unresolved issues and subconscious anxieties may arise and block our internal evolution. Sages and masters of the past who renounced the world were not motivated by fear; they simply had no further need to evolve through earthly experiences. To renounce the world from a positive place one must be confident and connected to the physical plane in a healthy way.

Our psychological completion is naturally tied to our participation in the world. Our interactions with the outer reality determine how we feel as a personality, and naturally need to be integrated into our experience of self. In order to feel complete, we must embrace the world and move beyond any fear of facing the challenges of life. By developing a harmonious connection to the world we begin to experience it as a place of fundamental goodness where we can reach spiritual awakening and completion.

the ending of karma

For many lifetimes we have given away our power to desires that we have been unable to satisfy. These desires have grown roots in our subconscious, influencing our thoughts, emotions and actions, and disabling us from reaching true rest. Apart from allowing us to discharge our desires for the sake of growth and freedom, evolution offers another strategy to emancipate us from attachments: it finally confronts us with our inability to satisfy our infinite cravings and wants and forces us to give them up. Life teaches us a natural humility by not allowing us to have everything we want. Through our disillusionment we learn that to reach freedom we have no choice but to renounce all false desires.

Our karmic roots bind us so deeply to the time-dimension, grace is required for our deliverance. Emancipation from karma is indeed a function of grace; it is the intervention of the beyond that cuts our last karmic ties. Divine intervention is an intrinsic part of our blueprint, without which the soul would never transcend her bondage. However, grace does not enter our life at random, but in accordance with our readiness to let go of our separate existence and transcend the plane of lower intelligence.

the human at rest

To reach completion is to arrive at a state of true existential repose. Upon completion, the human no longer creates a reality based on a personal agenda, but rests, free of the need to become someone other than self. When the human is at rest, the energy of desire, anxiety and boredom can no longer pull him away from his natural state of peace and harmony. He relaxes his existence into the presence of the soul, who reciprocates by enveloping him with the light of I am. The child is absorbed by his mother, and all separation between individual and universal dissolves into the immaculate.

realm of understanding

From the heart of the creator is born the ground of existence — being.
From being manifests consciousness; from consciousness, intelligence;
from intelligence, understanding; from understanding, pure knowing;
from pure knowing, beyond knowing; from beyond knowing,
the beyond itself.

Consciousness is the luminosity of being, intelligence is the
brilliancy of consciousness, understanding is the radiance of intelligence.
When understanding reaches its supreme flowering, pure knowing,
it returns to the root of being. As this spiral cycle of creation continues,
being again manifests consciousness, consciousness manifests intelligence,
and intelligence gives rise to a new expansion of understanding
before merging into the supreme state beyond knowing and not-knowing.

the mind

The mind is an instrument of intelligence through which knowledge and understanding are acquired. It has no objective essence of its own; it is no more than a subjective flux of impressions, associations and thoughts. The mind is linked to the soul through the sense of me, the essential quality that distinguishes it from artificial intelligence. Around the axle of me, the mind creates the coherent structure of identity that we experience as the personal self.

Initially, the mind developed as a tool for survival. However, through the evolution of intelligence, the functions of the mind have gradually extended into other spheres of reality, such as conceptual thinking and scientific understanding. Psychological processing that transcends the survival instinct has opened the doors to our conscious evolution, allowing the mind to expand and gradually awaken our spiritual intelligence. The highest endeavor of the mind is enquiry into the dimension of spirituality, as it initiates the actualization of its ultimate destiny — its own surrender.

the world of the mind

The ability of the human mind to observe and analyze its own activity is most extraordinary, and indicates a highly evolved consciousness. Also remarkable is that it does not rely solely on its individual capacity, but is capable of expanding through the conceptual knowledge that it gathers from the collective mind. The mind receives stimuli from the external world, processes the data in its internal world, and arrives at its own personal interpretations and conclusions. It is a self-programming thinking system that enlarges its inherent capacity for learning through the process of its own education.

A complex, multidimensional organism, the mind is composed of three basic interpenetrating layers: unconscious, subconscious and conscious.

The unconscious mind: The ability to think consciously manifests only on the mind's surface. It is similar to an ocean whose waves are visible on the surface while its depths lie hidden in the darkness beneath. The foundation of the mind is the unconscious, the store-house of all the memories and impressions we have gathered from our present and countless past lives. Our human intelligence actually could not function without the unconscious mind, for it is the inner ground of reality from which the conscious mind arises. Thus we can see that unconsciousness is not the polar opposite of consciousness; it is its ontological foundation.

The unconscious mind is individual, collective and universal. The individual unconscious relates to our personal history and past evolution. The sum total of the memories, knowledge and destiny of all humans and other species constitutes the collective unconscious. The universal unconscious is the existential root of the manifested universe — the original source of the phenomenal reality.

The subconscious mind: The subconscious mind is the link between the unconscious and the conscious mind, the subtle sphere of con-sciousness in which spontaneous thoughts, emotions and percep-tions manifest prior to the conscious mind becoming aware of them. 'Subconscious' signifies a low frequency of consciousness that oper-ates just above the unconscious level, and just below the conscious level. Unlike the unconscious, in the subconscious a degree of cogni-tion is active; semi-conscious experiencing and knowing are present.

There is a hierarchy of cognition that reflects the ladder of con-sciousness. The highest degree of cognition is the knowledge of I am, as it represents consciousness in its pure form. In the unconscious realm, cognition is zero. No one can actually experience the uncon-scious, because the knower is absent. The level of cognition inherent to the subconscious mind is sufficient to produce a subconscious experiencer, but too weak to crystallize a clear sense of ego. We can experience this clearly in the dream state, where the sense of me is present, but in too rudimentary a form to generate a lucid consciousness of its own. The lower the frequency and lucidity of me, the more subconscious its consciousness.

It is a common misperception that we experience the subconscious mind only while asleep or daydreaming. Most human beings actually live their whole lives in a subconscious state. Their sense of me is not truly conscious, for they are too busy frantically maintaining the insubstantial reality of personality to connect to their essence. In their ignorance, they mistake subconscious mental activity for conscious thinking, unaware that they are lost in a waking dream. Since the subconscious mind is the foundation of one's perception of reality, it is essential to become more aware of its nature in order to evolve towards higher consciousness.

The conscious mind: The conscious mind represents the stage in the development of consciousness in which thinking becomes self-conscious. It can be seen as a solidified ego that is able to focus the thinking process in a clear and directed way. This ability to focus attention and hold onto particular streams of thought is the chief characteristic that distinguishes the conscious from the subconscious mind. From a spiritual perspective, it is the conscious mind that performs self-enquiry and supports our awakening by establishing a connection between our lower consciousness and the dimension of pure subjectivity.

the mind and the sense of me

The mind operates within the objective reality, but serves its subjective host, for it cannot function without the presence of the one to whom it refers. Yet, the thinker is not the thought. The vital question then is: who is the thinker in separation from thinking? The thinker is the sense of me created by the mind that arises when the mind becomes self-conscious. In its essence, however, the thinker's sense of me lies deeper than the mind's self-consciousness; it points beyond thinking to the sense of I am. The thinker is not only a part of the mind, but also the bridge between the mind and I am. The thinker is in fact both this bridge and the one who crosses it. By first turning attention from thinking to the sense of me, and then from the sense of me to I am, the thinker discovers his true center.

How conscious we are directly reflects the strength of our sense of me. In the subconscious state, our sense of me is too feeble to become self-conscious. When we sleep or daydream, we cannot experience ourselves as separate from our fantasies at all — our identification with the wandering mind is total. In contrast, in the conscious state, our sense of identity is crystallized to a significant degree. Our me can recognize itself clearly as a knower separate from the known.

Within the conscious mind, me can recognize itself as distinct in relation to thought, but not in relation to its own essence. It senses itself as separate from thinking, but depends on thought to reflect its existence back upon itself. An ignorant me is just a shadow of the mind — it feels that it exists because it thinks. No thought, no me. Conscious me, or ego, does not possess true subjectivity; it has no quality of being or existence of its own.

the mind: friend or foe?

Thinking does not necessarily stand in opposition to spiritual illumination — it can be a creative expression of our true nature. If we are unconscious, the mind is unconscious as well; as we awaken, the mind becomes conscious. If we don't bring awareness into the mind, it is our worst enemy, a parasite that eats away at our spirit. But the moment we instill it with the qualities of presence, clarity and wisdom, the same mind becomes our ally.

The notion that we need to transcend the mind is correct, but this transcendence cannot be actualized until the mind itself has become highly evolved. Until we are ready to surrender it, the mind remains a fundamental component of our identity and our quest. Our goal is not to negate, but to transcend the mind through its integration as an integral part of our existence.

the illusory nature of the mind

The mind has no substance. It arises, but has no being. It merely creates the illusion of solidity by enveloping us in a net of endless thoughts. Blinded by a dark cloud of mental reality, we do not see the real world; a veil of thought separates us from reality as it is. Instead of being, feeling and knowing, we constantly think, think about what we think about, and think about what *to* think about. We are locked in the never-ending interpreting, checking, comparing and labeling commotion of the mind. The mind cannot rest, for it would cease to exist. It must constantly move in order to be.

We are prey to two false assumptions about the nature of the mind: that it has its own being apart from arising thoughts, and that it can capture the truth of reality. The mind is not an entity, and therefore has no identity. It is a mental flow devoid of any solidified sense of self. For lack of a true center, the mind can only grasp at objectified existence through thinking. It has no power to reveal the truth of reality, for it is always external to it.

Ironically, one can be intellectually convinced of the illusory nature of the mind, but remain fully identified with thinking. The mind can believe various concepts about its own unreality, but cannot actually experience itself as unreal. One cannot think about reality. Only in the absence of thought is that which is real revealed.

the power of the mind

Each thought is a unit of mental energy that carries an emotional charge — it has a force that affects reality. We must take responsibility for how and what we think, because that which the mind strongly believes and desires most often creates our future. Thinking is not a private affair limited to the headspace, but has karmic consequences that shape our lives and impact everyone around us.

Most humans think in circles, ruled by the mind's obsessive tendencies. When the mind cannot find something to think about, it will think about *anything* just to escape boredom. In this vacuum of purposelessness, the mind generates dull and depressing thought-forms and energies, utterly powerless to create anything positive. Unconscious, mechanical thinking is a misuse of energy and serves nothing.

The positive power of the mind is rooted in silence and presence. From a place of pure awareness and being, the mind is able to function with true creativity, intelligence and purpose. Abiding in mirror-like consciousness, an awakened mind reflects reality with clarity, and manifests the correct understanding and action.

intelligence

Intelligence is the creative power of the mind, the spirit of understanding that runs through our being and enlivens our existence. It is the mind's ability to use the energy of thoughts in an organized and purposeful way, and the secret link between the mind and I am. Intelligence is not thinking, it is the creative space between presence and arising thoughts; it is the uncrystallized movement of cognizance that precedes the gross manifestation of thought.

As the heart of consciousness and the dynamic force behind our journey to awakening, intelligence is the very essence and justification of our evolution. It is the only tool we have to uncover the meaning and aim of our existence. The mind without intelligence is like a car without a driver — it will idle, but it will never reach its destination. The expansion of intelligence leads to an increasingly higher perception and understanding of reality, liberating us from the false and revealing the truth of creation.

lower and higher intelligence

Intelligence is not always intelligent. There is higher intelligence, lower intelligence, and many shades in-between. Lower intelligence is bound by the unconscious energies and negative tendencies of the mind, whereas higher intelligence supports the wisdom of the soul and her evolution towards light. The capacity of our intelligence is not predetermined and static, but expands in proportion to our awakening to the realm of understanding; it is a direct reflection of the level of our evolution and the depth of our consciousness.

Intelligence is not efficiency of thought, but efficiency of consciousness. Humans who limit their intelligence by aspiring to nothing higher than intellectual sophistication serve only lower intelligence. No matter how erudite they become, they remain locked in the dimension of forgetfulness, for they misuse their intelligence by applying it solely within spheres that are removed from the heart of creation. Intelligence that is not rooted in the knowledge of the self is not conscious; it is in fact subconscious. It has a sense of me, but no sense of I am — it has no soul.

Until the mechanical mind is transcended, our intelligence cannot realize its full potential. Only a mind that is truly present — clear and awake — can be intelligent. Prior to the awakening of awareness, the intelligence of the mind operates in a space of confusion, without any center. Once I am is recognized as the true essence of the mind, our intelligence links itself to pure subjectivity and begins to act as an awakened agent of our conscious evolution.

the intuitive mind

Linear thinking represents only one aspect of the soul's intelligence, its analytical dimension. The discursive mind, which operates in the frontal lobe of the brain, is merely a self-conscious expression of our holistic intelligence. True intelligence, our higher intuition, is faster and much more direct than discursive thought. By the time the conscious mind draws its conclusions, understanding has already been reached in the intuitive mind.

Intuition is the soul's ability to gain direct insight into the nature of truth without the filtering of the linear mind. It is the most efficient faculty of holistic intelligence because it operates in a space of silence and emptiness that is directly linked to our higher wisdom. Intuition is therefore the aspect of intelligence most closely connected to the soul. It allows her to transmit her pure knowing to the mind, and through the mind, to formulate her understanding.

the power of recognition

The essence of intelligence is its cognizing faculty, the power of recognition. Recognition is immanent to consciousness; without it, the information of existence could neither be received nor registered. It is recognition that makes the growth of discernment and understanding possible. As recognition is not always spontaneously present, we often have to make an effort to activate it. We do so by deepening our discrimination, sharpening our spiritual perception and striving uncompromisingly for complete understanding. The refinement of our recognition directly corresponds to the evolution of our intelligence, sensitivity and inner experience.

Recognition has two main functions: it enables us to register and understand our experience, and it imbues our experience with meaning. As we have explained, one may have an experience but not recognize it, or one may recognize an experience but not see its existential value. We mature as both types of recognition develop; we grow in our ability to recognize various states of awakening, and also in our appreciation of their significance. On a certain level we could even say that recognition *is* the experience. If one has an experience but is unable to register it, the experience is valid, but empty. True awakening is the fusion of our inner realization with the depth of our recognition.

personal and impersonal intelligence

Intelligence belongs to no one. If we contemplate the laws of nature, the ecological systems of the earth, the tremendous wisdom of creation — we can clearly see that intelligence permeates the whole of existence. Impersonal intelligence is the foundation and fabric of the ever-expanding universe. Behind it there is no doer, no thinker, no agent. In the process of individuation, however, intelligence becomes personal. Within the infinite space of impersonal intelligence, countless beings, entities, creatures and individualized angles of perception have been formed. Personal intelligence is an individualized expression of universal consciousness that operates according to its blueprint within the boundless space of impersonal intelligence.

Although the ego can be seen as a form of personal intelligence, personal intelligence of a higher degree is the intelligence of the soul. As long as she is separate in her existence and lost in the ego, the soul's intelligence is able to evolve only in the mental dimension, within the bounds of personal memories, associations and perceptions. Only when the soul returns to the state of unity, and when her personal intelligence merges with universal consciousness, are its frontiers no longer constrained by her individual existence. Her personal intelligence does not dissolve entirely, but it is free to function in the impersonal space of pure subjectivity, constantly inspired by the beyond.

the luminosity of consciousness

What makes consciousness conscious, and how does consciousness know that it is conscious? In objectified consciousness, cognition is based on sensory perception, thought and emotion. The ego knows that it is conscious through checking, observing and processing incoming data. But on higher planes of consciousness, cognition does not require an object in order to know itself. Knowing is inherent to pure subjectivity. Intelligence is the heart of I am lit from within with the clarity of knowing; it knows beyond knowing that it knows — it is conscious without thought.

Intelligence is not thought. Intelligence *uses* thought to construct understanding, but is itself the primal cognizance that exists prior to the mind. The pure knowing of consciousness cannot be separated from intelligence. Intelligence is in fact what enables consciousness to be conscious; they are two aspects of the same reality. Pure intelligence is the self-illuminating radiance of consciousness, and pure consciousness is intelligence illuminated.

the essence of the soul

It is the soul who evolves. She owns intelligence and is the axis of its everlasting expansion. Her identity is being, and her essence is the pure intelligence through which she knows and can be herself. She is the light that emanates the knowledge of I am. Rooted in the space of pure subjectivity, the soul's intelligence constitutes the consciousness of her identity.

208

the light of understanding

Understanding and consciousness are inextricably tied — the higher our consciousness, the higher our understanding. True understanding is a direct experience-perception of reality — it is *being* understanding. In pure understanding, that which is comprehended reveals its meaning in the pristine mirror of pure consciousness, where there is no one who understands, understanding just is.

the purpose of understanding

Understanding is the nature of reality. There is no difference between being and knowing, no difference between understanding and love. Although it has many functions, understanding is a light unto itself. More than a means to attain spiritual states, it is their very essence. Not only does understanding bring us to our inner realizations, it saturates them with pure knowing. When intelligence merges with realization, understanding actually embodies the significance of that which has been realized.

the art of learning

Life is a never-ending process of self-discovery. Those who resist learning not only stop growing, but are bound to regress. Understanding is the essence of life, and like life itself, must continuously evolve. The art of learning is the art of living. In order to master it, we have to be truly awake, sensitive and highly intelligent in our encounter with life.

We must not take our lives for granted, leading a dull and lethargic existence. To grow in our understanding we must be open to learn. There are questions to be asked and answers to be discovered. We must enquire into the nature of our existence and seek the true explanation of its meaning and purpose. We must awaken from the amnesia of the collective mind and recognize the central problem of human existence — our forgetfulness. We are not who we think we are and life is not what it appears to be. To awaken from our unconscious condition and unravel the hidden truth of our creation is our ultimate reason to be.

evolution in time

Intelligence evolves through time. At the beginning of time, a seed of intelligence was planted in our soul so that we might grow towards our ultimate destiny and reach the optimal understanding reflected in our blueprint. Before becoming one with the inner realm, intelligence uses linear time as its vehicle. However, after shifting to the transcendental realm, intelligence enters 'real time'. Though often considered timeless, it is not true that there is no time in the dimension of universal I am. As long as consciousness and creation are present, so is time.

Real time is the time of universal consciousness. It is based not on a linear progression from past to future, but on pure evolution; it is the movement of intelligence within the motionlessness of the timeless. On the earth plane, time comes first and evolution follows, whereas in real time, evolution comes first and time follows. In this dimension, consciousness is ruled by time; in reality, consciousness rules time.

Universal evolution occurs ahead of time, on the other side of the now. In linear time, we recognize an experience because it has already happened in the past. In real time, we recognize an experience because it has already happened in the future. The one who knows the experience is ahead of the one who recognizes it. It is the position of the experiencer that determines the quality of time. If he is bound by the past, his experience of time is linear. If he abides in the now of reality, he is one with the universal flow of real time — his being precedes his becoming.

Time is the space of cognition between the recognizing consciousness and the recognized reality. If this space is absent, so are the recognition and sense of time. In linear time, the experiencer recognizes reality by referring to his last identifiable experience; he cannot experience the present. What he perceives as occurring in the present has in fact already happened in the immediate past. Only in real time is the experience truly of the present — it is instantaneous. Here, consciousness is one with the arising of each now, for the experiencer is merged with his timeless source.

Recognition in real time is a function of both the soul's being and her intelligence. Since she is merged with the pure consciousness of reality, the soul's total awareness of the now precedes the secondary recognition of that now within her intelligence. First she knows, then she recognizes. Her intelligence is non-abiding; it exists apart from the linear continuity of becoming in a state of constant surrender to the vertical reality. In real time, the experiencer is reabsorbed into the state of absence in each now, dissolved in every instant of recognition. He cannot distance himself from experience. He is one with it — one with reality.

Our evolution in this dimension depends upon the evolution taking place in real time; how fast consciousness evolves within universal I am impacts our linear time. As long as we are separated from the source, our consciousness is bound by the extremely low velocity of earthly time, but the more we merge with real time, the faster our evolutionary movement becomes.

the evolution of understanding

Our understanding evolves over the course of many lifetimes. In the dimension of forgetfulness, the evolution of understanding is slow and materialistic in nature, predominantly oriented towards serving our survival instinct and our desire to improve our worldly existence. It is only by connecting to the higher purpose of our intelligence that our understanding can evolve towards our ultimate destiny — spiritual awakening.

Even for a seeker on the path, the initial desire to understand is most often not based on a positive movement towards truth, but on a search for relief from unconscious living. In the state of deep unconsciousness, the highest attainment is in fact the recognition of the unreal and dissatisfactory nature of the unawakened reality. Having arrived at this stage of existential suffering, one can finally begin to open up to the spiritual quest.

Our understanding accelerates exponentially as we move beyond the dimension of ignorance. The more we understand, the more easily we can expand into further understanding. As we move closer to universal evolution, our understanding gradually transcends the boundaries of our human consciousness.

individual and collective understanding

Our evolution on earth has both collective and individual aspects. It is the singularity of our individual human evolution that places us above all other species. In pre-human forms of life, evolution is exclusively collective, but the progress of humanity has always been fueled by the creativity of individual minds. Ironically, however, the individuals who introduce new and revolutionary ideas to human consciousness inevitably struggle for freedom from the collective mind, for the herd mentality of mass-consciousness always seeks to restrict the freedom of subjective perception. True evolution can only take place independently of the collective mind. The deepest creativity of intelligence has its source in the realm of I am, and by nature expresses itself through individual souls.

Because the vision of spirituality is a part of the collective mind, it is inevitably tailored to reach the masses. Organized religion, however, though widely accepted, cannot bring transformation to the individual, because its message has to accommodate the unconsciousness of its audience. It opens the human mentally to the divine, but at the same time, locks it into a system of belief that is merely a sentimental substitute for real experience. 'New age' spirituality addresses a more sensitive group, but suffers the same limitation, because its popularity depends on the shallow level of the spiritual truth it presents. It affects humanity positively by opening it to the reality of subtler realms and alternative modes of transformation and healing, but it fails to point to the heart of awakening. Pure subjectivity is a dimension of existence totally incomprehensible to the collective consciousness.

The idea of spiritual illumination based on I am threatens the status quo of the collective unconscious. Humanity as a whole is afraid of confronting its own fundamental emptiness, the absence of sacred individuality. The invitation to awaken can only be extended to individuals who are sufficiently mature and conscious. For this reason, spiritual teachers of a higher order have never addressed humanity en masse, only individual seekers. Those who attempt to impact the collective mind by preaching spirituality and morality, or by commercializing the spiritual path, cannot bring true awakening, because they themselves are part of that mind.

complete understanding

Complete understanding does indeed exist, but not in the sense of knowing everything or having all the answers. Not all souls are destined to reach the same understanding of reality; each has a particular flavor of evolution and a unique vision of wholeness. The final understanding of each soul is reflected in the very nature of the completion through which she reaches the limits of her expansion within the realm of the known.

Upon completion, the soul can finally drop understanding. Her need to understand has exhausted itself, and she can rest on all levels. Understanding continues to evolve within her intelligence as a function of real time; however, it is no longer based on any inner deficiency or personal will to learn, but on the impersonal expansion of universal intelligence. The soul finally graduates from the dimension of understanding and returns to the original state of not-knowing. This is complete understanding.

beyond understanding

Spiritual evolution is a movement from not-knowing to knowing, then beyond knowing back to not-knowing. The initial state of not-knowing is ignorance; the ultimate not-knowing is freedom from the known. Understanding sets us free, but freedom itself is beyond understanding. To transcend the dimension of understanding one must be totally empty — one must be no one and know nothing.

the limits of understanding

To know what we need to know and to let go of what we do not need to know is wisdom. Understanding lights our way, but where we are going is beyond understanding. The moment we start clinging to the conclusions we have reached, they entrap us. Understanding is in fact the final barrier to the direct experience of reality, for it separates the knower from the known. Understanding *has* a purpose but it is not *the* purpose.

Certain traditions of enlightenment overemphasize the role of understanding as a tool for awakening, creating the illusion that through the power of self-knowledge or a sudden radical insight into the nature of reality we can instantly realize the self and complete our path. However, no matter how intelligent or spiritually sensitive, we cannot be transformed and illuminated through understanding alone. Many seekers gather extensive spiritual knowledge yet remain unable to realize true peace. Even the most profound spiritual revelations cannot tear down the walls of our separate existence and emancipate us from our deep sense of emptiness and suffering.

There is an enormous gap between understanding and reality, between knowing and experiencing. Although we may get in touch with the essence of our consciousness through understanding, without the total transmutation of our consciousness and the awakening of our complete self, we remain far from enlightenment. Our efforts to awaken through understanding orient us towards reality, but can never manifest as true self-realization. Enlightenment transcends understanding, for it is beyond the power of our intelligence to fathom the mystery of the self. True understanding is humble — it knows its own limits. While the final act of intelligence — the surrender into being — is indeed an expression of understanding, it points to the end of knowledge.

the burden of knowledge

Knowledge can be a blessing or a burden: it is a blessing when it enables us to progress on the path towards freedom; a burden if excessive or clung to when no longer needed. Knowledge is always of the past, for it is no more than an accumulation of memories, experiences and concepts. Though necessary to help us grow and live in the world, it cannot take us beyond it. In order to enter the dimension of the now, we must be empty, free of the totality of the past. Only in the absence of self is it possible to merge with universal presence. Knowledge, no matter how precious, crystallizes our personal identity — the known creates the knower. Even self-knowledge becomes a burden when it separates us from the realization of oneness and absence.

Knowledge can be seen as part of ignorance. In fact, without ignorance there is no knowledge; knowing requires the shadow of not-knowing. Only when both knowledge and ignorance are dropped can we enter the dimension beyond the knower and the known — the unknown.

letting go of understanding

Letting go is the essence of the spiritual path. To let go of understanding is the real key to freedom. Nonetheless, we cannot let go of understanding prematurely, as we must first enquire into the nature of reality. Only when understanding has fully ripened and been assimilated by our intelligence can it be transcended.

Letting go of understanding demands courage, for when we renounce the security of knowing, we become empty and exposed. Yet, we also become ready to be filled with the light of the self. We no longer require the crutch of knowledge in order to be. We are open to experience reality as it is, and in this pure state of existence, we regain our original innocence.

pure knowing is being

Pure knowing is the natural state of the spiritual dimension, yet it cannot be accessed until our personal consciousness has merged with the beyond. When we surrender knowledge and understanding to the non-conceptual ground of being, knowing and not-knowing transform into pure knowing. Pure knowing is owned by the supreme reality and revealed only to one who abides in the emptiness of the now.

divine ignorance

Our perception of reality before entering the path, and that after completing it, while dramatically different, are also mysteriously alike. To become a true sage is to become ignorant again, empty of all knowledge, intoxicated with the supreme alone. However, unlike ordinary ignorance, the ignorance of the sage is divine. It is a blissful state of freedom. In divine ignorance, one no longer knows through oneself — one knows through the creator. To enter divine ignorance we must return all of our understanding to its source. We no longer need the conceptual reality that supported our separate self — we leap into the dimension of no-support. With no place to abide, we lose ourselves in the boundless void of the unknown.

the state of not-knowing

Not-knowing is not antithetical to knowing. Although reflected in the mind, not-knowing points beyond all mental states — it is actually a state of existence. Not-knowing is the nature of the soul and the gate to the beyond. It is the meeting between the renunciation of the known and the knowing of the unknown.

Not-knowing is our ancient innocence. Nothing is more innocent than a small child facing the unknown world of infinite possibilities. That child-like innocence is within us all, beneath our empty knowledge and endless layers of mind. The dust of experiences we have gathered along our path has never touched its essence.

entering the unknown

'The unknown' is not an idea to grasp with the mind, but the pure reality beyond the known — the state of the universal now existing eternally prior to knowing and consciousness. Not-knowing is not the unknown itself; it is the final passage from mind to no-mind through which consciousness renounces knowing in order to enter the unknown. Entering the unknown through the gate of not-knowing, we surrender our knowing to the ancient source and merge with the eternal movement of universal intelligence. What was unknown to the mind becomes known to the soul as the bliss of samadhi and the state of love.

realm of oneness

To transcend separation and realize oneness is the supreme goal of our human evolution, by the power of which we come back to our original state and actualize our eternal identity. True oneness cannot be accessed prior to the awakening of the inner state, for without the inner state there is no existential bridge between self and reality. As we move into the states beyond the mind, our human consciousness gradually begins to surrender to reality as a whole. The expansion into no-mind, the awakening of integral consciousness and the return to the natural state are the major aspects of our enlightenment to complete oneness with existence.

Pure subjectivity is the only gateway to the one reality. Because it is the root of our perception and the source of me, I am must be awakened to provide the requisite ground from which we can embrace oneness. Our limited self can only be transcended through the awakening of the soul — the essence of our individual subjectivity and portal to universal subjectivity. By the power of soul-realization, we reinstate a perfect equilibrium between individual and universal and reclaim the ancient state of natural oneness.

unity and separation

As it is a universal experience that unity is bliss and separation is suffering, the attainment of oneness has always been the ultimate goal of all real spiritual paths and traditions of enlightenment. Although their means and teachings differ, they unanimously agree that separation is ignorance and unity is self-realization.

Unity is indeed the antidote to separation, but only from the standpoint of lower truth. The one reality transcends this division inherent to the realm of ignorance. It is within the undivided whole that we experience our dream of separation as well as our awakening to unity. In our evolution we journey between these existential extremes, shifting through a rainbow of diverse realizations as we draw ever closer to the realm beyond opposites.

The state of totality is not subject to divisions, for it is the absolute container of all possible and actual realities. To enter this great unknown, we must return to the natural state of selfless being and merge with the root of all things, the non-abiding realm of universal I am. Only after merging with existence do we finally rise above the dichotomy of unity and separation and realize the exalted state of oneness.

the state of oneness

In its most direct definition, oneness is the absence of separation. And while it is true that separation obscures the state of oneness, it is at the same time the very energy that makes the realization of oneness possible. Without separation, there is no oneness — without oneness, no separation. It is their complex interaction that constitutes the multilayered nature of both our awakening and the reality of oneness itself.

Just as the poles of ignorance and enlightenment are often misconstrued as having no intermediate reality, separation and oneness are commonly regarded as being fixed opposites. However, sensitive examination of the evolutionary process reveals that prior to our arrival at the ultimate state of oneness, various levels of separation still coexist with our growing experience of unity. Unification with the universal self is not simply the removal of separation, but the positive result of a process of evolution and expansion into the one reality. In the state of oneness, separation is not nullified, but transformed into the unity of individual intelligence within the ocean of universal I am.

the two dimensions of separation

Although existence is one, due to the human inability to experience it as a whole it is mistakenly viewed as being comprised of two distinct realms — inner and outer. This division is real, but only from the standpoint of an unevolved consciousness. As long as we operate in the plane of forgetfulness, the poles of inner and outer remain our primal reference points. Until unity with both inner and outer is realized, apperception of totality is impossible.

In actuality, the human being is painfully split from both the outer and inner realms — the planes of objectified reality and pure subjectivity — as if living neither inside nor outside of existence. He is locked in a netherworld, suspended between the reality of appearances and the reality of universal I am, experientially and existentially disconnected from both. From this rootless, painfully unstable place, our spiritual evolution begins.

The cardinal cause of our separation from both inner and outer is the exteriorization of our human consciousness from the dimension of pure subjectivity. The human sense of me is entirely uprooted from the internal space of the universal now, the ground of reality as it is. In fact, our sense of me is estranged from both the subjectivity of the soul *and* the subjectivity of the universal self. It has neither a stable sense of self, nor any abiding place in the inner realm — it is alienated from its own essence as well as from the fundamental reality.

The realization of oneness with phenomenal existence can only be achieved from a place of unity within the inner plane. The outer world is not outside of universal I am, but contained within its boundless space of pure being. Since creation dwells within the universal subjectivity of the self, there is no way to experience oneness with the external reality unless one becomes unified with the inner realm and the soul. When inner and outer are united and integrated in the consciousness of an individual, their duality is dissolved and the experiencer reaches the state of universal non-abidance and impersonality. Thus reality as a whole is divulged.

self and other than self

The essence of separation is friction between the experience of self and the reality external to self. Since the reality external to self is both objective and subjective, our experience of existence is determined by the quality of our simultaneous abidance in the world and in being. As long as we are lost in ignorance, our sense of identity is experienced only in contrast to the phenomenal world.

To possess a sense of self is perfectly natural and fundamental to all living things and does not in itself create a sense of separation. A bird feeling its sense of me is not extracted from its natural unity with existence; its sense of me is more or less dissolved in its environment. Since creation contains diversity-in-unity composed of infinite angles of perception, subject is by nature distinct from object, and can therefore clearly distinguish itself in thought and feeling. There is a natural equilibrium between individual consciousness and the reality that contains it. In the universal experience, subject and object are both embedded in consciousness, balanced in perfect harmony.

If we look deeper into the nature of reality, we can see that the balance between subject and object is actually intrinsic to pure consciousness. The very fact that consciousness is self-perceiving reveals that its absolute subjectivity includes a translucent objectivity that mirrors that same subjectivity back to itself. It is not the sense of me as such that creates the friction of separation, but the crystallization of identity that results from the soul losing its original transparency.

In the natural state of being, the cognition of oneself and the outer reality is unobstructed, freely interpenetrating, mutually inclusive and translucent. But in the human realm, consciousness has become unnaturally self-centered and alienated from the external world. This primal conflict between knowing oneself and knowing the world is the essence of duality and the source of our isolation from reality as a whole.

We arrive at the state of oneness not by eliminating the faculty to experience ourselves, but through the realization of the ultimate transparency between self and other-than-self. The ego alone can never reach transparency, because its very presence creates an existential knot in the openness of being. It is by nature in a state of perpetual contraction and self-centered attention. This crystallization of identity involuntarily translates as excessive self-awareness, and is responsible for the acute sense of separation between me and the world. In order for there to be transparency between self and other, we must first awaken the soul to regain the transparency inherent to our true being. When the soul awakens, she supplants the petrified ego and experiences herself in an expansive and pure way that mirrors the complete translucency of her abidance in the realm of pure subjectivity. From this place, her perception of the outer world is open, unhindered, all-pervasive, and free of any center. After she attains oneness, the soul continues to live in the world, but her identity is no longer constrained by a sense of separate self. She has no fixed boundaries and the world ceases to be external to her being and consciousness.

the root of separation

The root cause of our separation is our self-consciousness. The human mind perceives reality based on a split between subject and object, experiencer and experienced, observer and observed, knower and known. The perceived is external to the perceiver, who has no stable identity.

Lesser-evolved creatures have a sense of me just as we do, but one that is too weak to crystallize into a sense of separation. As humans, our sense of me has solidified in the mind, creating the illusion that our personality is an actual entity. This ego-entity is both excessively self-conscious in how it relates to the world and how it relates to the virtual reality of its own mind. By over-exercising its ability to think about itself, the ego has deformed our natural sense of me into a wound of separation.

Although self-consciousness is essential and fundamentally positive, the warped self-consciousness of the mind is responsible for our sense of isolation from both the natural state of being and the whole of creation. It has become a wall separating us from the totality of existence. Everything we experience is processed in the obstinately self-centered mind-construct of pseudo-me; we are conscious of ourselves only in contrast to everything that appears to be outside of our singular sense of I.

The human stream of consciousness constantly oscillates between subject and object, object and subject. Locked in a claustrophobic reality of mind, lonely and disconnected from the rest of creation, human self-consciousness has overridden the consciousness of the undivided whole. It is too conscious to feel unity with existence, and too unconscious to transcend the illusion of separation.

separation and unity

Most creatures below humans in the hierarchy of existence recognize neither unity nor separation — they are in an unconscious state of oneness. Above them on the evolutionary ladder, however, many possibilities exist for how beings can relate to unity, separation and their interplay.

There are those who recognize the presence of separation, but not the absence of unity — they are too asleep to question their existence, but conscious enough to suffer due to their separation. There are those who recognize both the presence of separation and the absence of unity — they have begun their evolution towards the realization of oneness. There are those who experience both separation and unity simultaneously — they have reached a relative realization of oneness, but have not yet transcended separation. There are those who are in a state of complete unity and have no concept of the presence or absence of separation — they live in a conscious state of oneness that bears no relation to the plane of illusion. Finally, there are those who are conscious of both their complete unity with existence and the absence of separation. These awakened souls have realized oneness while continuing to exist in the plane of ignorance.

the portal of perfect soleness

Before we can experience the world and self as one consciousness, we must first attain 'perfect soleness', complete separation from objectified reality. Upon entering the inner path, our identification with the world of perception is the fundamental distraction from realizing our essential self. For this reason, to awaken our true subjectivity, we must first disconnect our essence from the sensory, emotional and mental impressions that constantly invade our psyche and create the construct of the personal self. This need for internal focus may initially make us feel even more isolated from the world than in our previous, ordinary state of unconscious separation; but unless we regain solidity and stability within our true self, the illusory forces of the external reality and our own mind will continue to antagonize our integrity. By actualizing the soleness of I am, we lay the ground of being from which we can move beyond the polarities of inner and outer, self and other, I and you, here and now — and embrace the whole of existence as the undivided one.

misconceptions about oneness

We cannot transcend separation by negating our individuality, or through simplistic identification with the objective reality. These, the two most common misconceptions about oneness, actually lead us away from the reality of unity, for they presume that we must some-how disappear in order to merge.

Losing one's sense of self is not an experience of oneness, but the imbalanced condition of a split mind that is not grounded in the reality of I am. Although our individual consciousness is indeed responsible for our separation, it also serves as a base for the actu-alization of our union with the totality of existence. We do not need to eradicate our individuality, but to awaken its true subjectivity and surrender it to the whole. Only when our individual essence is awakened and then merged with the universal self can subject and object be embraced in one homogeneous field of reality.

To experience oneness with the external reality we do not aban-don our individuality. We do not *become* an object that appears in our field of perception — a chair, for instance. The perceiver does not become the perceived. Oneness does not stand in opposition to the natural presence of diversity and differentiation. The very existence of unity depends upon the polar dissimilarity of the subjective and objective modes of experiencing reality, without which there would be no way for consciousness to identify the manifested universe as an actual experience. To assume that one must actually become a chair in order to experience unity with it would degrade the con-cept of oneness to the level of 'mystical' insanity. The chair is just the chair, and the subject perceiving it remains just the subject. In the consciousness of unity, an object continues to be what it is, but ceases to be existentially external to the experiencer. The experiencer of oneness is absorbed in the inner realm, from which both subject and object spring forth in each instant of creation.

'negative' oneness

Oneness cannot be achieved by expanding or modifying the false self through altered states, emotional exhilaration or the suspension of consciousness. Though they sometimes create the illusion of oneness, such experiences are not grounded in pure subjectivity, and thus can be considered examples of 'negative' oneness. To experience oneness is to dissolve the boundaries of self, inwardly and outwardly, into the limitless translucency of the total reality.

In the realm of the mundane, the most common expressions of negative oneness are ecstatic states and human love, for both alleviate the pain of separation by transporting one beyond the boundaries of the individual self. The original meaning of ecstasy was 'standing outside of oneself'. This type of euphoric feeling can be induced by certain music, dance, and drug experiences, or by identification with a powerful idea or emotion. Here however, the very one who would constitute the foundation of unity is absent; hence, no positive experience of oneness can be attained. We may also sometimes temporarily lose our sense of separation when overwhelmed by intense beauty or compassion. But if we look beyond appearances, we can see that the experience actually points to our deepest longing for oneness with existence, not oneness itself.

For the average human, love as expressed in its many forms is the most accessible means of coming closer to a sense of unity with 'other'. However, though love is an attractive way to lose oneself, true oneness cannot be accessed by merging with an external being or object. Again, to lose or forget oneself is not a positive expansion, but an unproductive absence of conscious separation. Real oneness is actualized by first becoming one with oneself, next merging with the source of creation, and finally, embracing reality as a whole. Love is an imperfect oneness, while oneness is the perfect love. True love melts the duality between lover and beloved.

There are also more 'mystical' varieties of negative oneness, for example, to forget oneself by becoming spaced-out. Pure absent-mindedness goes beyond getting lost in daydreams or becoming distracted — it has no object. In fact, being spaced-out involves neither object nor subject; one does not know who, what or where one is. It is not a state signifying true freedom from separation, but a regression to a pre-conscious state wherein the conscious mind loses grip of both its internal and external reality.

It is possible that a spaced-out state mixed with certain energetic expansions can actually transport an adept into a mystical plane. There are in fact many spiritual paths that do not point to the grounded realization of pure subjectivity, but to various mystical states. Through mystical states the soul can connect to other dimensions and mental realms that present an alternate way of existing within totality, but she cannot realize herself and reach wholeness, for she remains alienated from her original nature and the vertical purity of being. Mystical states exist in-between the dimension of pure subjectivity and objectified reality, and as such, abide outside of the soul's essence. As altered states of consciousness they can be seductive for the mind, for they provide relief from ordinary waking consciousness and may even give us a *sense* of oneness. But as they are not founded upon the inner realm and the soul, they are unable to deliver us to the freedom and transcendence that is anchored in the self. Shifts to mystical states may give one an energetic experience, but they offer no real refuge from mental chaos, for they are merely relative dimensions of expansion peripheral to the source itself. They do not serve the realization of true oneness.

Negative oneness can be a dangerous pitfall on the path. We can lose our way by getting distracted by or even addicted to negative experiences of oneness. We must strive to move beyond illusive experiences of freedom and bliss in order to attain a true awakening that is rooted in the light of I am.

the essence of oneness

Is oneness an experience? While in any ordinary experience self is external to the object of experience, true oneness occurs in the non-experiential dimension, beyond the division of knower and known. It is experienced through one's own dissolution. The experiencer merges with the experienced — he is one with it. To experience oneness is to disappear into the beyond.

In essence, oneness is an expansion beyond oneself that is realized through one's positive absence in the presence of the total existence.

In the space of pure subjectivity, the truth of oneness is divulged, absorbing our sense of me, but not annihilating it. Through the realization of oneness, the core of our individuality — the light of the soul — is integrated into a complete experience of reality as a whole.

The complete state of oneness requires the motionlessness of being as its foundation. Although oneness encompasses both the inner and outer realms, it is primarily rooted in the vertical dimension of the now. In pure being, all-that-is reveals itself to the absorbed consciousness as the non-conceptual apperception of everythingness. To be one with reality is to dwell in the state of non-activity, the unconditional repose of existence. From the vertical profundity of being, the stillness of our essence, we expand horizontally into universal consciousness. Thus manifests the bliss of oneness.

levels in the realization of oneness

Are there stages leading to the state of oneness, or is the realization of oneness a singular event? Following an impersonal philosophy, we could deny the possibility of gradual evolution into oneness on the grounds that oneness signifies the sudden and absolute transcendence of individuality. But the logic behind this reasoning is overly simplistic. The realization of oneness is not the annihilation of individuality, but its transmutation.

Oneness itself has no grades, but the process of the unification of the individual with the universal is gradual. The journey begins with our evolution into the inner state and progressively deepens through the awakening of our true identity, our surrender into the beyond, and our expansion into the one reality. The more oneness increases, the more separation decreases, until by the cumulative power of our awakening, separation is no more.

The first level of oneness is accessed through the awakening of awareness, which opens the space of pure subjectivity. However, pure awareness represents a stage in the realization of oneness only if it is linked with the energy of being. If the state of presence is too crystallized and lacks surrender, it may temporarily intensify our self-consciousness and sense of separation. The natural state of presence is restful and transparent; it absorbs the sense of me in choiceless awareness.

The next level of oneness involves our expansion beyond awareness into being, which opens our connection to the universal source. By merging into being, the soul can dwell in the ground of existence, anchored in the unconditional state of repose. Through this absorption, she expands beyond herself and grows roots into the beyond. Only from the depth of being can the soul experience reality unmodified, as it is.

Absorption in being links the soul with the uncreated, but our further expansion into oneness takes place through the portal of the heart. In being, the soul is one with the source, but remains alienated from the external world. It is through the awakening of the heart that she reaches horizontal unity with creation, for the heart energetically and existentially bridges the inner and outer spheres of the one existence. The unity of vertical and horizontal expansion gives rise to a whole new experience of reality: when being and heart merge into one, they create a holistic field of energy that expands the soul into unity with both the source *and* creation.

After the awakening of the heart, the evolution into oneness progresses through the absorption of intelligence in I am, and the attainment of transparent me, in which the integration and unification of the soul and the inner state are completed. Beyond the state of transparent me, still deeper states of oneness manifest through existential shifts into the state beyond polarities and the transcendental state. The final and complete state of oneness is based on the samadhi of me, the transcendence of ego, the merging of the mind and the complete actualization of our eternal soul-identity.

the soul and the self

We must deeply contemplate the difference between the soul and the self in order to grasp the delicate balance between our presence and absence within the realization of unity. In our complete absence, one-ness cannot be experienced, for we are unconscious. In our ordinary presence, oneness cannot be experienced either, for our crystallized self-consciousness separates us from the whole. To realize oneness we need to transform our sense of me so that it can merge with absence while remaining present. As long as there is an experience, there must be an experiencer; but who we are as the experiencer is fluid, and changes according to the level of our awakening. Only our deeper self, not our human personality, can access the state of oneness. The dimension of me that experiences and recognizes one-ness is not a product of the mind, but an intelligent expression of the deepest consciousness of I am. It is the soul uniting her eternal pres-ence with totality. The light of recognition is inherent to the soul's intelligence and being. Her knowledge of being herself is uncondi-tionally merged with the consciousness of all-that-is.

The integral consciousness of our true self is steeped in the pure knowing of its own light, yet free of any self-reference. Such is the consciousness natural to all realized human souls. There are also var-ious beings of light that inhabit the space of universal consciousness, but possess no self-consciousness. They eternally dwell in a state of uninterrupted union with the beloved, but like humans, experience the light of creation in a way that is unique to their particular con-sciousness and level of evolution.

One must go deep into meditation to understand what it means to simultaneously experience one's complete presence and absence within the beyond. It is only by becoming our true self that we can merge with the ocean of universal presence and still remain con-scious. In this, the ultimate coalescence, that which merges is our illusory consciousness based on false individuality, and that which re-emerges is the pure consciousness of the soul based on the immor-tal light of I am.

The soul is an individualized angle of perception. She is an aspect of totality through which universal I am views its entire cre-ation, an infinitesimal sphere of I am that has a function and purpose within the totality of existence. The soul is not separate from the self, but exists within the space of universal consciousness, like a wave in the ocean. By becoming one with the self, the soul transcends her sense of separation, but not her existence and function. She continues her everlasting evolution within universal I am. Prior to her awakening, the soul evolved towards the state of unity, but now, from the point of her complete realization, she begins to evolve within the state of oneness, beyond oneness.

Oneness is not the final goal, but the true beginning of our expansion into the mystery of the beyond. Who is evolving? Who is expanding into the bliss of reality? Who is growing into deeper revelations of truth? There can be no final answer to this question because that one is eternally evolving and changing within his unchanging essence. There is no end to the awakening beyond awakening.

no-mind

In order to reach complete understanding, we must investigate the state of oneness from several complementary angles. Here we will examine the realization of oneness from the standpoint of the mind's presence and absence. What is the relationship between enlightenment and the transcendence of the mind, and what are the limits of that transcendence? Is the condition of no-mind the same as the state of oneness? Does 'no-mind' denote a complete absence of thought or is it an ontological dimension beyond mind? Is the state beyond the mind a single reality or is it multifaceted and multidimensional? What is no-mind?

beyond the mind

The limitation of the profound concept 'no-mind' is that it points to what is not, without indicating in any way what *is*. To truly understand the essence of this term, we must delve into the positive reality that lies behind it.

Since the reality beyond the mind is so subtle, and far beyond the grasp of ordinary language, some traditions choose to emphasize what it isn't rather than sully it with an imperfect understanding. However, if we avoid trying to understand what no-mind actually is, we leave the door open to its false interpretation and make ourselves vulnerable to numerous dangerous pitfalls.

Many seekers are stuck in their practice precisely because of their confusion about the state of no-mind. They either mistake various mystical or mental states for no-mind, or unskillfully resist thinking. They lack the understanding that no-mind is not realized by the negation or repression of thinking, but through a positive expansion into the highly intelligent dimension *beyond* the mind. We must have a deep intuitive feeling-understanding for what no-mind is in order to realize it, and we have to experience it before we can grasp its ultimate significance.

The knower of the state beyond the mind is in fact not the mind, but the soul. Even though the soul uses the content of the mind to formulate her understanding, she knows no-mind directly without the medium of thought. The aspect of the mind that has the ability to observe the condition of no-mind is not the gross conceptual mind, but the subtle mind that operates as the soul's intelligence. Thinking about non-thinking does not necessarily interfere with the thought-free state for the very simple reason that no-mind is existentially beyond thinking. No-mind is not the suspension of thought, but an energetic dimension of consciousness and being that transcends the mind itself.

beyond the presence and absence of thought

Since it is beyond the mind, no-mind is independent of both the presence and absence of thinking. If no-mind were based on the absence of thought, it would be confined to the realm of polarities. True no-mind is beyond polarities; it contains both the movement of thought and the stillness beyond thought.

The mechanical mind is transformed not through the suppression of thinking, but through an expansion into non-thinking. Trying to suppress thinking is a misguided approach, since thinking is a natural part of life. By consciously resting in no-mind, we stop fueling the energy of thought, and in due time, the mind becomes pacified and morphs into no-mind. The automatic activity of the mind doesn't fully stop; it gradually subsides into the tranquility of 'minimum thinking'. The natural state of mind is this minimum thinking, and no-mind is its existential foundation and container.

In meditation, we rest in a state beyond thinking, while allowing thoughts to manifest as they naturally do. The mind cannot be pacified directly, because any effort to change its condition only adds to its energy. Instead, we should remain completely unattached to mental content, or allow a relaxed, yet minimal involvement.

Gradually, as we grow roots into the dimension of no-mind, our sense of identity is freed from the mind. Once the state of no-mind is fully established, we can embrace the natural mind as a part of our multidimensional existence.

no-mind is our true self

Many seekers are conditioned by the impersonal vision of no-mind, which while not incorrect, is incomplete. For them, it is an unexpected revelation to realize that the state of no-mind is none other than being oneself. The understanding that to be in the state of no-mind is to be oneself liberates us. No longer do we strive to experience our state in an artificially impersonal way that conforms to our pre-conceived notions about no-mind. We can just be natural in the space of pure presence, beyond the coming and going of thoughts. Still, we must not limit our experience of no-mind to one of individual subjectivity; personal no-mind must be founded upon universal no-mind. Our pure subjectivity must be actualized in its primordial unity with the impersonal subjectivity of the supreme reality.

It is crucial to understand that the realization of no-mind is beyond the expansion into the inner state. Although the opening of the inner state is a precondition for transcending the mind, true no-mind is embodied in the shift of identity from mind to soul. Many seekers who have awakened the inner state are often still heavily identified with the mind. To be identified with the mind while abiding in the inner state does not mean that we are simply attracted to thoughts, but points to the fact that our sense of I am is still ingrained in the thinking intelligence. If this is the case, no matter what state we experience, our identity continues to be of the mind. Unless our identity shifts to the soul, the ego will continue to rule our consciousness as the illusory center of the mind. Prior to soul-awakening, it is the mind that is the primal knower and experiencer of the states beyond the mind; after the true awakening of no-mind occurs through an existential shift from the ego to I am, no-mind is known, experienced and owned by no-mind alone.

the non-conceptual state

The non-conceptual state reflects the surrender of the mind to the purity of no-mind. If the mind conceptualizes its experience of reality in any way, it veils the bare state of oneness. Any mental grasping creates a sense of separate self that obstructs the direct perception of that which is. To live in the freedom of the non-conceptual state is to transcend the fear of not-knowing and dwell upon nothing.

Ironically, the depth of the non-conceptual state is directly tied to the profundity of the previously gained conceptual insight. Intelligence does not become absent in the state of no-mind, but expands, penetrating the dimension beyond thinking with transparent knowing, and flooding it with the light of consciousness and truth. Only after the state of no-mind has been realized and fully comprehended can we move beyond understanding to embody supreme no-mind as the intelligence of the original void.

no-mind and oneness

True oneness is not realized solely through an energetic expansion beyond the mind, but through the dissolution of the very apparatus that externalizes the undivided reality by means of thought. Only when we are empty of self can all the illusory boundaries of our personal identity dissolve into the infinite space of the one reality. To enter the realm of oneness we must surrender our very existence. This surrender is the highest expression of human wisdom. It begins within our own intelligence, but ends in the beyond.

integral consciousness

Integral consciousness is another name for the unification of the mind with the inner state, and the ego with the soul. In our journey towards the realization of oneness we must merge our human personality with our eternal essence. Integral consciousness signifies this state of internal harmony. Through the integration of all aspects of our multifaceted existence, we give birth to a single state of consciousness. The attainment of this integral consciousness is the flowering of our spiritual evolution through which we realize true oneness with the soul and the supreme reality.

the split between the mind and the inner state

It is the experience of almost all meditators that the awakening of the state beyond the mind does not bring true peace. On the contrary, in most cases inner awakening has little or no effect on the fundamentally neurotic nature of the mind. In spite of reaching even a profound inner state, we continue to suffer a schizophrenic split between our human personality and the bliss of being — we remain fragmented and incomplete inside. Our personality is unable to follow the dramatic shift of awakening that has occurred on the inner plane; our level of consciousness as human beings is simply too low to recognize its immense value. We have our own unintelligent vision of happiness that has nothing to do with inner silence and the repose to be found in the beyond. Due to our basic ignorance, the mind persists in obsessively circulating thought-forms of desire and fear based on the reality of the earth-plane and the collective unconscious.

Seekers often wonder why, despite the presence of the inner state, they continue to be lost in the mind most of the time. It is essential here to comprehend that arriving at the state beyond the mind does not automatically transform our basic unconsciousness. To be truly conscious is much more profound than the awakening of any state, pure awareness included. One can be in the state of presence and remain completely unconscious. One can even dwell in the absolute state and remain hopelessly controlled by the mind. Shifting to a state beyond the mind does not guarantee that one existentially owns it as a new condition of being. Though it may have been realized on the energetic level, unless the inner state has become filled with the presence of I am, the consciousness of the soul cannot embody the inner realization.

To move beyond this debilitating divide between mind and being, a seeker must gain a deeper insight into the truth of his internal reality and merge with his essential identity. The integration of consciousness is the missing link between the awakening of the inner state and the awakening of the soul.

to go beyond the mind

What gives value to any state is our ability to see its transcendent depth. Only the power of our intelligence can distance us from the state of forgetfulness and bring real meaning to our abidance in the inner state.

In the state of ignorance, the intelligence of the mind is disconnected from that of the soul. Our responsibility is to develop a deeper wisdom and spiritual intuition to activate the intelligence of the soul. The awakening of this level of intelligence is far more complex than the awakening of the inner state, and requires a long period of evolution to clearly reflect the intrinsic wisdom of our higher being.

The intelligence of most seekers lags way behind their awakening to the states beyond the mind. The presence of the inner state does not give them enough motivation to renounce excessive thinking; they still habitually seek happiness through the mind. Furthermore, they cannot succeed in going beyond the mind by reaching other, even more profound states, because their problem lies elsewhere — they are asleep in their essence. The mind continues to constitute their fundamental identity. Their intellect may understand that they *should* be conscious and transcend the mechanical mind, but this conviction is purely mental and does not have the power to bring about a real change in their perception. It is the function of an evolved intelligence to align and integrate the mind with the realm of being. Integral intelligence still operates within the mind, but belongs to the soul and serves our higher purpose.

A seeker has to recognize that living in the mind is spiritual death. Unless we truly see the tremendous loss we suffer by forgetting our inner light and living unconsciously, how can we transcend the mind? The conversion of our perception is only possible when we finally recognize that there is no other way to exist than through continuous surrender to the inner realm.

merging the mind

Only the soul is able to recognize that in the absence of thought something infinitely more valuable emerges: our sacred presence. To surrender the mind is to open an inner space within which the mystery of being can manifest and absorb our separate self.

From the place of stillness to which merging the mind delivers us, thinking can still arise in a gentle and transparent way without causing an existential split between the human and the soul. Truly conscious thinking is an extension of the soul's intelligence, not an expression of the mechanical mind, and possesses the qualities of tranquility and bliss, for it is fully embraced by the light of awareness and being. Thinking that emerges from the depths of non-thinking is the natural creativity of silence. It is the soul abiding in the unbroken awareness of the self that bridges arising thoughts with the silence of being.

The merging of the mind is a gradual process of growing into the state of surrender. The mind still has things to think about, as the human has not yet completed his evolution and existence on earth — but a mind that is conscious during thinking does not disrupt the simultaneous awareness of the inner state. While pursuing the relative, it dwells in constant remembrance of its unchanging essence. It does not act outside of the self, but is contained within the all-pervading presence of I am.

becoming conscious

The process of becoming conscious is perhaps the most significant element of our evolution. We do not refer here to increasing the power of awareness, but to the illumination of the soul's intelligence. We can activate many components of our internal reality through practice, but we cannot awaken true understanding by means of meditation or mindfulness. Intelligence cannot be manipulated or activated from outside of self, for it represents the very consciousness of the soul. The evolution of our deepest intelligence is the result of an existential awakening to both our essence and our higher consciousness. The intelligence of the mind is something that we possess and can work with, but the intelligence of the soul is what and who we are.

Intelligence is the state of the soul's consciousness, the frequency of her light, and the pure reflection of her identity. To be conscious is to embody the existence of the soul on the plane of pure knowing — to honor and treasure our true nature by constantly abiding in the light of I am. This unremitting devotion to the self is an expression of our real awakening as the soul.

complete presence and the state of oneness

Integral consciousness is the consciousness of the soul fully integrated with the inner state, uninterrupted by the movement of thought. As the soul's awakening deepens through integral consciousness, not only does she dwell in continuous remembrance of the inner state, but also of her own holistic, undivided existence. Ultimately, integral consciousness is the soul's complete presence merged with unbroken awareness of the beyond — the state of being whole.

Through the awakening of integral consciousness, the split between mind and no-mind is transcended. Through the awakening of complete presence, the witness to oneness is absorbed into the consciousness of unity. When the mind surrenders to the inner state

realm of oneness

and our sense of identity shifts from thinking to being, we expand into the ultimate transparency of universal I am. From the heart of pure subjectivity, we dissolve through the realization of the soul into the supreme subjectivity of the undivided one reality.

the natural state

In the natural state, the frequency of reality has reached such immaculate clarity and openness that it can no longer be differentiated from the absence of experience. It is so fundamental to who we are and to what reality is, it has nothing to contrast with. The natural state is neither an experience nor an experiencer, but our true nature in absolute unity with the true nature of reality.

levels of attainment in the natural state

Any state of awakening we reach should eventually mature into its own dimension of the natural state. In our evolution towards the complete natural state, we move through the natural states of awareness, being, and heart, until we reach the natural state of the soul. The natural state of awareness is spacious, lucent and free of crystallized energy. The natural state of being has the characteristics of pure rest, non-fluctuation of energy, absolute transparency and unbroken absorption in the now. The natural state of the heart has the attributes of warm and tender expansiveness, deep and delicate sensitivity, and an unconditional sense of love and unity with creation. The natural state of the soul is a holistic and boundless experience of oneself that results from the integration of the inner state, the awakening of me and the surrender of the mind. In the natural state of the soul, one abides in a dimension beyond inner and outer, in complete union with the pure subjectivity contained in the space of everythingness.

Our further evolution into the natural state takes us into the state beyond polarities, the transcendental state, and samadhi. In these states, the sense of individuality and the construct of the mind gradually merge with the inner realm and the soul. The complete natural state can be defined as the absence of personal self within the presence of universal transparency.

natural absorption

For a state to be natural it must be linked with absorption in the vertical reality. Unless we are absorbed in the inner state, we cannot experience the necessary absence through which we can transcend self-referral. Natural absorption allows us to rest beyond our self-consciousness in unity with the dimension of pure subjectivity.

In the natural state, the soul is unconditionally immersed in the inner plane of being and non-being at all times. Her absorption is equally present during meditation and daily activities — beyond doing and non-doing, thinking and non-thinking, having the eyes open or closed. Natural absorption is the true goal of all mature paths, for it reveals the depth of reality without negating our ordinary existence on earth.

non-abidance

The ultimate reality has no support and no dwelling place. It abides upon everything and nothing, it abides upon itself. Non-abidance is the nature of reality — the formless, dimensionless foundation of the natural state. The natural state is one with the unoriginated consciousness of no support.

Non-abidance is the groundless ground of the now, the living depth of the enlightened reality. In non-abidance, one transcends the limiting need to have a relationship with existence. In truth, one can never 'relate' to existence as a whole. To experience the whole, one must get out of the way and dissolve into absence. In this absence, all is. In the state of separation, one dwells upon the external or internal reality through thought, experience or perception. In the state of oneness, one dwells upon nothing. To realize non-abidance is to merge with the natural state of existence.

Although the inner state is the gateway to reality, one cannot reach non-abidance through the inner state alone, for in the very act of dwelling in it there is an inherent duality in the relationship between one's individuality and the inner realm. To dwell in any state, no matter how profound, is to objectify it as external, even if this externality points inwards.

the stateless state

The natural state is unlike any ordinary state, for there is no one who dwells upon it. No one experiences the natural state, as the experiencer is no longer distinct from the state itself — he has merged with the inner realm. Because the natural state is not external to the one who knows it, there is no movement of energy and no direction of absorption. Natural absorption is everywhere and nowhere at the same time. It is not within or without, up or down, here or there. In natural absorption, no one is absorbed into nowhere. The natural state just is. This stateless state is neither the soul nor the beyond, but their undifferentiated unity — the dimensionless abode of the one existence — pure reality as it is.

nothing special

When we arrive at the destination of our inner quest, we realize that what we have reached is actually totally ordinary in its essence. The ego believes that behind the idea of enlightenment something absolutely extraordinary awaits. Bored with its own ordinariness and suffering a permanent inferiority complex, the idea of enlightenment holds a seductive charm, since it promises to transform its banal existence into a fairy tale of bliss and ecstasy. The ego looks to the path of self-realization as a way to gain spiritual power and collect all sorts of mystical experiences, but all of these projections are ultimately hollow. The ego cannot see the truth of the path unless it surrenders to it.

The natural state is nothing special; it is divinely ordinary and perfect in its simplicity. The ability to recognize its tremendous value comes from the surrender of the mind and the awakening of the deeper sensitivity of the soul. The soul does not seek anything special. She longs for truth, not intensity of experience. She seeks liberation from all that is false so that she can return to her natural state of peace, freedom and purity.

In its insensitivity, the ego is unable to even register the absence of the natural state until it gets so stifled by its own falseness that it is finally forced to recognize the lack of any internal space in which it can simply be. The natural state is like the air we breathe or the open space in which we live. No one considers space to be extraordinary, yet it contains all living things and is the very precondition of life. Only in the claustrophobic suffocation we experience when space is taken away from us are we able to see its priceless value. The natural state represents the basic goodness of existence, which is so primordial that we can identify it only when we lose or regain it.

If we do experience something 'special', it is not our natural state. As the mind cannot see beyond reality's surface, it only gets excited by shallow experiences that have no existential value. By surrendering to the natural state, we transcend our craving for experiences. In the emptiness of just being we merge with the transparency of reality and become free from seeking at last.

the natural state of oneness

The natural state of being is non-abidance. The natural state of consciousness is not-knowing. The natural state of the heart is kindness. The natural state of the mind is egolessness. The natural state of oneness is all-that-is, the one taste of existence. Dwelling in the natural state, the soul can finally rest in her original unity with the whole. The natural state of universal oneness is an ocean of pure bliss, the all-containing space of truth and love.

realm of transcendence

The aim of the spiritual path is the multidimensional awakening and expansion of our consciousness into ever deeper realizations of truth, love and understanding. From one angle, we evolve towards becoming more and more whole in the realm of the human and the soul; from another, we evolve towards a realization of unity with the one existence. But viewing the matter from the very root of our suffering and ignorance, the highest goal of our evolution is liberation from the realm of illusion.

Prior to transcendence, even the most profound states we reach are bound to ignorance for the fundamental reason that our personal self remains separate from the inner realm. The many awakenings we may have already experienced along the path still have not touched the core structure of our false identity rooted in the mind. Enlightenment is liberation from our false individuality. It is not our inner expansion, but the merging of our separate self with the beyond that crowns our evolution. Upon liberation, the soul actualizes her ultimate potential and becomes her divine self again, one with the very force that created her at the beginning of time. Thus, the circle is completed.

the state beyond polarities

The state beyond polarities represents an important level of our inner expansion towards the realization of oneness and transcendence, serving as a bridge between the awakening of the inner state and the surrender of our individual consciousness. Here, the soul comes closer to the realm of absence and the unconditional repose of the beyond and commences the most important stage in her evolution — her own surrender.

beyond polarities

Any state that is rooted in the vertical dimension can be said to be 'beyond polarities', because polarities belong to the horizontal plane of mind, personality and perception. The dimension of the inner state is by nature beyond the pairs of opposites that create the dynamics of the phenomenal world. However, prior to the realization of the state beyond polarities, the identity of the soul as she abides in awareness, being, or both, remains bound to the horizontal plane. In other words, one may abide beyond polarities, but not be beyond polarities oneself. Even in the absolute state our consciousness remains separate from the inner realm. Similarly, in the state of transparent me, although awareness is relatively integrated with being and the heart, it is not in a state of surrender; it coexists with the inner state, but on some level it is still embedded in the will of the mind. In order to move beyond polarities, the I am of awareness has to be pulled into complete surrender. Such is the function of the state beyond polarities. It is a state beyond any ordinary experience of abidance in the now in which the core of our consciousness finally becomes absorbed into the depths of the inner realm.

the deeper integration of the inner state

The nature of the shift to the state beyond polarities differs from one seeker to another, depending on which center or centers of the inner state are dominant. If awareness is gentle, and being or heart predominate, as in the majority of seekers, the shift is experienced as an overall integration of the inner state. One recognizes a dramatic change on the level of consciousness and energy as the three aspects of the inner state merge into one field of I am. If awareness is strong and solidified, the realization primarily affects the quality of our state within the headspace. Awareness undergoes a profound shift into the state of absorption and rest, and the sense of I am in the head is no longer felt as distinct and separate from the other aspects of the inner state.

In the state beyond polarities, the soul experiences herself and the inner state holistically for the first time. Whereas in transparent me the soul expands horizontally through the internal space of the inner state from within her pure subjectivity, in the state beyond polarities she expands within her unity with the inner state both vertically and horizontally.

the surrender of awareness

A person with strong awareness can control the unconscious flow of the mind with relative ease, but finds it difficult to surrender. The nature of awareness is simply contrary to surrender. Despite being beyond thinking, the state of pure awareness is nonetheless tied to the will of the mind, the very origin of our separate existence. It is so deeply rooted and crystallized throughout so many lifetimes that to transcend it, we must undermine the fundamental constitution of our identity. To truly surrender is to die as a separate individual.

The surrender of awareness in the state beyond polarities does not yet include the surrender of me. It is only I am in the mind that is pulled into the inner state; me remains external to it. For this reason, this state does not alter the human's experience of reality, only the quality of the soul's existence; she reaches the realization of relative absence by reconnecting with the original void that absorbs all individuality into impersonality.

The state beyond polarities is a phase of realization that serves as a passage between transparent me and the transcendental state. It is considered transitional because the soul remains largely identified with the ego and cannot reach complete absence; the I am of awareness is only partially freed from its intrinsic self-sustaining mechanism. At this stage, the experience of pure absence can only be accessed in deep meditation. Otherwise, the energy of the state cannot be fully contained.

entering the beyond

In the state beyond polarities the will of awareness surrenders to the vertical dimension of being and the soul becomes absorbed in the unchanging realm of the timeless now. Previously, the soul was expanding and awakening primarily within the dimension of time, on this, the manifested side of reality. Though linked with the beyond through the realization of the absolute, her consciousness could not cross the threshold of the inner realm. In the realization of the state beyond polarities, the soul finally begins the process of expanding into the universal dimension.

entering the realm of transcendence

When presence passes through the portal of absence, it is transformed into an ineffable unity of both the presence of absence and the absence of presence. To enter reality, our individuality has to surrender to its final limits and dissolve into the original void, the domain of the supreme self.

The surrender of awareness lays the foundation for transcendence, but its ultimate purpose is the unification of the ego with the inner realm. The ego cannot merge with reality unless awareness surrenders first, because awareness is the aspect of the soul's identity that links her existence with the mind. The spiritual role of the ego is to align itself with the surrender of the soul. As it enters the realm of transcendence, it begins the process of consciously dying into the beyond. Through its own surrender, the ego assists the soul in her return to the original state of non-being.

the transcendental state

The transcendental state is the gate through which the soul exits the plane of forgetfulness. The embodiment of this exalted state signifies the correct realization of the beyond. To transcend is to move beyond the whole history of human ignorance and re-emerge into the perfection of our original state. Through her shift to the other side of the now, the soul no longer only abides in the uncreated reality, as in the absolute state — she transcends the earthly dimension altogether and enters the realm of absence with her total consciousness.

Only a human who is merged with the soul and the beyond may pass through the secret gate between phenomenal existence and the transcendental realm — the portal of absence. It is the soul alone, in her primordial purity, that may enter the realm of absence, for this is where she originated. The transcendental realm is the great unknown, the land of mystery, the land of the source, the inconceivable womb of all creation — the very beyond.

surrender to the beyond

Over the course of eons of time, our personal will has solidified into a separate identity based on our memories and stream of consciousness. The moment the ego finally surrenders its will and yields to the beyond, our individual existence — our entire identity created by our infinite past — is nullified. When we move to the realm of absence, all that we have been is no longer relevant to who we have become.

To enter the dimension of absence is not the same as to become absent, for only by remaining present can we experience true absence. The presence that enters absence has been liberated from its separate existence. To experience absence, the experiencer of absence has to be in the state of absence himself, one with the original void.

The surrender of the ego has a profound impact on the surrender of awareness. Awareness and ego, though different, cannot be fully separated in our human consciousness. The ego supports awareness in its initial effort to surrender, but awareness itself cannot surrender completely until the ego has merged. In the state beyond polarities, the ego is still tied to the mind, which prevents awareness from becoming fully absorbed into absence. In the completely realized transcendental state, both ego and awareness are pulled into the realm of absence. The ego does not disappear entirely, but is transmuted into the identity and intelligence of the soul. Unlike the ego, the soul has no personal will; her consciousness operates in the pure space of universal I am. When she enters the other side of the now, the soul is released from her human personality and becomes free to embody her eternal self at last.

the second absolute state

Our first true surrender happens through the shift into the absolute, the dimension of the source. The unity between the being aspect of the soul and the absolute itself gives rise to what we refer to as the absolute *state*. Because it reflects our second entry into the realm of the source, the transcendental state is also called 'beyond the absolute state' or 'the second absolute state'. In the first absolute state, only the being aspect of the soul reaches the condition of no-will, or pure absence; in the second absolute state, her very consciousness enters the beyond. The moment the soul's consciousness reaches the condition of pure rest, she can be said to have truly surrendered. In the first absolute, the soul surrenders her will to be; in the second absolute, she surrenders her will to be conscious.

beyond oneness

The transcendental state is beyond the realization of oneness. The state of oneness is an experience of unity with existence, whereas the transcendental state is beyond both unity and separation. When the soul transcends the polarity of oneness and separation, she abides in neither condition. In the dimension of absence, human concepts and divisions no longer apply. These burdens have no place in the realm of transcendence. Unfettered by the mental reality, the soul now lives in the vast space of universal intelligence, embraced by a newness incomprehensible to the human mind.

pure reality

In the transcendental state there is just one reality — nothing exists between me and what is. The recognition of absence does not refer back to any experiencer, for there is no center of experiencing in the consciousness of totality. The observer has merged universally. In this pure reality, existence is self-illuminating, one with the intelligence of each now.

Only in the transcendental state can we know true freedom from individuality. Ego, mind, soul and beyond merge into one reality, released from both duality and non-duality. To encounter reality as it is, we must be in a state of non-perception, non-conceptualization and non-abidance. In the state of non-grasping, reality just is, for there is no one external to it. The human observer can never meet reality — reality can only be divulged to reality.

the state of surrender

To fully embody our transcendence we have to establish ourselves in the state of surrender. Otherwise, we are continuously pulled back down to the dimension of ignorance by the force of the subconscious. The final obstacle we face in our surrender is our identification with the mind-construct of the false self. In order to become aligned with the soul, our personal self must be renounced, surrendered and gradually dissolved. Through our ultimate surrender, not only do we gain access to the beyond, our whole being and existence move to the other side.

Although the transcendental state is itself the ultimate state of surrender, to complete it and merge our individuality we must pass through multiple layers of our own absence. An adept must be careful not to fall prey to the illusion that shifting into the state of transcendence is equivalent to reaching the state of surrender. Opening to the realm of absence is just the beginning of a complex process of ego dissolution. There are many layers of surrender leading to the realization of complete absence, each reflecting an increasingly deeper dissolution of the personal self in the soul and the soul's merging with the beyond. Our evolution into the state of transcendence is in fact an evolution into surrender. We must allow the whole superstructure of our separate existence to be dissolved by the gravitational pull of the source. The roots of conscious and subconscious me need to be extracted from the consciousness of our pure identity so that we can embody the timeless condition of absolute rest.

beyond surrender

Surrender presumes the presence of someone who is surrendered, so the transcendental state can be said to be beyond surrender, for the one who could surrender is no more. By merging her consciousness with the absolute, the soul sheds her earthly individuality and transcends her personal will at last. She becomes fully contained in the beyond, owned by the supreme consciousness and intelligence of universal freedom alone.

The deepest layers of surrender through which we must pass cannot be mapped by any teaching, for they are too subtle to be conceptualized. When we finally become dissolved in and by the transcendental state, we reach the ultimate limits of surrender, our very absence.

death in the beyond

The realm of absence is absent only from the viewpoint of personal presence. No one who is personally present can enter the beyond. Crossing over into the beyond, one must die to all that is not of the self. To spiritually die in this way is to enter the dimension of non-being while still in the body — to live through absence, relinquishing self-consciousness to the source of creation.

That which witnesses our absence is the impersonal intelligence of the soul. In the realization of absence, the soul does not disappear, but transcends the illusion that she owns her personal existence. She returns her individuality to her original creator, who alone owns the knowledge of I am. Through her death in the beyond, the soul awakens another, transcendental presence, actualized from the heart of universal subjectivity.

beyond illusion

It is not true, as described by certain traditions, that the world is an illusion in the sense of being the product of a hallucination. Although it can be considered unreal from the standpoint of the unchanging principle of the absolute reality, the world does indeed exist and plays an important function as the place where countless souls evolve towards awakening. The illusory character of this reality is due in large part to the fact that it belongs to a very low plane of consciousness and intelligence that does not reflect the truth of universal purpose and evolution. But what truly makes the world we live in unreal is not what it is in itself, but the limited and the existentially unstable position from which we perceive it. When the observer does not dwell in pure subjectivity, he is merely an element of his own phenomenal perception; the perceiver is the perceived — not in unity, but in ignorance. The disconnection from his true nature creates a false identification with the objective reality.

Unless we abide beyond the phenomenal world, we are unable to see through its illusory nature. Only from a place of absence can the soul experience reality in its true form. Through the imposition of his presence, the human observer necessarily modifies his perception of reality, coloring it with his constant interpretation. He cannot see reality as it is; for him, interpretation *is* perception. The soul's intelligence, our ultimate observer, is rooted in the non-conceptual ground of the absolute, the unmodifiable substratum of all realities. From the non-interpretive place of pure being, the world is seen for what it truly is — a time-bound expression of the cosmic void.

transcendence and soul-realization

The soul can be fully realized only in the state of transcendence. Because her nature is beyond self-reference, she must be in unity with the beyond in order to experience herself completely. Although free of self-awareness, the soul knows herself intimately as the light of I am; she is individual, but impersonal. She abides upon nothing within the universal self. To meet her within oneself, one has to be absent, empty of self. That which becomes empty and disappears into the beyond is the human, not the soul. When the human becomes absorbed into the state of absence, his energy merges with the soul so that she may reach the condition of absolute motionlessness in reality within which her primordial presence can finally awaken.

the expansion of the soul

Before returning to her home-realm, the transcendental state, the soul's evolution was slow, bound by the energies of unconsciousness. Once she has been reunited with her original state, she can start the process of expansion into her ultimate potential. Evolution does not end with the dissolution of individuality — it begins. True evolution takes place in the real time of universal intelligence, free of objectivity and separation. The soul can become whole only within universal wholeness.

the shift to the transcendental state

The shift to the transcendental state is purely a function of grace. No amount of discipline or self-enquiry can open the door to the other side. All our efforts, insights and spiritual practices cannot take us beyond the time-dimension, for they are confined to earthly consciousness. We cannot *attain* the state of surrender. We may try to surrender, but our very effort only reinforces our personal will and sense of separation. The gate to the beyond must be opened from the side of the beyond itself, where individual consciousness can be received by universal intelligence and emancipated from itself. Even so, without our deepest intention to surrender and die to the beyond, this gate will remain forever locked. This will-free, yet precise intention is what guides the energetic and conscious processes of existential letting go into the void of non-being.

Prior to the dramatic shift of the human into the transcendental state, the soul must already have reached a high level of maturity and completion within her earthly existence. Unless we are finished with the earth on a deep existential level, we simply cannot surrender — the opposing pull from the dimension of forgetfulness is simply too strong. Only when the timing in our evolution is right, and we are finally ready to let go of our earthly consciousness, is the passage to the beyond revealed by the higher power and grace.

Rarely does the shift to the transcendental state result in immediate union with the realm of absence. The initial shift signifies that the inner gate has opened, but the process of surrender must continue for the state to be fully embodied. The same laws of awakening, stabilization and integration that govern the awakening of the inner state also apply to the realization of the transcendental state. To transcend the dimension of presence — consciousness based on individuality — mind, ego, subtle bodies, and personal energies must all merge with the inner realm. The transcendental state, unlike other states, is fully intertwined with the surrender of ego-consciousness. Unless the ego is uprooted, transformed and dissolved in the soul, the realization of the transcendental state cannot reach its supreme culmination — complete freedom.

disidentification

The process of surrender is directly tied to disidentification from the flawed, false and negative parts of our psyche. Due to natural causes, the waking state often manifests mental, emotional, energetic and physical suffering. However, beyond the important task of disidentifying from our ordinary suffering lies yet a deeper challenge: disidentification from our false self, the crystallized sense of me in the mind. To disidentify from the false is to identify with the real — our timeless essence — to realize unity with the original light of I am.

Before we can understand the nature of disidentification, we have to look into the complex mechanism that causes our sense of me to identify with arising mental states and emotional moods. In the human mind, no gap exists between the experience of a mental state and its evaluation on the scales of pleasure and pain, like and dislike, positive and negative, and so forth. This involuntary, automatic interpretation solidifies our false self and creates the reality of how we think we feel. An experience and the interpretation of that experience are not the same, but in the ordinary mind they are inseparable. To disidentify is not to negate arising mental states as such, but to cut through our habitual identification with the mind's interpretation of those states. By cultivating the subtle art of disidentification, we loosen our ignorant bond to the mind and gradually separate our sense of me from our mental reality, sheltering it from psychological states that would otherwise constitute the very flavor of our personal self.

The disidentification of which we speak here is vertical in nature, founded upon the state of absence. It should not be confused with the horizontal type of mental exertion we make in our earlier efforts to disidentify, in which one part of the mind observes another in an attempt to dissociate itself from it. True disidentification is the natural result of moment to moment absorption in the non-conceptual state of pure being, which counteracts our mechanical identification with the mind's continuous evaluation of its own psychological states, and pulls the soul beyond the human realm into the state of freedom.

the last pitfalls

Due to its multifaceted nature and complexity, an adept on the path must be prepared to face numerous challenges and pitfalls as he approaches the realm of absence. It is of paramount importance that our mind and heart are sufficiently cleansed before we enter the transcendental state, for the state itself can magnify the ego's negative tendencies. Although the aim of transcendence is to leave the human consciousness behind, such a giant leap in our evolution is not possible unless the human himself is truly surrendered and no longer dominated by subconscious tendencies rooted in his lower nature.

Evolution into the inner realm must always be accompanied by the cleansing of the subconscious mind and the purification of intention. The nearer we draw to freedom, the more refined the snares of ego and the temptations that beckon us from the dimension of forgetfulness. As long as any trace of ego remains one is not on safe ground; hence the absolute requirement for constant ethical and spiritual prudence and deep honesty.

Arriving at the transcendental state, one is so close to the dimension of freedom that it is easy to translate the realization as an experience of complete freedom, while in actuality the state has neither reached its final depth, nor has the ego fully dissolved. There is still a long way to go before the soul can fully merge with universal intelligence and become emancipated from her human ego. Only by exercising extreme caution can a seeker protect himself from the pitfall of overconfidence after shifting into the transcendental state. After countless lifetimes of suffering in the realm of illusion, one must recognize the precious opportunity to reach the freedom bestowed upon us when we are granted entry into the realm of absence, and handle it with the utmost care. The soul is not permitted to enter the temple of the beloved unless she has become a luminous reflection of divine purity, surrender, humility, intelligence, honor, truth and love.

Though to begin the process of transcendence the ego needs to be partially uprooted, its basic structure remains intact until we are able to surrender our individual existence entirely. For this reason, prior to transcendence, we embrace the necessary coexistence of the ego with the soul in the movement of surrender, but remain vigilant of the threat of its presence. Before it is merged through the state of transcendence, the ego itself has to reach a level of maturity, understanding and purity sufficient to renounce itself.

When the soul initially enters the realm of absence, the function of intelligence loosens its grip and the mind becomes spaced-out, weakened in its ability to control its subconscious tendencies. At this time, deeply rooted inclinations may manifest even more strongly on its surface than usual. In certain cases, the subconscious ego may even begin to dominate the conscious ego, and instead of dissolving, crystallize into another false identity — another ego. If this occurs, the ego will actually abuse the transcendental state, further empowering itself on the human level instead of surrendering with ultimate humility to the beyond.

By intoxicating it with spiritual 'achievement', entry into the transcendental state may tempt the ego to resist its own dissolution. One can easily become entrapped in a web of spiritual materialism: an adept can grow arrogant by developing psychic powers and supernatural abilities, or by using the magnetism of his spiritual development to seek influence over others by assuming the role of a spiritual teacher too hastily. Such lower tendencies can enter into even the deepest states of self-realization. Blinded by arrogance, one may ignorantly cling to the idea of transcendence as an actual attainment, reconstructing the prison of ego, the very thing the soul seeks to dismantle. Freedom cannot be reached unless we have been tested on all levels and emerge fully prepared to surrender to our higher nature. The more one merges with the true reality, the more one begins to see that there is ultimately nothing to attain. The soul evolves not to gain something in particular, but to become herself in her eternal essence and drop the burden of unconsciousness.

Apart from the dangers present within the process of transcendence on the level of ego, we need to be aware of two other major pitfalls: over-accelerated 'transcendence', which puts the basic sanity of human consciousness at risk, and the distraction of mystical states. As we have already mentioned, evolution into transcendence is gradual in nature — one needs to pass through many levels of surrender before moving fully into the beyond. The shift to the transcendental state is so radical that to experience it too suddenly can create a deep crisis in our consciousness and even harm the functioning of our intelligence. As we move further into the inner dimension of surrender, our consciousness and energy need enough time to mature and adjust before they can merge with the realm of absence. The individual aspect of our consciousness must maintain its integral stability within the movement of its progressive dissolution into universal I am.

The final pitfall we would like to address is that of digression into mystical states, which give us a false sense of emancipation. Within the realm of transcendence, one can enter various altered states of consciousness that bypass the actualization of one's original self. The appeal of such states is that they allow us to disconnect from the human reality. We experience a relative freedom from our earthly existence, but it is a freedom rooted neither in the realization of the soul, nor unity with the source. These states may temporarily alleviate our suffering, but they do not enable the realization of wholeness. To avoid these evolutionary deviations, one must recognize the truth of pure surrender, which points to the samadhi plane of the soul and universal I am.

samadhi

To fuse individuality with universality is samadhi. To reabsorb the soul in the self is samadhi. Samadhi is the completion of the transcendental state, the final absorption of our personal self in the beyond — freedom itself. When our sense of me is merged with I am, and the soul is merged with the realm of absence, this is samadhi. To be and not to be simultaneously is samadhi, the exalted state of immobile and eternal union with the supreme reality.

entering samadhi

There are many kinds of relative samadhi, depending on the level of one's inner attainment and the depth of one's absorption. Each entry into the realm of pure subjectivity through the inner state can be viewed as a samadhi of some kind, such as the samadhi of awareness, being or the absolute. However, prior to merging with the beyond, no matter what state we are in, the experiencer is split from the inner dimension — the observer is external to being. Only in the deeper dimensions of transcendence are our mind and ego pulled into the universal now and dissolved into the realm of absence. True samadhi is beyond mere abidance in any state; it is the very absorption of our personal consciousness into universal existence.

Samadhi has a very clear direction of vertical absorption, but should not be confused with a trance-like suspension of consciousness. To forget oneself, space-out, fall into a stupor, drift into other realms, or become suspended in various states, has nothing to do with samadhi. These conditions of altered consciousness, or absence of consciousness, are not samadhi. They are states of abeyance that occur outside of the realm of I am, and therefore are devoid of spiritual illumination and have no transformative power. Samadhi can only be entered through the portal of pure subjectivity, and reflects a clarity of consciousness in which the essence of the soul is fully integrated.

264

Although fundamentally positive, it is also a misconception to view experiences of empty awareness, boundless consciousness, or other related conditions of transparency and expansion as samadhi, for they are horizontal in nature, and as such, do not point to the merging of the personal self. An adept enters the plane of samadhi only when his consciousness moves to the state of absence and is pulled into a natural absorption in the beyond. Samadhi is a state of pure freedom, emptiness and motionlessness that is rooted in the vertical dimension of the now. Samadhi in the inner realm is complete when our individual self, the relative me, merges with the source.

the samadhi of consciousness

Before we arrive at the samadhi of me, our experience of the transcendental state can be described as the samadhi of consciousness. Consciousness is none other than the pure awareness we experience in the headspace as the I am of the soul, our primal identity distinct and independent from our ego. Prior to the final immersion of awareness in the beyond, the soul's consciousness is separate from her being and heart, as well as from the inner realm. In the samadhi of consciousness, it is not me, but the soul who rests in unconditional absorption in the realm of absence. In the samadhi of consciousness, the transcendental state, the soul is in the state of surrender, but the human is still not merged. Although relatively absorbed, transparent and empty, the sense of me remains separate from the beyond. When fully established and integrated, the samadhi of consciousness has the same depth of complete repose whether we are in meditation or activity.

the samadhi of me

Only after establishing the samadhi of consciousness can the personal self be absorbed. Consciousness must first merge with the absolute for me to gain access to the beyond. In the partially realized transcendental state, the consciousness of the soul is in unity with the realm of absence, but her sense of me based on the mind has not yet dissolved.

In the samadhi of me, me itself moves into the absolute. The samadhi of me is the essence of our emancipation from our false individuality and the pain of separation.

In the samadhi of me, the ego is not relinquished, it merges with the integral consciousness of the soul; the human me returns to its origin and its energy begins to serve its source, the light of I am. The relative sense of me is pulled into itself, and then dissolves into the transcendental state and the soul. Absorbed in the homogeneous state of I am, our transformed me now begins to embody the condition of complete stillness. The samadhi of me resembles the experience of falling asleep while being fully awake; our sense of individual existence is submerged in the realm of absence, yet our consciousness remains clear.

The samadhi of me, like the samadhi of consciousness, is experienced in the headspace, and is initially reached in sitting practice with the eyes closed. First, the energies of me gather and become immobile in the front portion of the head, where they pass through the gate of absence. Once me and consciousness are fully integrated, their energetic distinction dissolves into a unified field that, while still experienced in the headspace, is encompassed by the whole body of the soul. In the samadhi of me, the samadhi of consciousness and our sense of me merge, manifesting the pure consciousness of the soul in her original state of absolute absorption.

The samadhi of me is experienced differently depending on whether the eyes are open or closed. When the eyes are open, the experience of me is transparent, lucid, and wakeful, for looking through open eyes activates our sense of me through its awareness of the world. When the eyes are closed, it is experienced as me moving into a state of deep inactivity. The samadhi of me with open eyes is like a vast, bright space of complete stillness; with closed eyes, like a deep pool of bliss.

Initially, the samadhi of me can only be experienced with the eyes closed, and only when the energy of me reaches sufficient stillness. When the eyes are open, one experiences the samadhi of consciousness and the transparency of me, but not the samadhi of me. Consciousness is in a condition of absence, but the sense of me is transparently present to itself. As the soul matures in her surrender, one begins to realize the samadhi of me immediately upon closing one's eyes, and gradually with the eyes open as well. As with the samadhi of me with closed eyes, in the samadhi of me with open eyes, me's existence moves to the absolute where it abides in the state of no-will. Still, a qualitative difference exists in the experience depending upon whether the eyes are open or closed. With open eyes, the samadhi of me can be said to be energetically in-between the samadhi of consciousness and the samadhi of me with closed eyes.

In the samadhi of me with closed eyes, me is absorbed through the front part of the brain; with open eyes, it is absorbed more through the central-vertical portion of the head. The difference is due to the fact that with closed eyes, me dissolves primarily through itself, and with open eyes, through consciousness. Once fully matured, there is no focal point for this samadhi, either in the headspace or in reality. It is all-encompassing, embracing inner and outer, seer and seen, in undifferentiated unity.

In the samadhi of me with open eyes, me is absorbed in the soul and the beyond, but remains transparently present to the outer world; intelligence is divided between its perception of the internal and external reality. When the eyes are closed, intelligence withdraws to the inner plane of being. Whether the eyes are open or closed, the lucidity of cognition and intelligence are sustained.

As for how the samadhi of me is actually felt — with closed eyes the inner bliss becomes intensified, whereas with open eyes there is more serenity. When the eyes are closed, our relative consciousness is absorbed and the horizontal sense of spaciousness is sucked into a deep sleep-like repose of non-dual bliss. When the eyes are open, the samadhi of me embraces the manifested world through the medium of the waking state, and is therefore imbued with the quality of open-space-consciousness; the unity of absorption and transparency infuses the inner bliss with clarity, giving rise to an experience of profound openness and peace.

the evolution of me into samadhi

In the realm of forgetfulness, the soul initially evolves only as me. Because she is dormant, she can only grow through her mind's identity. When me reaches a sufficient level of evolution and gains spiritual consciousness, it begins to assist in her awakening as the soul. When the soul is realized, me finally surrenders and merges with I am. The flowering of this intricate process is the unity of the soul and me — the samadhi of me.

The conscious mind has a sense of me, but no sense of I am, for I am belongs to the soul. However, the soul cannot realize her I am without me, who is intrinsic to her intelligence. The soul and me are in fact two sides of the same reality — two complementary aspects of our pure subjectivity. The soul is the I am of our existence and needs the sense of me as its conscious representation in the mind. Due to our ignorance, soul and ego are initially experienced as distinct from one another, but there is only one I am in the end, representing the fundamental unity between I am and me. In the ultimate definition of I am, I is me, and am is the soul. The realization of the samadhi of me reveals that what we had been calling 'ego' all along was none other than the unawakened me of the soul. Whereas the false me is in constant motion, separated from the inner state and the soul, the real me is motionless, one with I am.

Me can be by-passed or suspended in many ways, but to be in samadhi it has to move into absence through the gate of immobility where, in its own stillness, it can realize its true nature and become one with the wholeness of the soul. Only the real me can embody the light of pure individuality that is absorbed and embraced by the universal consciousness of the beyond. To realize the samadhi of me is to merge I with am, and me with the soul.

the samadhi of subconscious me

One cannot arrive at the samadhi of subconscious me before passing through the samadhi of consciousness and the samadhi of me.

Only then can the merging of the subconscious and the soul take place, the most subtle occurrence on the samadhi plane. Because the subconscious reality is hidden, it is much more difficult to penetrate and transcend than the conscious mind. When we speak about subconscious me, we are referring to a reality that lies deeper than arising thoughts, at the very root of the personal mind. It is the preconscious source of our conscious experience of me that controls all automatic functions, behaviors and mental formations.

Although the spontaneous manifestation of thought is rooted in the subconscious and unconscious layers of the mind, thought itself does not crystallize our sense of separate identity. The corrupting emergence of the I-construct within the originally pure flow of intelligence results from the ancient conditioning of our lower consciousness. From the point of our initial entry into the realm of forgetfulness, our lower consciousness habitually translates our otherwise transparent sense of me into a distinct personalized identity, thus locking us in an endless circulation of mind that recreates our false sense of self in each moment of active consciousness.

Within a consciousness that is not in surrender, each thought produces a subconscious sense of me, which when concentrated, becomes a conscious thought that in turn creates a conscious sense of me before dissolving back into the subconscious. This is how the ordinary human mind operates — from unconscious to subconscious, subconscious to conscious, and finally, from conscious back to subconscious and unconscious. Even in the samadhi of me, the subconscious automatically regenerates itself. It is as if there were two mes: one at rest, and the other actively reconstructing the personal self on the periphery of the mind.

To suppress thinking will not help us get beyond the split between me in samadhi and the incessantly self-perpetuating subconscious me, because that which we experience as subconscious thought is in fact a delayed expression of the false me that is constantly present on the subconscious level. We must go to the very root of the subconscious me, the origin of our separate self and

source of our personal mind. This pre-conscious sense of me existentially precedes its own continuous manifestation as subconscious me
in the mind. On an experiential level, this root is found and grasped
at the meeting place between the me in samadhi and the depths of
the mind from which the original impulse to think arises.

In practical terms, the samadhi of subconscious me is reached
through the organic expansion of the samadhi of me itself, which
gradually integrates and absorbs root-subconscious me. In actuality,
it is not that there are two distinct mes in our consciousness — me
in samadhi and subconscious me — rather that our me operates on
several parallel levels simultaneously. Initially, when core-conscious
me is in samadhi, subconscious me, the peripheral portion of this
same me, has no access to samadhi. Arrival at the samadhi of subconscious me is the function of a natural deepening of the samadhi
of me in which our true me embraces and absorbs its subconscious
roots in total surrender.

The channel through which subconscious me is absorbed into
samadhi is found at the back of the head. This area contains the space
that links the root of me and the manifestation of subconscious me in
the mind — it is where the pre-conscious processing of information
that prepares me to encounter the world takes place. Here we enter
the most profound dimension of samadhi, in which the core of our
personal identity, the essence of our subconscious me, merges with
the depths of absence.

The actual center from which root-subconscious me originates
is found in the medulla oblongata at the base of the head, the most
ancient part of the brain. When recreating our personal identity, root-
subconscious me has to travel upwards from the medulla to reach
the upper part of the brain where it becomes semi-conscious as subconscious me, and then conscious as conscious me. In order to reach
the samadhi of subconscious me, the movement of consciousness has
to be reversed so that it can be absorbed downwards within the back
of the head and pass through the medulla. In this way, consciousness

crosses the threshold of absence and pulls the root-subconscious me into absolute surrender.

the samadhi of intelligence

In deep samadhi, in addition to the sense of me becoming naturally absorbed, one may also experience the absorption of intelligence. As we have described, intelligence, the reflective consciousness that allows us to know directly that we exist in creation and gives us the ability to feel and to cognize, is a faculty of consciousness that operates on a more subtle plane than thinking. It both illuminates the realm of I am, and connects us to the world through the gateway of the senses. When intelligence is in samadhi, all mental functions are temporarily suspended, rendering it unable to distance itself from the experience by means of recognition — it is merged with pure consciousness in the stillness of oblivion.

To register sensory input, as in the act of visual seeing, active intelligence is required. It is therefore impossible to arrive at the samadhi of intelligence with open eyes unless, as a result of total absorption, one does not register one's surroundings. To be in the samadhi of intelligence with open eyes is to see nothing, for the moment we begin to see, our intelligence is reactivated. Although we see 'nothing', the samadhi of intelligence is not a condition of blankness in which recognition is entirely absent. The cognizing intelligence is suspended, but the non-dual self-luminous knowing of the unmanifested essence is spontaneously present, as in the condition of a dreamless, awakened sleep.

The soul expresses itself through two centers of identity in the human form. Her natural center in creation is the heart, but the essence of her consciousness is in the head. When her essence withdraws to an unmanifested condition, as in the samadhi of intelligence, the soul recedes to the state of primordial consciousness. Even though from the view point of the experiencer the samadhi of intelligence is beyond bodily reference, if we analyze it objectively, we can see that the last conscious connection between the soul and her absence is experienced in the head.

The presence of intelligence is intrinsic to the creative existence of the soul and essential to her further evolution. The samadhi of intelligence is therefore not something to be consciously sought or desired during waking or in meditation. We have addressed it here only to enable the seeker to correctly perceive and understand the experience when it manifests spontaneously.

transparent ego

When the core of me is in samadhi, the intelligence that operates in the open space of inner repose gives rise to a secondary sense of me as a relative point of reference. To activate the observer, intelligence utilizes the central portion of the brain, which usually is reserved for spontaneous or subconscious thinking. It cannot use the frontal lobe, where the conscious mind and will operate, for that is where root-me is absorbed.

Since intelligence is present in all types of samadhi except the samadhi of intelligence, 'minimum ego' must also be present to maintain our human consciousness. Minimum ego is the portion of the soul's energy that is still linked to the mind after the sense of me has been absorbed in samadhi. This minimum ego generates very little thought-energy; hence the big difference between ordinary thinking and thinking in samadhi. In samadhi, not only is the ego absorbed into the state of absence, but the mind moves to the other side as well. Thinking, whether subconscious or conscious, occurs in emptiness and absence, free of any effort or will that could create a sense of separation or crystallize personal identity. The observer can still recreate himself within the thinking process, but he is transparent, merely functional. In samadhi, intelligence moves freely in an open space of pure consciousness that has no center of I. Although the relative sense of me naturally arises as a point of reference within the flow of intelligence, it is entirely owned by the I am of the soul into which it dissolves in each now.

272

arising thoughts in samadhi

Samadhi does not fully arrest the activity of the mind. The intermittent arising of thoughts in meditation functions as a sort of 'screen saver' on the screen of our personal consciousness. Our relative consciousness cannot remain entirely static, even while contained within the stillness of samadhi, for it is our link to creation. Intelligence has to move whenever it receives inspiration from the subconscious mind. Unless it is suspended in a trance-like absorption, it constantly awaits and processes input from the world through mind and senses; hearing a sound, feeling the body, even assessing the depth of samadhi, are all expressions of the subtle mind. A trance-like absorption in which all thoughts and bodily impressions are suspended is not a natural state, because the watcher is absent; it compromises the movement of life and intelligence through which we embody our human reality and the complete experience of me.

the samadhi of the observer

There are three layers of identity in our consciousness: the observer, me, and I am. The observer is the ever-shifting, functional center of our intelligence; me is the light of pure individuality that illuminates itself as the transparent self of our personal identity; I am is the light of impersonality, the root of our being unified with the universal self. In order to arise, the observer borrows its sense of me from our fundamental me, similar to the way in which our fundamental me borrows its sense of I am from the soul.

In reality, consciousness manifests from I am to me, and then to the observer; in the state of ignorance, where neither I am nor me is awakened, the process is experienced as if in reverse. Prior to our awakening as the soul, we are only the observer — we have no other vehicle through which to reflect, understand and evolve. Me awakens through the observer by linking the observer to the soul, and the observer, in turn, links the mind to me.

The observer is another name for the ego. Lacking both I am and pure me, he is a mere shadow identity. The ego is an aspect of me limited to its functional expression as thinker, checker, observer and decision-maker — it is the dynamic aspect of me that watches, evaluates and manages thoughts, emotions and experiences. In the absence of awakening, the ego operates as our false center, masquerading as our real me.

In the state of forgetfulness, the observer is the only experiencer and knower of reality that one has. Even if we are in touch with the state beyond thought, unless we are truly awakened, the moment the observer stops paying attention to that state, both the experience and the recognition of the experience are forgotten. Only upon awakening do we realize that the soul, as the primal experiencer, is inseparable from the experience of reality. The observer, the secondary experiencer, processes experiences in the mind, but the soul feels and knows them directly, prior to thought and reflection. After her awakening, even if the observer does not pay attention to our inner reality, the soul dwells continuously in the self-evident recognition of I am. The continuity of consciousness that we experience through the inner state is not a function of the observer, but of the soul's I amness. The main problem we encounter after giving birth to the inner state is that our primary and secondary experiencers are disjoined. When, through the process of surrender, the primary and secondary experiencers merge, our internal experience of self is magnified in its depth and intensity, because the soul finally becomes whole.

The process of transcending the observer is complex and takes many turns, for though he is the cause of our separation, he cannot simply be discarded; his presence is essential to our evolution. Awakening to me, one actualizes a deeper consciousness of oneself that is not observing or thinking, but being. The moment me ceases to operate as a mere function of the mind and begins to experience itself as pure subjectivity, it is transformed into the me of the soul. This stable, fundamental me exists apart from intelligence, but is still partially connected to the mind through the observer, who now moves to the periphery. However, even though his position has changed, our identification with the observer persists, and as a result, we continue to suffer the same existential split between our fundamental me and our ego in which we have been entrenched from time immemorial. Despite entering the transcendental state, the observer continues to separate us from our absence; he is the single part of our identity that cannot enter samadhi.

Even after reaching a profound state of being one remains powerless to rid oneself of the observer for the very simple reason that one still *is* this observer. Although not our fundamental me, the observer still operates as a parallel sense of me that can neither be repressed nor ignored. He is not a thought, emotion or attitude from which we can disidentify, but the very one doing the disidentifying. Initially, we have to accept the observer as a part of our multilayered existence so that we can mature as this observer as well. The observer cannot be merged unless he himself grows into an understanding of how to cooperate in the process of his own surrender and dissolution.

In meditation, we come closest to the condition of being a unified whole and experiencing minimum ego during those moments when the observer pays complete one-pointed attention to the space of our inner abidance. The moment the observer is distracted, we drift away and become identified with our ego-self again. Our fundamental problem with the observer in meditation is that by nature he cannot maintain constant focus on the inner state, or any point of reference for that matter. He simply has limited powers of concentration. He must, now and again, divert his attention away from his object to circulate energy and consciousness, either by initiating a conscious thought process or by getting lost in subconscious thinking. We experience this division between the soul absorbed in the beyond and the observer isolated in his mind-identity not only in the ordinary state of meditation, but in the samadhi of consciousness as well. Only in those moments when the observer makes a conscious effort to rest in the transcendental state does his identity become somewhat united with the soul. And even then he is not merged; his sense of separation is merely pacified.

To transcend the observer is perhaps our greatest challenge, for it strikes at the very root of the false individuality through which we have been living for countless incarnations. To merge the observer, we first must reach the samadhi of me, which in its full maturity and integration dissolves the I-construct into itself. In the initial stages of our entry into this samadhi, before the mind is fully transformed and absorbed, the habitual observer still maintains his identity based on personality. Prior to arriving at the state of pure absence, it is not the whole of me that abides in samadhi: its core is absorbed, but the sub-conscious mind automatically recreates a parallel sense of me as the observer on the outer layer of our consciousness. As we mature into surrender, our subconscious identity gradually drops and merges with our fundamental me, which is already in samadhi.

Practically speaking, in order to unite with me, the observer must arrive at a condition of no-will, or absolute rest. In our journey towards the ultimate repose, the different aspects of our existence surrender, one by one. First, our being reaches the state of no-will by shifting into the absolute, followed by our consciousness when it enters the realm of absence. Next, our me surrenders by reaching samadhi — and finally, the observer merges with me. In terms of the movement of energy, because the samadhi of me occurs in the front part of the brain, which is normally reserved for conscious thinking, the conscious observer must shift his activity to the upper-central portion of the head in order to function. When the observer is pulled into absorption, this is the region of the brain into which the samadhi of me expands.

Freedom from the observer does not imply a complete absence of the faculties of reflection and observation. As we have explained, minimum ego is a natural component of our multidimensional existence. However, the observer experienced in the enlightened state is fully merged with the soul. He abides in absence, free of will; his compulsion to recreate a sense of a separate self has been fully uprooted. The observer that arises in samadhi is of the soul. Although he naturally possesses a dynamic sense of me within the movement of intelligence, this sense of me is entirely contained in the beyond.

samadhi: deep sleep in waking

For an ordinary human, dreamless sleep is the deepest possible repose, for awareness is completely suspended. In the awakened reality, however, the dimension of deep sleep is always present, independent of both the presence and absence of consciousness. As the ground of being, it underlies both the waking and sleep states. It is only because of our ignorance that we have lost our conscious connection with the fundamental reality of the source.

In the waking state, both the human and the soul are alienated from the repose of sound sleep, whereas in the dream state, although the human is lost in the subconscious realm, the soul becomes unconsciously reabsorbed into the original absence. In spite of the commotion of dreaming, one has a sense of rejuvenating rest. Only in deep sleep, however, is our rest absolute, for the human is entirely absent, dissolved in the soul.

Deep sleep is the absolute reality in primordial darkness prior to its illumination by the light of consciousness. It is through deep sleep that humans and other forms of consciousness, even those that are unrealized, can temporarily return to the source and experience unconscious unity with the beyond. However, due to the lack of consciousness, it is a negative unity. In universal consciousness, the light of self-luminous cognition together with the original absence create a single body of existence that forms the foundation of the manifested universe; the absolute and consciousness are undivided. In ignorance, when the soul retreats to deep sleep and loses her waking awareness, she cannot access the original consciousness of the beyond and recedes to a nothingness-like absence within absence.

The condition of samadhi allows us to enter the reality of deep sleep during waking; our consciousness is in absolute rest while still conscious. To obtain the state of absence within the waking reality is to become present in the beyond. Our experiences of forgetfulness and remembrance are confined to waking consciousness, in which ignorance is absence of presence, and awakening is presence of presence. In order to move beyond the frontiers of the waking state, our presence must enter the realm of absence. To be present in absence *is* samadhi, deep sleep in waking.

samadhi in sleep: turiya

Turiya, 'the fourth state', is the name traditionally given to the unconditional state of being beyond waking, dreaming and deep sleep. In the waking state, we experience the ordinary conscious state; in the dream state, the subconscious; in the deep sleep, the unconscious. Turiya is usually defined as the super-conscious state that dwells at the root of all states of consciousness as well as absence of consciousness, the transcendental reality underlying the plane of illusion.

Commonly understood to be both universal and impersonal, from the ultimate standpoint, turiya is not actually the substratum of all possible states, but the meeting point between the individual soul and the transcendental reality. It can be described as the natural samadhi of the soul in the universal self. The realization of turiya results from a dual absorption of the soul: in her individual essence, and in the beyond. She abides in her fundamental nature and the realm of absence simultaneously. Turiya is the consciousness of the soul in her original form in unity with the beloved — the soul in timeless repose.

Although the state of turiya experienced in sleep is none other than the soul, it is only her unmanifested essence. For the realization of wholeness and the actualization of her complete multidimensional existence, the soul needs to enter the reality of creation through the gate of one of the many waking states that exist in this or other universes. The waking state for an awakened soul is no longer in conflict with turiya. On the contrary, it is a plane of reality necessary as an environment for the expansion of her consciousness and intelligence.

Turiya is beyond all relative states, but in order to manifest as a conscious experience, it must first be realized in the waking state. For a human being, the waking state is the only gateway to reality. However, although we may realize various levels of awakening during waking, none should be mistaken for unconditional turiya. Unless turiya is realized, any awakening or 'enlightenment' that we attain is confined within the boundaries of our waking reality; no matter how profound, it is no more than an 'expanded waking state'. To transcend the waking state in waking is a function of our passage to the realm of absence through the gateway of presence. Although turiya is realized within the waking reality, it itself transcends the waking dimension by establishing our soul in the ever-present consciousness of universal subjectivity.

The state of turiya is experienced in its primordial isolation only when the soul is in the samadhi of both me and intelligence, as in an awakened deep sleep state. When experienced in conjunction with waking or dream states, although beyond them, the flavor of turiya is colored by their presence. In the waking state, turiya is infused with an active consciousness that illuminates one's inner and outer worlds; it is positively integrated with the conscious mind and the experience of the soul in the body. In deep sleep, turiya withdraws to its unmanifested seed and recedes to the bliss of absolute rest. In dreaming, turiya coexists with the subconscious activity of the mind. For someone who has reached the samadhi of me, to open the eyes is to experience turiya in the waking state, and to close them is to experience turiya in the intermediate state between sleep and waking.

From the standpoint of our evolution through the inner states, turiya can be said to be synonymous with the transcendental state. Turiya experienced in the waking state is our ultimate natural state. However, to avoid confusing turiya with the transcendental state and the natural state, we narrow its definition here to the consciousness of our essence in sleep. In other words, turiya is 'awakened sleep'.

Even for one who has reached the transcendental state, it is quite rare to be able to transfer the consciousness of that state into sleep.

Since our conscious evolution takes place primarily during the waking state, our spiritual attainments are naturally more integrated with our waking consciousness than our sleep. The recognition of our transcendental presence in the sleep state requires a further awakening that crosses the boundaries of our waking reality, thus empowering our consciousness to pierce through the layers of our subconscious and unconscious self.

The state of turiya does not register or even relate to subconscious activity in sleep. It is a parallel sleep reality. Just as turiya in the waking state coexists with the parallel waking state of activity, turiya in sleep is present beneath the simultaneously occurring dreaming. In turiya in sleep, the soul consciously dwells in the bliss of being (though not conscious that she is conscious of being conscious), while subconscious me experiences dreams or dissolves into dreamless sleep. Turiya is aware of nothing but itself; it is the consciousness of pure bliss, the inherent quality of being, the soul's original form of absolute unity with the beloved.

Falling asleep is the temporary dissolution of conscious intelligence. In ordinary sleep, intelligence first dissolves into a subconscious state, manifesting dreams, and then into an unconscious state. However, in the kind of sleep in which turiya is present, intelligence is consciously absorbed into the samadhi of me. In the dreaming phase of awakened sleep, dreaming can occasionally occur, whereas in deep sleep, the subconscious is absorbed and only the consciousness of the self remains. The latter state is similar in nature to the samadhi of intelligence in the waking state.

The phenomenon of turiya in sleep is not the same as lucid dreaming. To bring awareness into the sleep state as it is most commonly practiced is nothing but an expansion of certain faculties within the ego itself. By exercising an artificial type of mindfulness we may be able to transfer a portion of our conscious waking mind into the subconscious reality of sleep, but the dreamer, dreaming activity, and consciousness of dreams remain functions of our personalized ego-identity. In lucid dreaming, the soul is neither conscious of her pure subjectivity nor rests in absorption. She is fully identified with the dream reality and absent to herself. Ego alone is aware of dreaming. In turiya, the soul abides in her pure subjectivity *and* unbroken absorption in the source. It is the state of true samadhi; no one is aware, awareness just is.

In our existential challenge to become fully 'awake', it is not the conscious waking mind that we need to incorporate into the sleep state, but the essence of the soul's consciousness. In order to succeed in this task, we must first reach a state of complete surrender during waking through the cultivation of the samadhi of me, for it is the samadhi of me that bridges the consciousness of surrender with the depths of the sleep state. Awakened sleep is actually an extension of the samadhi of me. When me in samadhi fully merges in the beyond, it 'locks' itself into the original state; its continuity becomes unbroken, even as our relative consciousness dissolves in the process of falling asleep.

There are two common misconceptions about turiya. The first is that it is realized as the natural outcome of being established in pure awareness. Although an important achievement, continuity of the state of presence is an attainment limited to waking. The second misconception is that turiya can be actualized through an effort to maintain awareness while falling asleep. However, because the effort to be aware is horizontal in nature, it interferes with the natural process of falling asleep, which requires the dissolution of the conscious mind. In contrast, cultivating the samadhi of me and vertical awareness while falling asleep is in complete harmony with the need to dissolve our waking consciousness. The realization of turiya is the flowering of the pure awareness of waking merged with the absolute surrender of sleep.

Turiya is realized by establishing a state of constant surrender that in its complete maturity becomes merged and integrated with the consciousness of the soul. Only then can pure awareness be transmuted into the eternal presence of our timeless essence. It is the gravity and inertia of our absolute surrender that enable a continuity of self to root itself beneath the dreaming and sleep states. By reactualizing the consciousness of our unborn self, we transcend all states, and finally become embedded in the true reality beyond waking and sleep, life and death.

The practice of awakening the turiya state during sleep is very sensitive, and should not be initiated prior to reaching the level of samadhi in which both consciousness and me have fully surrendered in the waking state. Although it is unlikely that premature practice of turiya in the sleep state would be harmful, it could potentially interfere with the dreaming and sleep processes. By imposing artificial awareness on the sleep state, one may hinder the natural release of the subconscious mind, depriving oneself of essential physical and psychological rest.

consciousness of consciousness

In our journey towards the realization of our essential nature we travel through deeper and deeper experiences of awakening and surrender into the final depth of the original self. Our first step is to recognize the state of presence, to become aware of consciousness. Our second step is to remember the state of presence, which is awareness of consciousness. Our third step is to abide in the state of presence, which is awareness *in* consciousness. Our fourth step is to become the state of presence, which is consciousness of awareness. Our fifth step is to surrender the state of presence, which is consciousness of awareness resting in consciousness. Our sixth and final step is to merge presence with absence, which is consciousness of awareness immersed in consciousness absorbed in the absolute.

All of these stages of awakening and transcendence are contained within the space of our waking dimension and depend upon awareness as their driving force. However, the deepest penetration of the original state can only take place when we transcend the frontiers of the waking reality through the actualization of our primordial consciousness. In our ultimate absorption we experience a state of being in which awareness is entirely absent, but consciousness stays awake, as in samadhi within sleep or the samadhi of intelligence. We enter the original awakened consciousness, devoid of me — consciousness of consciousness.

beyond turiya

The term 'beyond the fourth' or 'turiyatitta' denotes the ontological foundation of turiya, the transcendental space upon which turiya dwells. Turiyatitta is the ocean of the universal beyond within which the realized soul abides and expands into the divine reality. Through realization of turiya, the soul merges with turiyatitta, but she does not become it. Turiyatitta is always beyond. Its origin is the absence beyond absence, the void beyond void, the boundless beyond. Turiyatitta lies beneath the first three states as well as the fourth — it is the inner realm, the dimension of universal consciousness, the source.

Turiya can also be said to be the substratum of the first three states, but only from the standpoint of an awakened soul, not the universal self. Traditionally, it is assumed that turiya exists independently of our experience and recognition, and remains hidden from our consciousness only due to our forgetfulness. However, unless turiya is awakened, it can neither be experienced nor recognized, for it does not exist in separation from our individual consciousness. Since turiya is the soul at rest, if the soul is not in samadhi, turiya is simply absent.

Turiyatitta represents a higher plane of existence than turiya, for while the state of turiya must be awakened in order to manifest as our conscious experience, turiyatitta is ever present, irrespective of our enlightenment or ignorance. Although in turiya the soul does experience unity with the universal, she is merely on the cusp of the infinite; the immense reality of the original self remains hidden in the beyond. Turiya is the individual's point of entry into the universal, and turiyatitta is the universal itself. Turiya is the individual impersonality; turiyatitta is the impersonal universality.

the dimensions of the surrendering self

Surrender is not a singular event, but a multidimensional process that absorbs various aspects of our existence, one at a time. To embrace surrender as a whole, we must address the different dimensions of the surrendering self: the soul, consciousness, intelligence, mind and me. Although close consideration of these various aspects of our identity may seem to complicate the simple reality of surrender, we must understand the essential role that each plays in our transcendence.

The soul is the I am of our inner being that needs to be remembered, awakened and merged with the divine. I am, the manifestation of universal I am, is the individual impersonality felt as the core of our being prior to manifesting as me. Me is the knowing superimposed upon I am through which the universal light of individuality becomes embodied as the consciousness of oneself. Consciousness is the I am of awareness and functions as a bridge between the soul and the mind. Awareness is the soul's true nature on the level of consciousness that contains her pure intelligence. Consciousness and awareness are essentially the same, but consciousness refers more to the soul's essence, and awareness to her intelligence and the mind. The human mind operates through the ego, which is the sense of identity parallel to the soul that is responsible for creating and sustaining our personal sense of me. The sense of me is the root of our human self, and so long as it is not merged, we remain alienated from the soul.

The mind is the natural movement of thought that recreates the functional center of identity that we translate as I, moment to moment. When the sense of me is absorbed into the soul, the mind continues to operate, but without any center. It is embraced by the consciousness of the soul and transmuted into the light of her intelligence. The ordinary mind serves the false me, or ego; the mind in surrender serves our higher being.

The ego is the part of the soul's sense of I am that she invested in the mind when she entered the state of forgetfulness. Our ordinary sense of me is but a lost soul who has forgotten her true identity in the process of becoming human. As long as the soul remains ignorant of herself, the ego owns our sense of me in the mind. The ego's unreality can be penetrated and exposed only upon the soul's awakening, for she alone owns the light of me.

When consciousness surrenders into the state of absence, the soul merges her awareness with her being. However, prior to transcendence, there is still a split between the soul, who dwells in the freedom of absence, and our human identity, which continues to perpetuate a secondary sense of me in the mind. Even after the soul surrenders and merges her consciousness with the beyond, the core of our false self has still not been uprooted. In order to reach a state of true wholeness, the human has to submit his existence to the soul — our sense of me has to dissolve into the beyond.

We must see the difference between consciousness and me to understand the difference between the samadhi of consciousness and the samadhi of me. Since consciousness is the primary sense of I am that exists prior to arising thoughts and their subsequent identification with the personal me, the samadhi of consciousness enables the soul's identity in the headspace to move into the state of absence. The samadhi of me transforms the essence of self-awareness in the mind, merging it with the soul. Prior to its complete surrender, the ego is peripheral to consciousness, operating as the observer who confirms that consciousness is in samadhi. When it finally surrenders itself, the ego is absorbed by the soul and the beyond. The inherent ability of intelligence to think and observe is retained, but now, as the ultimate observer, our pure intelligence flows in unity with the cosmic whole.

the natural samadhi

True samadhi is not a trance or disappearance, but natural abidance within universal reality as it is. It is everywhere and nowhere. It does not occur in relation to the inner, nor in contrast to the outer. There is no coming in or going out of samadhi. It does not move, it does not change. It is clear, luminous, pristine, conscious, and still, like a diamond mountain. It is the state of the self, the end of becoming. To reach the natural samadhi signifies that the soul has arrived at her destination. Through the blessing of the natural samadhi, she is absolved of her ignorance and emancipated from the wheel of separation and suffering to become reabsorbed into the absolute source from whence she originally emerged. Freed from bondage and remerged with the vastness of the transcendental realm, she can be her ultimate self at last.

liberation

The bone and marrow of the spiritual path is the deep recognition of the limited, unsatisfactory and unconscious nature of human existence. Unless we recognize the basic suffering of human life that is rooted in the forgetfulness of our eternal nature, the longing for spiritual emancipation will never awaken. The desire for freedom is encoded in our higher being, but we must consciously recognize our ignorance, or else it will lie dormant. The moment we become conscious enough to realize our unconsciousness, we are ready to begin the journey towards transformation. Before initiating the process of liberation, an intense urge and unquenchable yearning for true freedom needs to take birth within our human intelligence.

Liberation is the ultimate destination of all true seekers on the path to spiritual enlightenment. Beyond any ordinary concept of enlightenment, liberation is the total dissolution of the false. It is our ultimate release from the dimension of ignorance, the final opening into the beyond.

Due to our lower tendencies, impurities, and the very existence of ego, even after reaching unity with the inner realm, we are still a long way from deliverance. To remove all that stands in the way of our freedom, we must dissolve the construct of our infinite past — our identity based on the mind. This most significant and difficult task is completed according to the intricate science of transcendence as revealed by the wisdom of higher intelligence and grace.

the goal of liberation

One cannot penetrate the essence of liberation intellectually, as it is a sphere beyond human existence into which the mind cannot enter — indeed it is the very freedom from the mind-based reality. Not a state, but the removal of everything that separates us from our original purity and wholeness, liberation is the essence of transcendence.

It allows the soul to leave the totality of her history in time behind so that she can return to her ancient perfection.

Only within the dimension of absence can the past self be uprooted from the soul's original purity. The completion of the transcendental state is interlinked with the soul's emancipation from the ego; unless the core of the mind is dissolved through liberation, the state itself cannot reach its final depth. Liberation from our false self and the shift of our existence into the beyond are interdependent aspects of our transcendence; liberation is founded upon the transcendental state, the transcendental state upon liberation.

Liberation is not another shift deeper into the inner realm, but an event that strikes at the very root of our human existence, the ego. Prior to transcendence, the ego was an indivisible element of our inner evolution, coexisting with our spiritual attainments; our evolution did not challenge the structure of our personal identity. In all of the states beyond the mind, the ego was left intact, untouched by our inner expansion. It could enjoy the inner experience or simply become bored. Either way, it was always there, safe and secure, checking and watching or even ignoring the environment of the inner state. But in the state of transcendence, the ego-identity is confronted, its essential structure threatened. It can no longer maintain its cloistered position as spectator, but must enter the fire of absence and surrender itself to the unknown. For the transcendental state to be realized, the ego must implode into the void of non-being — it must die for the soul to be free.

the dissolution of ego

The ego-identity is a multifarious subconscious reality that encompasses all of the mes we have accumulated over the course of our past incarnations. In each lifetime we create a new sense of me, and when that lifetime ends, that particular me ceases to be conscious and moves to the subconscious layer of the soul's existence. What we experience as our conscious me therefore reflects the identity and stream of memories only of the present lifetime. However, for conscious me to operate, it has to draw from the subconscious memories and knowledge accumulated by all the past mes stored in the unconscious. The ego is therefore not a simple entity, but a complex organism created out of countless thought-forms and psychological impressions gathered since the beginning of our personal time, each one imbued with a separate sense of me that, put together, project the illusion of a solidified individual.

Liberation is not of the ego, but *from* the ego. The soul cannot transcend unless she is existentially disconnected from the ego-construct of the mind. The ego can neither dissolve itself nor dissolve into the beyond; it can neither attain reality nor abolish its own unreality. Thus ego-dissolution is not a function of will. In fact, the highest act of our free will is to surrender, and even here, our powers are limited. The only way the mind's intelligence can cooperate with the dissolution of the ego is for it to consciously rest in the transcendental state.

In order to prepare the ground for the ego to surrender we must attain a maximum purity of mind by cultivating sincerity, honesty, humility and heartfulness. The refinement of these qualities opens the mind to a higher perception that reflects the unreality of ego and the truth of the soul. The ego must be exposed in its falsehood before it can be renounced. For the ego to dissolve, all the layers of me-identities in the subconscious mind that have been superimposed upon the soul's true nature must be scraped away so that she can re-actualize her original experience of herself in the timeless now.

In the process of its dissolution, the ego becomes increasingly transparent and weightless until it finally dissolves into the soul. The ego does not disappear with the event of transcendence, it simply ceases to link itself with the associative centers in the brain connected to self-reference that are responsible for the fabrication of the false center in the mind. The observer, the checker, the experiencer, the thinker — the individualized points of reference in our consciousness — are all a natural function of the soul's existence in time. The ego is not false in itself, but in the unconscious way it has operated over the course of our evolution. Due to our ignorance, the ego split from the soul's essence and became identified with lower intelligence, the intelligence of the false me. It began to exist as an autonomous entity, solidifying into our separate self.

In transcendence, the ego is transformed into the open intelligence of the soul. It surrenders to the primordial intelligence of universal consciousness and becomes decentralized, de-focalized and dissolved into a field of open consciousness, merged with our original self. The 'open ego', our ultimate observer, is still linked to the individual soul, but has no center of individuality, no me of its own — it is liberated from itself. It is part of the whole — it is of the soul.

The process of ego-dissolution is based on the evolutionary intervention of a higher wisdom. It is the grace of the soul and the beyond that finally allow the liberation from ego to take place. Without the love and grace of the divine, no human being could ever be emancipated from the earth plane. Only the supreme creator, the one who holds the blueprint of the soul, has the power to actualize her ultimate potential and freedom.

leaving no traces

The existence of a liberated soul is not based on psychological continuity, but on a continuity of unbecoming. Awareness that is built into the state of absence does not create a sense of personal self. For a soul rooted in the dimension of the now, everything that arises in time leaves no traces in the immaculate void of her consciousness. All that manifests in her consciousness is simultaneously dissolved in the natural state of emptiness and non-abidance. Thoughts continue to manifest, but they are erased by the power of absence as they arise, unless consciously processed.

The soul of an awakened being abides in the unbroken continuity of the timeless now, but her human expression abides in each integral 'moment' of earthly time. A moment is the meeting between the consciousness of the now and the consciousness of the here; it is how each now is experienced on earth. A moment of each now is an externalization of the timeless into the here that enables the soul to expand into creation through the doorway of her human intelligence. While abiding in the now, there is still enough space in each moment for the soul to experience her human consciousness in earthly time. In the moment, even while absorbed in the beyond, an enlightened being can feel sadness and joy, desire and aversion, excitement and boredom — but none of these emotions leave any traces. As the soul's identity returns to the condition of unbroken samadhi, each moment that arises from the now is fully experienced, but becomes instantaneously reabsorbed into the void of the now from which the next moment manifests.

For the movement of becoming to leave no traces in our consciousness, the will to grasp at psychological continuity in time must be entirely uprooted from the consciousness of the soul. Only one who is in complete surrender can live in the continuity of becoming, but dwell in the continuity of being. For the awakened soul, to leave no traces means not to be here; for the awakened human, it is to be total in each moment. In this total moment of the human absorbed in the now of the soul, each experience burns to ashes in the sacred fire of absence, leaving an open space for a new moment to emerge.

Though he leaves no traces, even an awakened human requires a minimum of continuity in empirical time in order to function. There is still a coherent flow of intelligence through which each moment connects to the next. However, the logical unfolding of becoming and the integral movement of life are not based on personal will, but on the impersonal intelligence of the universal spirit that runs through the whole of existence. The self-realized being has become an open channel for the flow of this intelligence, the wisdom of becoming. He is rooted in the unchanging ground of the timeless now, and from this place serves the purpose of existence in time.

the ending of our earthly identity

By completing our earthly existence we conclude but a small portion of universal evolution. Prior to transcendence, our identity is human — but our soul is not human in her essence. No human can truly conceive of the soul without first transcending his human consciousness; to know the soul is to become the soul. To end her earthly identity, the soul must leave the shell of her human mind behind and reemerge within the state of universal intelligence.

To attain freedom, the soul first needs to resolve her karmic ties and reach completion within her human existence, a process governed by her evolutionary destiny, her alignment with the path, and the elements of timing and grace. Only when she is at peace with her human experience can she let go of her earthly consciousness. Otherwise, the entire net of desires, attachments and subconscious tendencies that link her to the human realm will continue to pull her down into the plane of forgetfulness with irresistible gravity. Only when she is relieved of her karmic burden can the soul uplift her existence to universal evolution. Transcendence is the outcome of the soul's completion, which requires human completion as its existential foundation.

from personality to universality

Liberation goes beyond mere abidance in any of the inner states, the state of transcendence included. No matter what state we reach, there is always a sense of I that personalizes the experience and claims it as his own. It is the dissolution of the I-construct that is the secret of real transcendence. In transcendence, it is not that there exists a personal self that experiences his own absence as abidance in the transcendental state. The experiencer is no more. One dwells in a reality beyond self-reference and, in place of the personal self, something absolutely pure and universal emerges.

freedom

When she leaves the dimension of forgetfulness behind, the soul becomes one with the supreme transparency of pure existence and reaches freedom, the unknown realm that lies beyond the perception of the human mind. Who then is free? No one is free, for freedom is the state of reality, and cannot be owned by any individual. In the absence of the one who is in bondage, even freedom is transcended. No one has parted, no one has arrived, and no one has realized his immortal essence. The cost of freedom is the very death of our separate self — a small price to pay considering that the majority of our human experience is suffering.

the soul and the self

In transcendence, the soul merges with the universal self — individuality dissolves into the ocean of universal being. To realize the state of oneness is to transcend self while remaining an indivisible part of that realization. Though dissolved, the soul continues to exist, but now in a new, transcendental way; the beloved allows her to return to a state of conscious unity with the undivided whole so that she may continue her everlasting evolution as an angle of perception within that unity. Oneness is not an inert reality, but the eternally occurring reunion of the soul and her creator within the space of totality, an everlasting journey of love and individual expansion into the divine reality.

our ultimate self

The purpose of evolution is the transmutation of our personal individuality into the impersonal distinctness of the soul's unique existence within the undivided whole. Liberation is the ending of our past self and the beginning of our expansion into the supreme beyond. To become our true self is to awaken all aspects of the soul's multidimensional existence and surrender to the wisdom of the supreme reality. The soul in her ultimate form is a being of light whose only purpose is to serve the expansion and evolution of universal I am.

To be free is to embody the natural state of existence, the ultimate humility and simplicity of egolessness. A liberated soul has dropped the burden of spirituality and become profoundly ordinary. Beyond enlightenment and ignorance, presence and absence, being and non-being, knowing and not-knowing, here and now — she is free, and beyond freedom.

the end and the new beginning

From the perspective of higher intelligence, human enlightenment is limited, barely scratching the surface of the eternal truth. The bliss of freedom, peace of liberation, and joy of transcendence are the last emotions we feel in the plane of forgetfulness — and though they point to the beyond, they are nonetheless still tied to our human consciousness. Only when these relative experiences are left behind through the power of absence can we be reborn into our universal existence.

There is an immense difference between our evolution on earth and our post-transcendence existence in the beyond. Upon entering the domain of universal consciousness, the soul becomes one with the eternal expansion of light and intelligence. Evolution is no longer her private affair; it is universal and infinite. Evolution within the state of wholeness is by nature impersonal, because the soul in transcendence no longer owns her individuality — it is owned by her creator. It is the divine who evolves, experiencing the realm of creation through countless souls, beings of light and forms of consciousness.

One who has not transcended his human reality is not meant to know what lies beyond it. It is not the destiny of human consciousness to cross the boundaries of the known. Only the eternal heart of the soul is allowed to enter the unknown.

never-ending evolution

Evolution has no end. We may believe that the need for evolution proves the existence of imperfection, and this is so — but only in the phenomenal universe. Within universal I am, evolution is not based on the transcendence of imperfection, but on the expansion of perfection. While on earth, we evolve from imperfection to never-fully-achieved-perfection; in the true reality, it is perfection itself that evolves towards an eternally ascending frequency of consciousness and truth. The universal imperative to evolve and expand is not driven by the individual's sense of lack or incompleteness, but the natural expression of truth, bliss and light.

the mystery beyond the known

In our ignorance, we unconsciously assume that our longing for spiritual transformation is based on an essential need to reach personal well-being and release, when in truth it is existence using our self-centeredness as fuel for its own expansion. We do not evolve for our own sake, but for the sake of the eternal whole. It is the will of the divine that all beings and forms of intelligence expand into the sacred heart of creation.

What is the crowning goal of evolution? To meet the unknown source of our existence is our highest aim, the secret destiny of our intelligence and love. But what is the purpose of universal evolution if wholeness and freedom are the natural state of existence? Evolution ultimately has no goal apart from itself. It is the nature of existence to everlastingly unfold the profundity of the self. Evolution is a never-ending exploration of consciousness, intelligence and love within the ever-expanding universe. Evolution is the very meaning of creation. It is our only reason to be.

glossary

Absolute: the dimension of the source; the realm of absence; the unborn; the uncreated; the heart of the now; the primordial isness of reality; the original void; the ground of creation; the unmanifested essence of the beyond; the being aspect of the supreme reality; the final depth of the inner realm.

Absolute State: the final depth in the realization of being; the state of pure rest and unconditional absorption; a state of freedom from energetic fluctuations; the unification of the soul and the absolute on the level of being.

Absorption: the experience of being pulled into the inner plane; the fusion of self and reality; the amalgamation of relative consciousness with the absolute existence; the unconditional repose of the soul in the beloved; samadhi.

Awakening: a radical shift of consciousness into a higher state of existence; a sudden opening into one of the states beyond the mind.

Awareness: the radiance of cognition; the true nature of intelligence; the pure knowing of consciousness channeled through me that brings the phenomenal world into recognition or, when internalized, illuminates the knowledge of I am.

Being: the aspect of the inner state that links the soul with the vertical plane of the source; the ground of existence; the pure isness of the supreme reality; the fundamental support of consciousness and all that is.

Beloved: the heart of the supreme reality; the divine; the creator; the all-embracing love-essence of the god-state.

Beyond: the inner dimension of universal I am; the divine realm; the unmanifested.

Blueprint: the design and plan for the completion for each soul; the evolutionary destiny of the soul and final vision of her wholeness.

Completion: the arrival at maximal wholeness within one's human existence; the ending of root-karma; the actualization of the soul's full potential; the enlightenment of the soul.

Complete Me: the unification of pure me and the human personality.

Conscious Me: the sense of presence experienced in the mind; self-attention within the thinking process; the ego.

Conscious Mind: the level of consciousness at which intelligence can sustain a relatively clear sense of me.

Consciousness: the light of cognition intrinsic to creation and being; the source of awareness; the primordial knowledge of I am.

Creation: the totality of manifested consciousness; the entirety of the phenomenal world and the inner plane of universal consciousness.

Cultivation: methodical practice directed towards perfecting a previously awakened state, or towards preparing the ground for a further stage of awakening.

Divine: the heart of the absolute reality; the domain of grace and love.

Duality: in ignorance, the state of separation; in reality, the natural polarization of consciousness into being and knowing.

Ego: the self-consciousness of the mind; the sense of me based on personality.

Enlightenment: the complete transcendence of ignorance; the dissolution of the false self; the awakening of the soul; the soul's return to her original state of oneness and wholeness; the complete inner state; the merging of the mind; the unification of me with the soul and the soul with the ultimate reality.

Emptiness: a content-free state of consciousness; no-mind; non-abidance; the state of absence.

False Me: a subconscious sense of me fully identified with the mental realm; a superficial sense of individuality alienated from one's true nature; the exteriorized self-consciousness of forgetfulness; me disconnected from I am.

God: the supreme reality; the absolute heart of existence; the mind and being of all-that-is; the cause and ultimate goal of creation.

Grace: evolutionary intervention from the beyond or from a human guide that manifests as a sudden acceleration of our awakening, healing and purification, or a release from karmic ties.

Gradual Enlightenment: a concept according to which enlightenment is reached by elevating one's level of awakening through many stages of gradual inner progress.

Gradual Path: an evolutionary journey towards enlightenment involving the gradual completion of many levels of awakening.

Healing: the transformation of human pain into love and wholeness.

Heart: the sacred core of individual consciousness; the seat of the soul; the soul's gateway to the divine; the divine realm.

Here: the horizontal plane of existence made known by the senses and the mind; perceptual reality; that which appears to be arising from the now; that which comes and goes, lacking the fundamental quality of being; the time-space continuum.

Horizontal Plane: the here; the relative expression of the now in the linear time-space continuum.

Human: the vehicle of the soul on the earth plane; the soul's extension in creation; a temporary identity based on mind and personality that has a sense of me, but not of I am.

I am: the soul; the light of pure subjectivity; the essence of true individuality; the centre of higher intelligence; the fundamental nature of universal consciousness.

Inner State: the state of pure subjectivity beyond the mind as experienced through awareness, being, heart, or any combination thereof; the energy-body of the soul; the soul's portal to the beyond.

Integral Consciousness: the state of unity between the mind and the inner state; the unbroken consciousness of the inner state and the soul; an undisrupted state of complete awareness and presence.

Integration: full maturity, transparency and naturalness within a previously awakened state.

Intelligence: the living spirit of existence; the coherence and purposefulness of the thought-process; a movement of understanding linked to the sense of me and the soul.

Karma: the interconnectedness of all elements in creation; the law of cause and effect; the law of justice in the plane of relativity.

Negative Karma: the net of illusion that holds the majority of souls in a state of lower consciousness; a lack of evolutionary support caused by one's resistance to awaken from the collective ignorance.

Positive Karma: being true to the inner call of the soul and taking responsibility for one's own awakening, manifesting as assistance from existence.

Liberation: the final step in the journey towards self-realization; emancipation from human existence; the ending of karma; freedom from self; entry into reality.

Me: the sense of personal individuality; the personalized light of pure subjectivity tied to individual purpose, blueprint and destiny; the first and foremost expression of the soul through which she reflects her identity in the mirror of pure consciousness; the human sense of individuality arising from the fundamental I am; the human sense of I am; the cognizing essence of the waking state through which the soul enters creation; the link between the I am of the soul and the mind of the human.

Meditation: a natural state of absorption in reality; abidance in the inner state; a condition of surrender to the now; just being; the unity of I am with the beyond.

Meditation Practice: a training of concentration upon self and letting go of self that aims at achieving the natural state of pure subjectivity; the internalization of attention; an expansion and deepening of consciousness towards unity with the beyond.

Mind: an organism of mental reality composed of the conscious, subconscious and unconscious, inseparable from intelligence and the intrinsic sense of me.

Mystical State: an altered state of consciousness not rooted in the reality of I am and the soul.

Natural State: effortless abidance in reality as it is; natural absorption in being; the state of perfect emptiness; an experience of transparency between the soul and the beyond.

No-mind: a dimension of consciousness and being that exists beyond and independently of the mind; a profound level of realization wherein the sense of me in the mind is absorbed into the state of emptiness; the surrender of the mind to the consciousness of the soul.

Non-abidance: an experience of non-separation in which the division between here and now is dissolved; a level of realization in which the soul abides in the reality of all, beyond any reference to creation or the uncreated; transparent unity between consciousness of oneself and consciousness of the totality that transcends the self-limiting notions of 'who' and 'where.'

Non-being: non-abidance; the realm of absence; the state of transcendence; a condition in which me has merged with the beyond; the dissolution of self in the absolute through which being is transcended; the absence of a knower through which being reveals its non-abiding depth.

Non-conceptualization: the natural state of being; a condition of abidance in reality free of veiling mental constructs; the unity of the knower and no-mind.

Non-doing: a state of surrender; pure meditation; the original stillness of being.

Non-thinking: natural absorption in the light of consciousness and being that is not touched by arising thoughts, yet includes the transparent movement of intelligence.

Not-knowing: the thought-and-content-free dimension of being and consciousness.

Now: the vertical reality of being; the timeless ground of reality; the meeting-point between time and the beyond; the source of the present moment; real time.

Oneness: a condition of existence devoid of a sense of separation; a level of realization in which the individual consciousness is merged with the consciousness of all; a state of unity through which the ultimate transparency between the soul and the one reality is realized.

Over-soul: the aspect of universal intelligence that bridges the soul and her destiny; the force of grace that oversees and directs the evolution of each soul.

Personality: a structure of human consciousness composed of the physical, emotional and mental bodies; the psychological frame of ego-consciousness; the sense of self based on the mind.

Pure Me: me in itself as reflected in the light of I am; the luminous consciousness of oneself beyond the mind and senses; awakened me.

Pure Subjectivity: the realm of I am; the dimension of the source and the soul; the ground of consciousness; consciousness in its original non-objectified form.

Purification: the cleansing of the mind; the removal of negative tendencies; the alignment of the human with the soul's essence and purpose.

Real Time: the non-linear flow of the timeless now; the transcendental time of the beyond; the becoming of being; the process of cognition merged with non-becoming.

Samadhi: the natural absorption of human consciousness into the soul and the beyond; the merging of I am and me in the state of absence; the dissolution of me in I am.

Self: the self-evident, self-radiant, self-knowing, fundamental nature of reality; the non-dual consciousness of existence in itself, by itself and through itself; in its higher meaning, universal I am; in its lower meaning, the soul; in its most basic meaning, the sense of me.

Self-attention: in its highest meaning, I am conscious of I am (consciousness of consciousness); in its higher meaning, me conscious of I am (awareness of consciousness); in its lower meaning, me conscious of itself (awareness of awareness).

Self-remembrance: mindfulness of I am; the effort to maintain constant awareness of pure consciousness; unbroken recollection of the state of presence; the horizontal unity of me and I am.

Separation: a state of ignorance and forgetfulness in which the condition of conscious oneness is absent; a low level of evolution wherein individual consciousness experiences itself as existing apart from the one reality; an existential friction between self and the total existence; the sense of me alienated from both the inner realm and creation.

Soul: the essence of impersonal individuality linked to the eternal evolution of light and consciousness; an individualized angle of perception endowed with the intrinsic knowledge of I am.

Dormant Soul: the soul in its seed-potential, entirely disconnected from me.

Active Soul: the soul unaware of herself, but inspiring her evolution through the intuitive dimension of human consciousness.

Awakened Soul: the soul conscious of her own identity.

Soul-awakening: the realization of I am; the meeting with the light of one's pure subjectivity.

Soul-realization: the complete actualization of the soul's identity; becoming one's eternal self; the culmination of the individuation process; the birth of the complete state of I am, our ultimate individuality.

Source: the absolute; the unmanifested; the original emptiness.

Stabilization: the relative completion of a process through which an awakened state becomes fully established; a stage of awakening in which the need for further cultivation of a particular state becomes unnecessary.

State Beyond Polarities: an early stage of the process of transcendence in which awareness reaches a level of relative absorption and absence.

State of Presence: the state of self-attention; pure awareness; consciousness in itself; the turning back of consciousness upon itself; the centre of the soul's intelligence; the I am of the mind.

303

Subconscious Me: the subliminal sense of identity; the diluted sense of me experienced below the threshold of conscious me; a dream-like, unfocused sense of self experienced when lost in the mind or spaced-out.

Subconscious Mind: the semi-conscious arising of thoughts in which the 'thinker' is not present to himself.

Subconscious: a subtle realm of lower intelligence present below the conscious reality; the processing sphere of mental impressions that serves as the foundation of the conscious mind.

Sudden Enlightenment: instantaneous arrival at the enlightened state through a sudden and dramatic shift of consciousness and being.

Sudden Path: the path based on the principle of sudden enlightenment.

Time: the movement of becoming as reflected in consciousness.

Transcendence: liberation; the final level in the realization of the transcendental state wherein one is released from the dimension of ignorance.

Transcendental State: the state of absence; a level of realization in which the consciousness of the soul merges with the absolute.

Transcendental Me: the realization of the soul from within the transcendental state; the complete experience of me merged with the realm of absence; me abiding in the natural, unconditional samadhi.

Transparent Me: a level of soul-realization in which me is met and actualized holistically within its translucent unity with the inner state.

Turiya: samadhi in the sleep state; I am integrated with sleep; awakened sleep; the fourth state — beyond waking, dreaming and deep sleep; the soul absorbed in the beloved; the natural samadhi.

Turiyatitta: the substratum upon which the soul abides in samadhi; the beyond; the state of the creator.

Unconscious Mind: the matrix of memories, impressions, and tendencies that lies beneath the subconscious and conscious mind; the non-conscious source of the subconscious mind; the impersonal wisdom at the root of individual consciousness.

Unconscious: the storehouse of universal, collective and individual mind-content; the ontological foundation of manifested consciousness.

Understanding: the clarity of knowing; the unity of discrimination and wisdom.

Universal Consciousness: the self-illuminating aspect of the whole of existence; the impersonal I am of totality; the fundamental nature of the absolute now.

Universal I am: the consciousness of the god-state; the overseeing awareness of all-that-is; the supreme reality.

Universal Intelligence: the wisdom of totality; the mind of universal consciousness; the intelligence of the supreme reality.

Wholeness: the soul's evolutionary completion, including her spiritual enlightenment and human completion; the realization of our evolutionary potential; the embodiment of our ultimate self; the complete and multidimensional awakening of our soul-identity.

Witness: the background consciousness beyond perceptual reality; the state of presence; the condition of natural non-involvement founded upon consciousness of one's true self.

**MANTRA
BOOKS**

We publish books on Eastern religions and philosophies.
Books that aim to inform and explore the various
traditions, that began rooted in East and
have migrated West.

Swami Shddahcnanda —

3 stages of Being

— The personal (Most of us are here)

— Knowing that one is beyond (awakening
body   people)

— Living from a state of
conciousness of
a Jiva mukta. enlightened
being